Understanding Imperial Russia

UNDERSTANDING IMPERIAL RUSSIA

State and Society in the Old Regime

MARC RAEFF

Translated by Arthur Goldhammer
Foreword by John Keep, University of Toronto

New York Columbia University Press

Library of Congress Cataloging in Publication Data

Raeff, Marc.
Understanding imperial Russia.

Translation of: Comprendre l'ancien régime russe.
Bibliography: p.
Includes index.
1. Soviet Union—History—1613–1689. 2. Soviet
Union—History—1689–1800. 3. Soviet Union—History—
19th century. I. Title.
DK113.R3413 1984   947   83-26241
ISBN 0-231-05842-X
ISBN 0-231-05843-8   (pa)

Title of the original French edition, *Comprendre l'ancien
régime russe,* © Editions du Seuil, 1982

Columbia University Press
New York and Guildford, Surrey
Copyright © 1984 Columbia University Press

PRINTED IN THE UNITED STATES OF AMERICA

c 10 9 8 7 6 5 4 3
p 10 9 8 7 6 5 4 3

Pour
Alain et Maria Besançon
and to my students

CONTENTS

FOREWORD

To understand the apparent strangeness and durability of the
Soviet system we need to know about Russia's past: not just
the decades that immediately preceded the Revolution of 1917,
but the distant epoch that saw the emergence and consolidation of the empire of the tsars. That is not the only reason
for examining the subject, but in our unhistorical age it is a
common one, and in no way discreditable.

It has been said, no doubt a little facetiously, that Stalin's
rule combined features characteristic of the reigns of several
of the Romanovs: Peter the Great's ruthless drive for progress at any price, Catherine II's flair for public relations and
'news management,' the arbitrariness of the tyrannical Paul
and the oppressive regimentation of the militaristic Nicholas
I. Of course we need not assume that Stalin was conscious of
these precedents; still less would any responsible historian
waste time trying to demonstrate continuities of such a kind.
Yet continuities there are—patterns of institutional and social behavior—that it does make excellent sense to examine.
There are also important differences, not only between pre-
and post-revolutionary Russia, but also between successive
phases of the Imperial era—the period from the early eighteenth to the early twentieth century that is treated in this
book.

Marc Raeff is one of the foremost historians of Russia in
the United States today. Born in Moscow, he spent his early
years in western Europe, whose languages and cultures he

knows well. He completed his formal education at Harvard University in 1950 and then embarked on a brilliant academic career. Since 1973 he has been Boris Bakhmeteff Professor of Russian Studies at Columbia University in New York City. A teacher, he has also written prolifically on almost every aspect of his subject. A recent bibliography listed more than 200 books, articles, and reviews by his pen.[1] Intellectual life, territorial expansion, minority problems, peasant revolts, historiography, and particularly public administration—all these topics, and many more, have been illuminated by his erudition and incisive judgments. He has also edited several valuable anthologies on various themes for use by students in the classroom.

Nor has Raeff confined his interests to Russia or the world of the Slavs. He has tackled a task which few of his colleagues would be brave enough to attempt: to place Russian history firmly in the European context where it properly belongs. Since the present work first appeared in French in 1982 he has published a study that will surely become a classic: *The Well Ordered Police State: Social and Institutional Change Through Law in the Germanies and Russia, 1600–1800* (New Haven: Yale University Press, 1983). Together these two volumes offer a distillation of his views on the dynamics of the historical process in central and eastern Europe during modern times.

Raeff's insights into this process have shaped the thinking of a whole generation of scholars in North America and western Europe. If we now know incomparably more than we did 30 years ago about the workings of the Imperial bureaucracy, in particular, as well as about a host of hitherto neglected individual thinkers, mainly on the right or in the center of the political spectrum, this is due in no small measure to his seminal influence. This influence would doubtless have extended further eastward than it has if Soviet his-

---

1. E. Kasinec and M. Molloy (comps.), "Marc Raeff: A Bibliography," *Russian Review* (1982) 41:454–71. (To August 1982).

torians were free to respond to intellectual stimuli from abroad, to analyze evidence objectively, and to say what they think in print. For what Raeff offers is nothing less than an original conception of the motive forces that have determined their country's past—one that applies the findings of modern philosophers, psychologists, sociologists, and historians to the great body of factual knowledge accumulated by prerevolutionary and Soviet specialists.

To understand this contribution, we have first to consider the interpretation of Russian history that was current before the revolution, one which in large measure also informed writing on the subject outside the Soviet Union—at least in the English-speaking countries—until the early 1950s. In the late nineteenth century Russia developed a rich historiographical tradition, marked by such eminent names as Sergei M. Soloviev, Vasilii O. Kliuchevskii, and Pavel N. Miliukov. After 1900 the discipline expanded further; the grand schemes of earlier writers were refined and there was vigorous investigation into a number of more specialized domains. At the risk of some simplification the prevailing view might be described as "liberal." Scholars could not remain indifferent to the struggles which at that time ranged through educated society, together with elements of the popular masses, against a government that claimed to be autocratic and often behaved in an arbitrary manner. Although the monarchy had its defenders, most historians felt that, whatever services it had rendered to the nation in earlier centuries, it was now on the side of "reaction." It was concerned mainly with defending its own interests, which were no longer those of the general public; the people needed a share in power and social change—in a word, "progress." Among educated Russians of the day the debate was not about the desirability of progress as such, but about the pace of advance and the methods to be used in securing it. In this controversy reformers were matched against revolutionaries, industrializers against agrarians, westernizers against nationalists, and so on.

There was also a shift of interest away from political, and particularly legal, problems which had preoccupied earlier historians of the so-called "juridical school," toward social and economic history. These historians identified progress with economic development, and more especially with social leveling as means of overcoming mass poverty. For them the miserable condition in which most of the tsar's subjects still lived was in large measure a heritage of serfdom. This shameful institution, they reasoned, had lasted for two and a half centuries, from *circa* 1600 to 1861; it had symbolized Russia's backwardness at a time when Europe was forging ahead; akin to slavery in many ways, it had involved cruelty and hardship for those subjected to it; it had been eliminated only at the cost of bitter conflict; and its consequences lived on into their own time, not just in economic backwardness but in the minds of the descendants of former serfs and former masters.

Here then, as it seemed, was another legacy of the past to contend with. Almost automatically the two major obstacles to progress were seen as connected: after all, serfdom and absolutism had come into being simultaneously, to serve a common need, so did not the abolition of one necessitate the disappearance of the other? Logic and experience suggested that the self-interest of the court must be connected with the self-interest of the landowning nobility; from this it followed gratifyingly that those who opposed them must be altruists concerned solely with the public good. Accordingly progressive historians deemed it to be their prime duty to register the sufferings and achievements of the common people *(narod)* and of the intellectuals who stood up for them, the intelligentsia. These notions were rooted in the positivist spirit of the age, when men by and large believed that the scientific study of factual data sufficed to lead one to the truth.

This comfortable outlook was shattered by the cataclysms of the twentieth century: World War I and, for Russia, the violent revolutions that brought devastation in its wake and swept away all the old familiar landmarks. There resulted a situation in which adherents of only a single historical school were free to practice their profession. Intellectually Soviet Marxist historiography owed a good deal to its predecessor; but it turned what had been no more than assumptions into dogma. At every turn writers were required to assert an optimistic belief in the cause of progress, as this was now interpreted by the political authorities; their works had to reflect the doctrine that history was made by "the masses," that change came about through class struggle, and that foreign influences had played a negligible role in Russia's past, which was thus reduced to a kind of overture to the glories of the present.

The obvious exaggerations of this school were challenged by western liberals, who perhaps did not realize the extent to which they stood on common ground with their opponents. For example, both believed that men, individually or collectively, were motivated in large degree by self-interest, and that history was mainly about their struggles for power: how to "divide up the cake." This prompted others, who stood aloof from the controversy, to ask themselves whether there might not be better ways in which to look at the past in the hope of resolving some of these vexing issues. Why not, so to say, rebake the cake?

This is not the place to explore the philosophical underpinnings of the school of thought which plays such a prominent role in western, especially American, historiography today.[2] We may simply mention two of its more obvious practical implications, so far as they are relevant to this book.

In the first place, these writers abstain more rigorously than most of their predecessors from moral judgments. Not for them impassioned denunciations of abuses of power by cor-

2. We are referring not to the partisans of quantification, but rather to those who might be termed neoconservatives, had this term not acquired misleading political connotations, or as neohistoricists or neostatists—except that they have rejected the determinism of the nineteenth-century historicists and moved toward a relativistic standpoint.

rupt officials or the "idle rich"—once the stock in trade of
bien-pensant liberals and radicals. Superficial readers might
construe this as amoralism, but they would be wrong: it is
rather an awareness that moral judgments are usually anachronistic and lead one on to treacherous ground that it is better to avoid.

In the second place, these historians are fully cognizant of
the complexities and ambiguities of human behavior, and thus
of the difficulties that stand in the way of its scientific analysis. Where every concept or sentiment may contain its opposite, where every attraction implies an element of rejection, there can be no certainties. Perhaps we are all relativists
now. The idea of a single unilinear course of development
seems childishly naïve—a product of the railroad age; so, too,
the notion that any one historical factor should be singled out
as in some way "basic" or "determinant." Instead, one tries
to size up each factor individually, in the knowledge that its
weight will vary over space and time and that its relation to
other factors will differ in each concrete situation. Nor can
cause and effect be neatly isolated, for they are interlinked in
the proverbial "seamless web" of action and reaction. Powerful individuals or groups may believe that they are shaping
events, but they do not act in a vacuum; their wills are con-
ditioned by countless antecedents as well as by the institutional context in which they operate.

For the same reason these limitations make it difficult to
predict what may be the consequences of a specific act: however well prepared, much will depend on the way it is implemented and the imponderable responses of those to whom it
is addressed. Every measure, every idea once translated into
action, has its positive and negative aspect, which renders any
absolute judgment on it simplistic; for if something is given
something else is surely taken away—for every winner there
will be losers. To take a concrete example: the Russian annexation of much of Poland in the eighteenth-century parti-
tions brought the empire an important accession of territory

and population, yet it also led to the growth of nationalist sentiment and ultimately to problems all too evident today in relations between the two countries. Or again: the so-called "great reforms" of the 1860s presented the Imperial government with demands for still greater concessions which it could not grant without committing suicide.

History is replete with paradoxes—and few have a finer sense of them than the author of this volume. Readers will find a number worth savoring and lingering over: the state sought to encourage private economic initiative yet hampered it by retaining extensive supervisory rights; its efforts to reform the judicial system in 1775 delayed progress toward a *Rechtsstaat*; serfdom entrenched social privilege yet permitted a measure of peasant mobility that helped to narrow the gap between the classes; and radical intellectuals perpetuated the tradition of personal authority established by the very autocrats they sought to overthrow. The central paradox for Raeff is that between the appearance of personal rule and the reality of its institutionalization (chapter 7). This "led Russia into the revolution of 1917," for the tsars were forced by their very own policies to undercut the basis on which their authority rested among the common people: their archaic patrimonial image. Elsewhere the author illustrates the antinomy between personal and institutionalized power with reference to a single individual, one of the most colorful in Russian history: Catherine II's favorite Prince, G. A. Potemkin.[3]

By applying this challenging conceptual approach to his subject Raeff manages to illuminate familiar problems from a new angle, to pose provocative questions, to demonstrate the limits of our knowledge, and to make us reconsider what had hitherto seemed to be incontrovertible truths.

3. Cf. pp. 96–97; and M. Raeff, "The Style of Russia's Imperial Policy and Prince G. N. Potemkin," in G. N. Grob, ed., *Statesmen and Statecraft in the Modern West: Essays in Honor of Dwight E. Lee and H. Donaldson Jordan* (Barre, Mass., 1967), p. 42.

Central to his argument is the view of absolutism as the major force working for change in modern Russia: "it was the state," he writes, "that took the lead in efforts to create a more dynamic society, better equipped to exploit available resources in a rational way" (p. 53). The idea itself is of course not new; indeed it is as old as Peter I and his advisers. Nineteenth-century historiography familiarized us with the idea of both Peter and Catherine "the Great" as innovators whose plans were too radical for the society of their day to absorb. For some (Soloviev) the state had been the demiurge behind the country's development since the dawn of recorded history. But this view was too extreme and failed to convince; and in reacting against it writers extended to the whole institution the discredit that attached to certain less successful rulers.

This controversy now has to be hoisted to a higher plane, as it were: it is not the deeds or misdeeds of individual monarchs that are under discussion, but the role which the central *vlast'* (power) as a whole—monarchs, advisers, executants, and groups co-opted into its service—marked out for itself, under the influence of western thought. Looking at matters in this way involves a certain abstraction from reality, for we can all think of individual rulers, officials, or aristocrats who do not quite fit this picture, in that they were less concerned with changing Russia than with bolstering their power or enriching themselves. Whether the exceptions invalidate the concept may be a matter of opinion. Raeff refines our view of the "tutelage" which the central *vlast'* exercised for so long, directly or indirectly, over the peoples of the empire; he shows that its achievements were greater in some fields than in others and explains why this was so.

One reason was the nature of the bureaucracy, the principal element in the state's power structure and the main instrument for effecting change. This is a second major theme: we are introduced to its leading representatives, whom the

older historiography often slighted or ignored, without overlooking the humble clerks who toiled away in countless offices and tried to cope with the mountains of paper that built
up each day in this highly regimented administration. We learn
of their successes, which were often considerable—the com-
pilation, as early as 1830, of a *Complete Collection of Laws
of the Russian Empire,* in 55 stout volumes, is an extraordinary achievement by any standard—and also of their failures,
the reasons for which are to be sought primarily in the educational field.

Similar shortcomings were also for a long time characteristic of the landowning nobility, from which the higher (rank-
holding) bureaucrats may be said to have seceded to form an
independent social group. This cultural backwardness was
primarily responsible for the durability of serfdom—treated
here not as a consequence of the masters' egoism but as a
mutual relationship that imposed disabilities on the powerful as well as on the powerless. Serfdom, Raeff insists, was
not a "system"; it had almost as many variants as there were
serfowners; informal arrangements were of its essence; and
in practice there were many ways of evading its most harmful and demeaning restrictions.

Again, there is room for argument here, both as to the place
which serfdom ought to occupy in the history of pre-reform
Russia[4] and, more particularly, as to the degree which self-
interest and sheer inertia affected the elite's stance. The per-
vasiveness of physical violence in Russian rural society (and
in the military), it seems to me, deserves to be stressed. It
produced an equally brutal response, which earlier historians
were sometimes prepared to condone. Today few would share
the mythopoeic and anachronistic view that the rebel bands
who followed the cossack chieftain Emelian Pugachev were
popular heroes struggling valiantly for the people's rights, for

4. Raeff states justly that serfdom shaped the character of authority throughout
Russia, but this does not appear to be central to his argument.

Raeff has exposed the fallaciousness of such an approach.[5] Nor is it now generally believed that an egalitarian redistribution of land in or after 1861 could have radically improved the peasants' life-style—an opinion common among intellectuals at the time.

The errors of this class of men constitute a fourth theme of this book. Those whom earlier generations regarded as the natural leaders of society are here downgraded to marginals, alienated from both the government and the masses, prone to unrealistic abstract thinking, attracted by the last word in foreign intellectual fashions, and even tempted to sanction terrorism. It is a formidable indictment which may not convince all members of the jury.[6] In defense it might be contended that the vices of the "men of the sixties" are less characteristic of other generations; but few will contest Raeff's point that the intelligentsia has received a disproportionate share of attention from historians, given their relative ineffectiveness in putting their ideas into practice.

An exception has to be made for those active in the literary or artistic domain, and whose accomplishments are among the glories of nineteenth- and early-twentieth-century European civilization. *Understanding Imperial Russia* pays tribute to their achievements (and to those of scientists, too), so far as its modest compass allows. It also brings out the richness of everyday cultural life, symbolized by the "thick journals" that were read by educated persons across the length and breadth of the empire. In our age of struggling newspapers and canned entertainment such sustained attention to serious issues seems little short of marvelous. Moreover, Raeff argues that this 'high culture' rested on a solid basis, in that the educational system maintained high standards in its up-

5. Cf. p. 86; and M. Raeff, "Pugachev's Revolt," in R. Forster and J. P. Greene, eds., *Preconditions of Revolution in Early Modern Europe* (Baltimore-London, 1970), pp. 161–202.

6. Objections to Raeff's assessment of the intelligentsia mentality were raised by M. Confino, "A propos de la noblesse russe," *Annales: économies, sociétés, civilisations* (1967) 22:1163–1205; cf. Raeff's reply in *ibid.* (1968) 23:1178–9.

per echelons, whatever might be said about weaknesses at the base. Orthodox Christianity, too, often dismissed as intellectually sterile, inspired men and women at all levels in society. Given the pettifogging secular control to which the official Church was subject, this was a significant achievement which explains the religious renaissance that occurred in Russia during the early years of the twentieth century. It is in the light of this cultural efflorescence that the empire's political history needs to be set—a rare virtue, alas—if it is to be evaluated correctly and valid comparisons made with the situation in our own day.

These themes, it appears to me, are among the most important in this volume, but no summary can do justice to the subtlety with which they and others are treated. We are offered here both a developmental "model," to use a term that the social sciences have made familiar, and a study in depth of the various ways in which human beings sought to apply that model or to adjust their lives to it. For those who seek to thread their way through the complex flow of events Marc Raeff is an expert guide, and one cannot ask for more than that. "Understandest thou what thou readest?" inquired the apostle of the man from far-off Ethiopia.

"How can I," he replied, "except some man should guide me?"

When it comes to modern Russia, are our needs any less?

John Keep
University of Toronto

PREFACE

This essay owes its origin to a series of seminars I conducted at the *Centre russe* of the *Ecole des hautes études en sciences sociales* in Paris in 1980. I am most grateful to Fr. Furet, President of the *Ecole* and to my friend Alain Besançon, director of its *Centre russe,* for inviting me, and to the participants of the seminars for their stimulating and judicious comments.

Dr. B. Sapir, Professor I. de Madariaga, and Dr. J. P. Le-Donne kindly pointed out several factual slips and unclear statements, which I have endeavored to correct in the English version. I am much indebted to Mr. Arthur Goldhammer for his felicitous rendering of the original French text, to Professor R. Wortman for recommending publication in English, and to Professor J. H. L. Keep for kindly introducing the book.

Marc Raeff
September 1983

Understanding Imperial Russia

1
THE MUSCOVITE BACKGROUND

*B*Y the middle of the seventeenth century the political culture of Muscovy had reached a pinnacle of development. The institutions on which that development was based received their definitive form with the promulgation of the law code of 1649 *(Ulozhenie).* Shortly thereafter, however, Muscovite civilization began to falter and soon entered upon a period of rapid decline, which, within the space of one generation, culminated, upon the death of Tsar Alexis in 1676, in a serious cultural, social, and institutional crisis. In turn, this crisis helped to lay the groundwork for the radical, indeed revolutionary, changes carried out by Peter the Great. ·

What, then, can we say about the Muscovite Empire in the year 1650, in that brief moment when it seemed that the regime had succeeded in consolidating its cultural base and in surmounting the difficulties of the Time of Troubles (at the beginning of the century), thus setting the stage for what seemed to be the likelihood of further progress? This question is not at all easy to answer, because the seventeenth century is one of the most neglected periods in Russian history. Apart from certain specialized questions (such as the religious crisis and peasant and urban uprisings), the tendency among historians has been to explain the period, in an almost mechanical way, in terms of factors whose origins can be traced back to the reign of Ivan IV (the Terrible) in the sixteenth century or, alternatively, to view it as a mere precursor of the eighteenth century. There have been few serious

studies of seventeenth-century Muscovite society and civilization of the sort that might help us to understand Muscovy
in its prime and to explain its subsequent rapid decline. Although I cannot hope to fill this gap, I shall here try to give
a brief picture of Muscovite political culture, subject to re-
vision in the light of subsequent research.

The Symbiosis Between Church and State

Among our sources one in particular is especially illumi-
nating in regard to Muscovite political culture after 1649: the
Complete Collection of the Laws of the Russian Empire,
whose first volume contains the code of Tsar Alexis. In addition, we must of course look at both public and private law
and at contemporary literature before we can begin to say what
civic life in Muscovy was like. In examining legislative and
court records, the first thing that strikes us is the remarkable
symbiosis between church and state. This does not mean, of
course, that in the political realm the church was not subordinate to the state (especially after the Patriarch Nikon was
deposed in 1666). It is clear, however, that the Muscovite regime—or, more precisely, its sovereign, the tsar—never conceived of itself as existing outside an ecclesiastical framework, separate from the church hierarchy and its leader, the
patriarch. Furthermore, in contrast to western and central
Europe, where, even before the Reformation, there was constant tension between society and the church, between religious norms and secular law, in Muscovy religion served both
as a cultural underpinning of the regime and as a principle in
terms of which Russia was able to define itself as a nation.
Specifically, the tsar and his subjects defined themselves as
members of the Russian Orthodox Church, whose teachings
functioned as what we would nowadays call an ideology. It
should come as no surprise, then, that any challenge to or
conflict involving the rituals and teachings of the church had

profound repercussions on the political and cultural life of the nation and struck at the very roots of Muscovite national identity and spiritual unity. The schism involving the so-called Old Believers was one such case, to which we shall return later on.

One indication of the church–state symbiosis mentioned above can be seen in the fact that the patriarch and other members of the church hierarchy took an active part in various political functions, including public ceremonies involving the tsar. Among the ceremonies in which religious figures participated on an equal footing with political dignitaries were the baptism and confirmation of royal children, royal weddings and funerals, and of course the anointment of the tsar. In these ceremonies, according to the order of precedence established by custom, the patriarch outranked all other dignitaries except the tsar himself. Important legislative acts and public proclamations were drawn up in the name of the tsar (after consultation with the boyars) and the patriarch (with the consent of the ecclesiastical synod or *sinklit*). These practices were similar to those employed by other traditional monarchies claiming to rule by divine right, and except for the survivals of Byzantine ritual there is nothing astonishing about them. It is important, however, to stress the active role of the patriarch and the Church in the legislative process itself.

In any comparison between Russia and Western countries in the seventeenth century, one fact stands out: in Russia we find the government and administrative authorities acting without regard to any distinction between the temporal realm and the spiritual realm. For example, it was the government that ordered that religious ceremonies be held in order to ward off epidemics in certain areas or to secure God's grace in time of famine or natural disaster. What is more, the civil authorities not only ordered that ceremonies and processions be held but actually organized and staged them; ecclesiastical personnel played a subordinate role, merely following orders is-

sued by the government. To give another example, governors
(voevoda) were required to take icons and reliquaries with
them on their propitiatory rounds; these relics and icons were
selected by the Moscow authorities and made available to the
governors in order to ensure that this essential public service
would be carried out. In the juridical realm, acts of private
law (such as contracts of sale and exchange) as well as public
law (such as convocations of synods, measures of ecclesiastical discipline, and religious ordinances issued by the patriarch or metropolitans) enjoyed the same status as acts of the
tsar. Proclaimed and promulgated in the name of the patriarch in the same manner as acts of the temporal government,
these acts were included in compilations of law on an equal
footing with acts of the tsar and the boyar duma. These aspects of the church–state symbiosis are worth emphasizing
because they abruptly disappeared in the early years of Peter
the Great's reign. From that time on, all legislative acts were
strictly secular in form, even those involving affairs of the
church.

The Legitimacy of the Tsar

As in the Byzantine system, the tsar was actually an ecclesiastical personage in the same sense as the patriarch and
played a hieratic role in certain church rituals. The tsar's legitimacy stemmed from this hieratic role as well as from the
fact that, since the fall of Constantinople to the Ottoman
Turks, he was the only independent Orthodox prince. The
notion of a unified and continuous ruling dynasty, partly
Scandinavian in origin and partly borrowed from the Khans
of the Golden Horde, no doubt played an important part in
shaping the autocratic character of the Muscovite rulers. Yet
according to both popular tradition and official mythology, the
major influences on Muscovite political ideology and practice were, first, the idea of Moscow as the Third Rome,

whereby the tsar, as heir to the legacy of Rome and Byzantium, claimed the legitimate right to rule, and, second, the hieratic conception of the tsar's power. It should come as no surprise, then, that the tsar could be approached only in an attitude of fervent devotion. As if to underscore his hieratic role, the tsar seldom appeared in public, and then almost always in connection with religious occasions and ceremonies. The tsar, along with his family and court, lived apart—one might almost say cut off—from the society of the capital (to say nothing of the fact that the tsar's visits to the provinces were very rare indeed, excursions outside the Kremlin being justified only for pilgrimages or visits to nearby monasteries). Muscovy knew virtually nothing of the pomp and circumstance, the splendid entries, and the triumphal parades that were the inevitable hallmark of public life in the absolute monarchies of central and western Europe during the baroque era. The physical isolation of the tsar, together with the court's lack of involvement in the daily life of the capital, created a gulf between court and society far wider than that between Paris and Versailles in the time of Louis XIV, whose courtiers, as we know from contemporary evidence, led an active life both at court and in the city. This observation helps to clear up another puzzle: we know that some courtiers of Tsar Alexis adopted European fashions and customs: they dressed in Polish costumes and took to shaving, for example; the tsar's children were taught European languages and literature; and plays were staged within the walls of the Kremlin.[1] Yet outside those walls none of these western innovations caught on. This was not merely because these western imports were, in the eyes of many, far too radical and contrary to Russian religious traditions and teachings but also because few people on the outside saw or even knew what

1. Tsar Alexis was an avid hunter and frequently hunted in sparsely populated areas near Moscow. He also took part in several military campaigns against Poland. These moves were a harbinger of things to come: his son, Peter the Great, was a frenetic traveler.

was going on at court.[2] Such western customs as penetrated the walls of the Kremlin had few repercussions outside and played only a limited role in the cultural transformation of the country.

Given the symbiosis of church and state, the most important function of the tsar (and his government) was to ensure the perpetuation of Orthodoxy. This role was set forth in the preambles to important pieces of legislation as well as in the official titles borne by the tsar. For a sort of "proof by contradiction" of the importance attached to this function, we need only cite Peter the Great's decree of December 22, 1697, which eliminated the "theological" *(bogoslovie)* epithets from the tsar's titles and replaced them with a straightforward declaration of the tsar's divine right: "We, by the grace of God, most radiant and powerful great lord."

THE ROLE OF THE GOVERNMENT

In keeping with this "medieval" conception of the nature of government, the tsarist administration was essentially negative or passive in nature. To perpetuate orthodoxy the government had only to maintain order and preserve domestic tranquillity, administer justice, and defend the country against foreign enemies. It is not surprising, then, to discover that the government took no part in exploiting the country's resources or developing its productive capacities, tasks that had by this time become the main concern of most European states. We find no Muscovite legislation (or other measures) comparable to the *Polizeiordnungen* of the German and Scandinavian countries or the *Grandes Ordonnances* of Colbert.[3] This is not to say that the tsarist officials took no pos-

2. A parallel may be drawn with the cloistered life of the Soviet elite.

3. The notorious *Novotorgovyi ustav* or new commercial code of 1667 contains not a single positive clause. It encouraged commerce by establishing a system of tariffs and tolls and set up a schedule of fines for infraction of commercial regulations.

itive steps that had an immediate impact on society. But unlike most western countries, in which administrative tasks were normally carried out by various organized, autonomous groups, in Russia the imperial government had to mobilize and organize the population in order to carry out its twofold mission, to maintain order and administer justice on the one hand and to perpetuate Orthodoxy on the other.

Perhaps the most striking characteristic of the Muscovite political system was the universality of state service. Society was divided into two groups: those who gave of themselves (nobles and their retinue, who served in the army and in the bureaucracy) and those who gave of their property by paying taxes (mainly peasants and ordinary townsmen). The government's main task was to see that these obligations, in principle incumbent upon everyone, were discharged in an orderly way. In consequence, the government became involved in the life of almost every one of the tsar's subjects—or at least every one of the tsar's subjects that the administrative apparatus was in a position to oversee directly (in practice this exempted much of the peasantry). Village communes acted as state agents to require services and dues of free peasants and state or "black" peasants,[4] and landowners did the same with regard to their serfs.

Human and fiscal resources were mobilized exclusively for the benefit of the central government in Moscow. The administration was not really concerned with establishing a local tax collection system. The governor, the tsar's direct representative in the major provincial cities, was responsible merely for sending to Moscow men and revenues from the region. As representative of the tsar in his capacity as judge, the *voevoda* or governor did, it is true, have jurisdiction over some minor cases; more serious cases (civil as well as criminal) were the responsibility of the Moscow chanceries. Rel-

---

4. The *chrnososhnye krestiane* were peasants living on "black," or taxable, land and were popularly known as "black peasants."

atively autonomous local bodies must therefore have played
an important role in day-to-day local administration. Unfortunately, we know next to nothing about how these bodies
operated. The few bits of information we do have all pertain
to free peasant communities in the northern Dvina region, a
sparsely populated area not at all typical of Muscovite society in general.[5]

It is worth noting, however, that the policy of the Moscow
government in regard to the organization of local administration changed over the course of the seventeenth century. Following the Time of Troubles the government reestablished
the system of local elected officials *(gubnye liudi)* introduced
by Ivan IV. After the tsar's authority was firmly reestablished
throughout the country, these officials were replaced by the
voevoda, who was appointed by the central government. In
the second half of the century the *gubnye liudi* were briefly
revived and granted limited authority, only to be supplanted
once more by *voevodas* nominated by Moscow. These policy
changes are in themselves indicative of the low priority attached to regional administration by Moscow administrators.
Further proof of this is afforded by the limited authority that
Moscow granted to local administrative bodies, including such
things as the power to organize auxiliary militia, to collect
certain taxes, and to judge minor cases. The lack of a logical,
consistent policy with respect to local administration is evidence of the gradual decline and dislocation of the Muscovite
system in the second half of the seventeenth century.

Muscovy, as P. B. Struve has remarked, was a liturgical state.
To put it another way, every member of Muscovite society
was required to serve the state by giving "of himself" and "of

---

5. See Hans-Joachin Torke, *Die staatsbedingte Gesellschaft im Moskauer Reich:
Zar und Zemlija in der altrussischen Herrschaftsverfassung 1613–1689* (Leyden: Brill,
1974), which shows the weakness of local social organizations. The standard works
of B. Chicherin and M. Bogoslovsky on local administration in the seventeenth century are based mainly on the area of North Dvina.

his property." Organizing this state service was therefore the administration's primary task. Once the Code of 1649 had stiffened the laws pertaining to the institution of serfdom, the tsar's officials ceased to take much interest in the condition or activity of the peasant classes. Peasant affairs henceforth came within the purview of private law, and the state intervened only in complicated and controversial cases, and then only upon request of the parties involved. It is true that, during the reign of Fedor and the regency of Sophia, a number of laws pertaining to the repossession of fugitive serfs were promulgated. In my view this legislation in itself shows that the traditional structure of Muscovite society had weakened: since traditional rules and customs were no longer as effective as they once had been, the state was forced, not without misgivings, to intervene. By contrast, the government always showed great interest in the state service activities of all categories of "nobles." The state mobilized nobles in time of war and called them for maneuvers in time of peace. It took charge of the assignment and classification of nobles (razbor) and oversaw the distribution of land as compensation for service (pomest'e, votchina[6]) as well as other material rewards. Any number of laws and administrative decrees attest to a lack of enthusiasm for state service on the part of those required to perform it. These laws and decrees provided sanctions against anyone who failed to heed the call or who turned up late or without the required equipment. Punishments (which could be revoked if the guilty party turned himself in) ranged from confiscation of lands and other property to imprisonment and reprisals against relatives and servants of the derelict party. In other words, the noble called to perform state service was nothing more than a serf, indeed a slave, of the sovereign.

6. The *pomest'e* ("benefice") was an estate granted for life to a member of the state service. The *votchina* ("allod") was an estate of which ownership was hereditary.

The Subjugation of Society

We should begin by pointing out that the subjection of
Russian society by the tsarist government started at the top.
"Nobles"—boyars, servants of Moscow, appanaged princes
(udel'nye kniazia) and their retinues—were transformed into
nothing less than the serfs or servants of the sovereign. They
were not vassals endowed with certain rights by bilateral
contract (notwithstanding the actual inequalities that frequently accompanied such contracts in the West) but servants or *kholopy* (really little more than serfs) of the tsar.[7]
Only after the imperial government had subjugated the elite
did it attempt to extend its dominion to the peasantry. The
lot of the peasant under serfdom in the seventeenth century
was not yet particularly harsh, since landowners, themselves
servants of the central government, were frequently obliged
to spend time away from their estates and were therefore unable to add to the burdens imposed by the tsar. Paradoxical
as it may seem, the upper strata of Muscovite society were
more fully subjugated and had to bear a heavier burden than
the lower strata. Of course this does not mean that the masses
were better off than the elite in a material sense, but they did
enjoy greater freedom of action in daily life. Some writers
(mainly liberals and Marxists) have argued that peasant resistance to serfdom was the most important factor in the history of Muscovy in the seventeenth century. The foregoing
remarks cast doubt on this line of reasoning, which is usually supported by pointing to the frequency and scope of
peasant uprisings, particularly those of Bolotnikov and Stenka
Razin. In fact, however, these revolts erupted in outlying areas
among social and ethnic groups that had traditionally enjoyed a measure of autonomy, which the imperial government was attempting to eradicate. In what is properly termed

7. Thus the term "feudal" is not applicable to Muscovite Russia, despite the as-
sertions of Soviet historians and their *marxisant* bourgeois emulators.

Muscovite territory serfdom actually took hold via a slow and gradual process, and the implications of the serf system were not fully appreciated until enserfment was complete. It should not be forgotten, moreover, that peasants frequently chose voluntarily to become serfs (i.e., to accept restrictions on their freedom of movement) because they saw certain advantages in doing so: serfdom made it possible to avoid still greater burdens and presumably offered protection against famine and violence, protection which, it was thought, great landowners were in a position to provide.[8]

The main practical problem that the Moscow government faced in the second half of the seventeenth century was the following: How could the government extract taxes and services from those of its subjects—primarily peasants—located at great distances from the seat of power, beyond the reach of the tsar's direct representatives? Was it necessary to delegate this responsibility to local "nobles"? If so, would this not reduce the obligations of those nobles to the central government? Would it not lead to the development of local forms of solidarity and local autonomy which in turn would weaken the central government's control over its recruits? If, on the other hand, administrative tasks (such as monitoring the discharge of service obligations and the payment of taxes) were delegated to traditional communal bodies, as was done before the middle of the sixteenth century, would this not run counter to the requirements of total mobilization, reducing the tsar's effective control over the country and resulting in material losses for "nobles" recruited to the tsar's service? The government never managed to overcome this dilemma, which explains why Muscovite policy in the second half of the seventeenth century looks so much like a hesitation waltz.

The practices of the liturgical state and the imposition of

8. The concept of "second serfdom," which does not work very well as an explanation of economic and social developments in Poland, eastern Prussia, and Bohemia in the fifteenth and sixteenth centuries, can be applied to Muscovite Russia only with caveats so numerous as to deprive it of all explanatory value.

service obligations on the entire population had psychological as well as political implications. Universal service requires (or engenders) a consensus as to the fundamental nature of the national political culture. When certain facets of
that culture are challenged by segments of society, the result
is likely to be a "moral crisis" (in the sense attached to that
term in the eighteenth century) that can do far more harm to
a country than any foreign enemy or natural disaster.

State service in the Muscovite regime was highly hierarchical in nature. The highest ranks comprised the *boiarskaia
duma,* or council of boyars,[9] below which came the Kremlin
courtiers among whom the leading administrators and gen-
erals were recruited. Still farther down we find various categories of provincial civil servants. In order to prevent the formation of a powerful and autonomous aristocratic oligarchy
while still honoring the privileges of birth, Muscovy in-
vented the *mestnichestvo* (order of precedence) system, which
took account both of services rendered to the state by a man's
ancestors (thus giving heredity its due) and of services rendered by the man himself (thus rewarding merit). No one was
required to serve under any person whose rank in the service
(associated with both the family and the individual) was lower
than his own (except by express order of the tsar). Service lists
were kept up to date by means of an involved calculus, at least
for persons connected with central government bureaus or
involved in court ceremonies. This system had two consequences: first, it insured that the tsar would have ultimate
effective control over all nobles in government service, because their rank depended on duties and titles that only the
sovereign could bestow; second, it guaranteed that there would
be permanent conflict between the families of nobles in service, particularly those attached to the court and eligible for
entry into the *boiarskaia duma,* and thus prevented the for-

9. *Boiarskaia duma:* boyars' council. Boyar was the highest rank in the service
hierarchy. The title was reserved for courtiers and eminent members of the most
prominent families in the tsar's immediate entourage.

mation of a common front, of stubborn allegiances that might
have posed a threat to the absolute power of the tsar. Because
of these internal divisions, cleverly maintained by the *mestnichestvo* system (whose abolition in 1682 merely gave official sanction to the fact that many civil servants had been
promoted to high rank who had no direct affiliation with the
old aristocratic clans), the high Muscovite nobility never really
constituted itself as a true "order." For nobles in state service, it is obvious that *mestnichestvo* was a source of insecurity and instability, since an individual's rank ultimately
depended on the tsar's favor and willingness to recognize
meritorious service.

The danger that the *mestnichestvo* system might have involved for Muscovite political culture and society was in large
part compensated, if not entirely outweighed, by customs that
made it possible to externalize the conflicts generated by the
system. Disputes over precedence were resolved by a whole
range of ritual forms, culminating in judgment by special
"tribunals" (commissions made up of members of the *boiar
duma*) whose decisions were then ratified by the tsar as final
arbiter. Judgments were rendered and executed in accordance
with strict forms: any person found guilty of violating or re-
fusing to abide by the order of precedence was delivered over
to the mercy of the person offended.[10] The offense was then
purged in a ritual of insults and offensive oaths, which restored harmony and settled disputes without recourse or
dueling or other forms of violence (such things were not unknown, but remained within ritualized and accepted limits).
This calls to mind the forms of social control and systems
for the settlement of intracommunal conflicts brought to light
by recent studies of the accusation and trial of witches in the
West.

10. The "guilty party" was required to go to the home of the person offended to
make a public apology and then had to allow himself to be beaten by the latter's
domestics. This abject submission to corporal punishment was the result of the absence, under the Muscovite regime, of a code of honor and a notion of individual
dignity among the "noble" service class.

It is clear that the *sine qua non* of such a ritualized system
is absolute acceptance of the society's fundamental norms.
Any deviation from the social norms automatically implies
rejection of the system and hence renunciation of the tsar as
supreme protector. Indeed, deviation was seen as tantamount
to social treason. This gave rise to a Manichean world view:
one was either a subject of holy Moscow or a foreigner and,
by definition, an enemy. To accept other norms, tolerate innovations, challenge or show skepticism toward established
traditions was literally as well as figuratively to become an
outlaw in the eyes of Moscow. The words used to describe
those who became outlaws indicate what was at stake: con-
federates of Khovanski and Shaklovitov found guilty of "treason" ceased to be referred to in legal documents by their ordinary names and were designated instead by diminutives
together with insulting epithets emphasizing their "disgrace" and their expulsion from Russian society. Though
shocking today, perhaps, this verbal violence served as a safety
valve by allowing conflicts to be resolved without recourse
to political violence: the use of insults helped to quell tensions that might otherwise have rent the social fabric.

The Decline of Muscovite Society

Russian society had to cope with a number of significant
dangers. Bear in mind that Muscovy in the mid-seventeenth
century was a multinational empire incorporating several
peoples with different languages, religions, and civilizations,
including peoples that were not even Christian let alone Orthodox. Without going into detail about this vast and still in-
sufficiently explored subject, we may say simply that the
tsarist government used two methods for dealing with the
threat of disintegration posed by alien and foreign populations: first, it tried to isolate those populations to the maxi-
mum possible extent, which, given the primitive technology

of the day and the vastness of the territory, was usually not terribly difficult, particularly for populations residing on the borders of the empire and in Siberia; and second, it tried to convert, baptize, and integrate the alien elements. Individuals and peoples converted and baptized were automatically assimilated into Orthodox society, regardless of their native language or customs. Converted alien elites were easily integrated, not to say absorbed, into the class of "servants of the tsar" and hence into the Muscovite elite. There were of course cases in which isolation and integration proved difficult, the Ukraine being the first prominent example. The impracticability of traditional methods in these cases raised serious new problems, which helped to accelerate the decline of Muscovite culture and the onset of the final crisis that paved the way for Peter the Great.

No society can remain static for long. Every culture is subject to influences—whether from outside or from within—that gradually change its nature. Firmly rooted societies and cultures adapt to change and tolerate innovation while preserving their basic character and deep-seated identity. But declining societies and decadent, drifting cultures can be undermined and destroyed by external influence or internal turmoil. In the case of Moscow, scarcely a generation after the essential outlines of its political culture had been laid down by the Code of 1649, that culture had fallen into disarray, society had lapsed into crisis, and the state itself was tottering on the verge of collapse. In retrospect we can see that, during the second half of the seventeenth century, fragile Muscovite culture disintegrated as one shock after another battered Russian society, creating a vacuum that facilitated the radical changes made by Peter the Great. What factors explain the collapse of Muscovite political culture? The facts are generally well known, so that a brief review of the subject will suffice.

At the head of the list we must place the *raskol* (or schism of "Old Believers"), simply because of the importance of the church–state symbiosis discussed above. The schism, which stemmed largely from disputes over church organization and ritual, led, in the 1660s, to a breakdown of religious consensus. The Old Believers refused to accept innovations in liturgical rites and texts, innovations which were based on Ukrainian and Greek models introduced into Russia by the energetic Patriarch Nikon. They therefore split from the official church and became the object of prosecution as well as persecution by the temporal authorities. They proclaimed themselves champions of the true Muscovite orthodoxy and asserted Moscow's preeminence as the Third Rome. They looked forward to the coming of the Antichrist as a precursor of the final victory of Christ and the Last Judgment. By rejecting the state authorities as traitors to orthodoxy and servants of the Antichrist, the Old Believers excluded themselves from the public life of the nation; this brought them into contact with discontented groups driven to rebellion for social and economic reasons. In this way they contributed to the disintegration of Muscovite society and, by rocking the traditional foundations of Muscovite civilization, also weakened the state. Ultimately, the *raskol* produced division within the masses, resulting in the almost total alienation of the Old Believers (peasants and merchants) from the cultural and political life of the nation. It is highly likely, moreover, that because large numbers of people who played an especially active and enterprising economic role rallied to the Old Faith the progress of trade and industry within the Empire was adversely affected. The active role played by Old Believers in the modernization of the Russian economy in the nineteenth century, after the legal situation of the schismatics had improved, is indicative of the enormous human potential that was allowed to go to waste in the previous century.

Second among the causes of collapse of the Muscovite regime was the prevalence of social and economic conflict. Such conflict was not new, of course, but the resurgence of violent protest by both peasants and townsmen helped to undermine Muscovite society. The importance of these rebellions is difficult to gauge. Were rebellions more frequent and more violent in the second half of the seventeenth century than in the first? If we except the Time of Troubles in the first decade of the century, this would seem to have been the case. Uprisings occurred in the country's oldest and most prominent cities (in 1648, 1662, and 1682, to name a few of the most important), reflecting both economic and cultural unrest. These were sometimes provoked or accompanied by mutinies of professional soldiers or *streltsy*,[11] many of whom had rallied to the Old Faith. This in itself shows that economic, social, religious, and political phenomena were intertwined and suggests that Muscovy was sinking into a latent state of crisis. The great peasant uprising of 1670–71, led by Stenka Razin and characterized as a "peasant war" by Soviet historians, shows that many traditional social bonds had been weakened or destroyed. It also revealed the degree of unrest prevailing among such marginal social groups as the Cossacks of the Don and Volga regions, the alien populations of the southeastern steppes, and the frontier garrisons, to say nothing of fugitive serfs and criminals. Government attempts to stamp out these revolts militarily resulted in a marked increase in government outlays and heavy new burdens on taxpayers. The political and ideological repression that followed cast doubt on the justness of the tsar's rule and on the belief that the ruling elites and the masses shared a common political culture.

Third among the causes of collapse we must mention the role of foreign trade, particularly the import of foreign goods and the influx of foreign individuals. Foreign goods, imported both to meet the needs of the military and to satisfy the taste of courtiers for luxury and novelty, gradually transformed the tastes of the Muscovite elite. New decorative motifs, of European inspiration, found their way into Russian architecture and painting (both icons and *parsuny*[12]), as well as the clothing and hunting accoutrements of the court nobility, and

11. The *streltsy* were professional soldiers who had another occupation besides the military and engaged in business in the cities where they were garrisoned.

12. *Parsuny:* portraits (derived from *personae*).

books, plays, and musical composition. Thereby they helped
alter traditional forms of behavior and life styles. The influx
of foreign visitors who established themselves temporarily or
permanently in the "foreign suburb" *(nemetskaia sloboda)* of
Moscow obviously had an impact on the appearance of the
capital, in spite of the restrictions imposed by the timorous
ecclesiastical authorities, who feared that the example of foreign ways of life constituted a temptation and a threat to the
orthodoxy of the populace. This fear only reinforced the feeling that traditional orthodoxy was vulnerable and unstable and
that customary practices could easily be undermined by outside influences. Of course, the important role played by foreigners in certain areas of Russian public life meant that
Russians had to enter into contact with foreigners and accommodate to foreign ways. Even more important, however,
was the fact that the existence of the foreign suburb represented a breach in the impregnable walls that had cut Moscow off, culturally and economically, from the rest of Europe
after the Time of Troubles. Similarly, trade relations with
Holland and England were more important for their cultural
than for their economic impact, in that they facilitated contact with the Western world and introduced new influences
into Muscovite life.

Expansionist aims frequently have an unforeseen negative
impact on societies whose governments adopt them. And so
it was with Muscovy when it extended its frontiers toward
the southwest, and especially when it gained control of the
Ukraine, extending its dominion to the territories on the left
bank of the Dnieper and to Kiev, a region that had previously
been controlled by the Cossack army camped on the Sich. For
one thing, this annexation made it possible for a new spirit
to make its influence felt in Muscovy (more on this later).
For another, it placed a heavy military, political, and administrative burden on the limited resources of the Muscovite
government. To mention one problem whose far-reaching
consequences became apparent only later on, Moscow found

it difficult to absorb the Ukraine, with its complex social structure consisting of a hodgepodge of different groups, classes, religious sects, and armed militias and its inextricable mixture of customs, languages, and social roles. The Muscovite officials felt themselves obliged to aid the wealthy ruling classes in the Ukraine, particularly the Cossack "officers" (starshiny), in their efforts to subjugate the peasantry and consolidate their local base of power. This did not fail to arouse resistance, in some cases quite violent resistance, among the masses, and the whole effort represented a considerable drain on Moscow's economic and military resources.

What is more, in the last few decades of the seventeenth century and the first few decades of the eighteenth, the tsarist government waged an open and loudly heralded campaign to win over and assimilate the Ukrainian ruling elite (military, religious, and social). Ukrainians who went over to Moscow became members of the Muscovite service elite. In this way Russia slowly absorbed the culture and world view of the Ukrainian elites, which had been shaped by the intellectual atmosphere of Kiev. To what degree this influx of new and alien elements into the ranks of the Muscovite (and later the imperial) service class played a part in the transformation of Russian political culture in the eighteenth century is a question that has yet to be studied in detail. One thing is certain: the Ukrainians who became servants of Moscow brought with them Western notions of politics and administration and thus laid the groundwork for the changes undertaken by Peter the Great. Meanwhile, the men and ideas imported from the Ukraine weakened and undermined Moscow's traditional political culture by destroying the spiritual and moral consensus on which it was based. Muscovite civilization in the last few decades of the seventeenth century began to show signs of Western influence, such as the so-called Moscow baroque style, which is related to Polish baroque and which was largely a product of Ukrainian influences, transmitted to Moscow by members of the religious and temporal elites who came from the Ukraine. What was most important of all, finally, was that the annexation of the Ukraine and the intellectual influence it exercised turned Muscovy away from the East and directed its attention toward the West. Moscow found itself increasingly involved in diplomatic and military conflicts centering on Poland and the regions to the west of the Black Sea (Moldavia and Walachia or the "Balkan slopes"). This political reorientation coincided with the renewal of efforts to drive the Ottoman Turks out of Europe following their defeat at the gates of Vienna in 1683 and also coincided with the decline of eastern influence in technology and the arts.

The combined effect of the *raskol*, of social and economic conflict, and of cultural importations from the West, mainly by way of Kiev, was to induce the Muscovite religious and temporal elites (especially the court and service nobility) to abandon the old Muscovite traditions step by step, with each stage following very quickly on the preceding one. In the sixteenth century the high service nobility had looked to the East as an example in matters of armament, luxury articles, dress, and even such customs as the *terem*.[13] But in the seventeenth century, and particularly after 1650, leading figures in the Kremlin looked to the West and above all to Poland for their inspiration. The vogue for things Polish not only led Russian nobles to dress like their Polish counterparts, learn their language, and take up certain of their tastes and amusements (most notably the theater) but also fostered interest in what Poles were thinking and writing about. This interest was not limited to *belles-lettres* narrowly construed but extended to journalism and political tracts. Now and then we notice signs of curiosity about "political freedom" and even a desire to emulate such Polish forms of corporate organization as the *szlachta*. It was, quite naturally, the Ukrainian elite that was most attracted by these fashions and most influenced by

13. *Terem:* the residence of the wives and daughters of the tsar and the boyars, where men were forbidden to enter.

Western borrowings. But Moscow was subject to a sort of secondary influence that threatened to alter the traditional relationship between the tsar and his service nobility. The resulting latent tensions came to the surface in the crises over the succession to the throne that followed the death of Tsar Alexis.

The clergy was subject to influences from two different sources—influences that varied in range, power, and chronology. With respect to church ritual and administration, first of all, the Russian clergy moved away from the neo-Byzantine and proto-Renaissance models which had guided it in the second half of the fifteenth and the early part of the sixteenth century and which had left their mark on Muscovite religious and spiritual life. This was accompanied by increasing ritualism and rigid formalism, enforced by a centralized, hierarchical administration wholly subordinate to the needs of the temporal authorities. With respect to intellectual matters, on the other hand, the Russian Church fell more and more under the sway of European neoscholasticism, thanks to the efforts of the Kievan schools of theology. Ties between the Russian Church and the metropolis of Kiev (theoretically under the jurisdiction of Constantinople but in fact autonomous) preceded Moscow's gaining political control over the Kievan region, and Kiev's academic and ecclesiastical influence had long been transmitted to Russia, primarily by way of the city's Slavo-Latin Academy. The annexation of the Ukraine and, with it, of Kiev in 1667 only added to Kiev's importance as a source of intellectual and ideological influence and gave new importance to Polish and central European influences on the one hand and to Orthodox influences stemming from Mount Athos and Constantinople on the other hand (all transmitted through Kiev). With the subsequent decline of Muscovite culture, the waning of Moscow's sense of internal insecurity owing to the Time of Troubles and the religious and moral turmoil associated with the *raskol*, Kiev became the focus of intellectual revival. What Kiev offered

Moscow was not merely an Orthodoxy brought up to date by a blending of the influence of Mount Athos and contemporary Greek practice, but also a judicious fortification of its ideological and ecclesiastical arsenal with new Western ideas that could be used to combat the Catholic Counterreformation supported by the Wasa dynasty in Poland and by the Catholic magnates and high clergy in the Ukraine and eastern Poland.

These Western ideas were translated into forms of logic and rhetoric based on the neoscholastic philosophy then taught in Polish and Roman Catholic schools of theology as well as in German universities. We still know very little about how these ideas were transmitted, nor can we fully gauge their character or date their arrival in Russia with any precision. Merely listing a few of the adademic centers in which we find Russian- and Ukrainian-born students of theology, however, will help to give some idea of the nature of Western influences absorbed: the Basileum in Rome, the University of Padua, the faculties of theology and philosophy in Germany (Catholic as well as Protestant). Thus, indirectly and unwittingly, the new generation of Russian clerical scholars was laying the groundwork for the introduction of philosophical rationalism, the logic of Port-Royal, scientific knowledge, and new philosophical ideas (i.e., natural law). This intellectual armament would later aid in the triumph of Western administrative, political, and economic methods under Peter the Great.

The intellectual, moral, and political innovations we have been discussing were almost exclusively confined to the Moscow elites, the court entourage, and the high political authorities in the Kremlin. The rest of the populace (including much of the traditional and provincial service elites) felt none of their influence. Thus a gulf began to form—a gulf destined to widen rapidly—between the popular world view, circumscribed by the traditional culture, and the constantly broadening world view of the Kremlin elite. It is of course true that there always was a gulf between the elite and the populace (notwithstanding the slavophile myth to the contrary regarding Muscovy in the period before Peter the Great). Nevertheless, if we leave aside a few exceptions (such as the orientalism of the Moscow court in the sixteenth and first half of the seventeenth century), we can say that the differences between elite and popular culture were mainly of a quantitative order: in a deep sense elite and populace shared the same culture, rooted in an Orthodoxy accepted by all. It was this deep unity that was disrupted in the last few decades of the seventeenth century. The Muscovite elite learned to speak a new language, a language that drew its inspiration and substance from contemporary Western civilization. At the same time it acquired a new civilization whose strength grew by leaps and bounds, sustained by intellectual elites which looked forward to a transformation of the material world that would liberate the creative powers of the individual. In short, this was a civilization that no longer feared novelty and even sought it out, a civilization that rejected the immobility of traditional society and accordingly attempted either to eradicate tradition or bend it to its will. To the extent that the Moscow elites were imbued with the leading ideas of Western civilization in this period, those ideas had revolutionary impact, by virtue of their radical antagonism to popular traditions, to a degree unknown in central and western Europe. As a result, elite and populace ceased to speak a common language and this new factor must be added to the various conflicts and identity crises discussed above. Taken together, all of these things led to the collapse of Muscovite political culture and paved the way for Peter the Great's "revolution."

To sum up this discussion, we may say that, in the second half of the seventeenth century, owing to innovations of a material as well as spiritual and intellectual nature, Moscow suffered a cultural crisis. The populace responded by clinging stubbornly to static traditional forms, cutting itself off from all outside influences and innovations, while the elites ex-

perienced a fundamental reorientation of their mental outlook and social and cultural patterns. This cast doubt on the
traditional norms of Muscovite political life, and a series of
crises of succession threatened the legitimacy of tsarist rule
and of the Kremlin "establishment." The decline of traditional norms and practices paved the way for the acceptance
of new ideas and methods from central and western Europe.
Systematic and powerful, these new ideas were suitable for
export and capable of being adapted to the conditions prevailing in Muscovite Russia when Peter I assumed personal
power early in the 1690s. The coincidence of the decline or
collapse of traditional tsarist culture with the availability in
Europe of a systematic set of political ideas and social practices set the stage for Peter's "revolution," which brought
Russia into the concert of "modern" European powers.

The West European Model

By the end of the seventeenth century the states of western and central Europe all shared a fairly homogeneous system of administrative practices and political (as well as social and economic) ideas, which can be subsumed under the
concepts of "cameralism" and "the well-ordered police state."
Derived from practices dating back to the sixteenth century,
this "system" was molded by seventeenth-century philosophy and science and their new views of man and nature. The
general outlines of the system are well known and can be
found in most political and economic histories of modern
Europe. Still, it may not be out of place here to discuss certain features of the system that are generally ignored, particularly since these were the features whose introduction led
to nothing less than a political revolution in the West, a revolution of which today's world is the direct heir (using the
word "revolution" here in a broad sense, as in "industrial
revolution," to refer to the long-term effects of changes whose
pace and scope varied from one country to another).

What, then, was novel and revolutionary about the notion of the well-ordered police state, and the cameralist practices associated with it, before that notion was transformed by *philosophes*, physiocrats, and enlightened absolutists into an ideology of progress in the second half of the eighteenth century? Convinced as I am of the truth of Goethe's aphorism *"Es ist der Geist der sich den Körper baut,"* it seems to me that we must look to the intellectual and spiritual history of western Europe in the sixteenth and seventeenth centuries for the sources of the cameralist system. The broadening of humanity's intellectual horizons in the sixteenth century spelled an end to the "medieval" conception of a closed and finite universe. To the men of the seventeenth century, persuaded by recent scientific discoveries that the new world view that had begun to take shape in the previous century was indeed the true one, the world seemed boundless and infinite. The best minds immediately drew the practical conclusion that the potential of available resources was also limitless, at least in comparison with what the men of the Middle Ages had imagined.

If, moreover, men took the trouble to study nature closely and discover its laws, that potential could be determined and harnessed. Human reason could, by reflecting on observations of nature, determine the fundamental laws governing the natural world. Then the limitless resources of the boundless universe might not merely be measured but explored and exploited for the benefit of mankind. Man had only to bend the environment to his will and turn his productive prowess to the harnessing of nature. Thus, not reason alone but also human creative will and energy are the prime movers in organizing society and determining policy.[14] Combined, reason

14. Note, in this connection, the influence of neo-Stoicism, which underwent a dramatic renaissance in France and the Low Countries at the end of the sixteenth and beginning of the seventeenth century. From there it spread to the German-speaking countries, especially Prussia. See L. Zanta, *La Renaissance du stoïcisme au XVIe siècle* (Paris, 1914); G. Abel, *Stoizismus und frühe Neuzeit: Zur Entstehungsgeschichte modernen Denkens im Felde von Ethik und Politik* (Berlin: De Gruyter, 1978); and the articles of Gerhard Oestreich collected in the volume *Geist*

and will give man the strength to see into the future: the future becomes the projection of the present according to immutable laws that can be discovered by empirical science. If the future can be predicted, man can organize his present efforts to prepare for it. He can shape tomorrow's social world to replace today's social reality. As Ilya Prigogine and Friedrich von Hayek have shown by studying the history of the natural and social sciences, and as Michel Tournier has discovered through imagination and literary intuition, the fundamental trait of modern man is his determination to organize society rationally for the purpose of achieving ever greater productivity. Once this idea has taken hold of man's behavior and thinking, the individual—made ready to assume his responsibilities by the Protestant Reformation and individualistic philosophy—becomes the agent of a ceaseless dynamic of expansion and development: there is no end to the growth of knowledge and to the creativity of production, which brings to mankind one new benefit after another, improving his material well-being and intensifying his spiritual life. Convinced that this was the case, late-eighteenth-century intellectuals and men of action came to see progress as a positive value and an end in itself; in other words, they came to believe in an ideology of progress.

So much for the intellectual and philosophical background. What about the political applications of these ideas? Government's first task was to discover the untapped potential of spiritual, human, and material resources that society had to offer, in order to enhance the wealth of the state and contribute to the prosperity and well-being of society as a whole. The eighteenth century added a further goal: to en-

und Gestalt des frühmodernen Staates: Ausgewählte Aufsätze (Berlin: Duncker and Humblot, 1969), and, by the same author, "Calvinismus, Neustoizismus, und Preussentum," Jahrbuch für die Geschichte Mittel- und Ostdeutschlands (1956) 5:157–81, and "Die Bedeutung des niederländischen Späthumanismus für Brandenburg-Preussen," Humanismus und Naturrecht in Berlin-Brandenburg (Berlin: De Gruyter, 1979), pp. 16–27.

hance the happiness of society and of its individual members.

Now, to achieve these goals, the first obstacle to overcome was the traditional notion that resources are limited, parcelled out once and for all at Creation. In this view, scarcity is inevitable, so that it makes sense to attend to the needs of the moment and let the future take care of itself. Before change could occur, people had to be reeducated and disciplined and social structures had to be created in order to harness individuals to regular productive labor and induce them to invest with an eye to future returns. The government's role was therefore to organize social activity with a "high time horizon,"[15] so that the fruits of current activities could be harvested later on. This necessitated policies aimed at breaking down the traditional peasant mentality, with its "take life one day at a time" attitude and its squandering of resources in public and private consumption.

The investment of surplus resources in the hope of increased future profits can be envisaged only if reasonably reliable predictions of the future can be made on the basis of known "laws" and trends. Accordingly, government's second task was to eradicate prejudices and superstitions (usually of religious origin) that might stand in the way of attempts to explain the universe rationally and to influence the course of events. By the early seventeenth century modern science had overcome the tendency to believe in magical explanations and miracles, and this proved to be an essential prerequisite to the adoption of administrative methods aimed at efficiently organizing social action so as to capitalize upon available resources.[16]

Government, together with the political elite, therefore had

15. See Alexander Gerschenkron, "Time Horizon in Balzac and Others," *Proceedings of the American Philosophical Society* (April 1978) 122(2).

16. See R. Lenoble, *Mersenne, ou la naissance du mécanisme*, 2d. ed. (Paris: Vrin, 1971); Charles Webster, *The Great Instauration: Science, Medicine, and Reform. 1626–1660* (London: Duckworth, 1975).

a decisive role to play: to reeducate the populace and to organized new social institutions. Active government participation in the renovation of society was the great political innovation of the seventeenth century (for which the groundwork had been laid in the previous century). As the French jurist Maurice Hauriou has rightly noted, "administration is the foundation of society," where "society" is defined as a coherent structure of institutions and groups organized with a view to effective long-term action. It is not, however, entirely accurate to say that the new role of administration was embodied primarily in centralized rule by the sovereign and his advisers. It is more correct to speak of an extension of the state's role as guide and organizer of public life. Like God, the state (or the sovereign) served only to give an initial impetus to the machinery that actually organized society and developed potentially available resources. It is quite clear that no state (in the sense of central administrative apparatus) in the seventeenth century had the technical or material resources to organize and govern society on its own. The political elite, the sovereign's traditional advisers, could define administrative objectives and offer practical guidance, but they usually lacked the means to translate their ideas effectively into practice. The state was therefore forced to rely on the services of various social groups, classes, "estates," and "orders"—or, to borrow a phrase, it was forced to rely on the "intermediary bodies" with which the *ancien régime* in Europe abounded on account of its "feudal" origins. Seventeenth-century governments also extended their reach by involving new groups in the work of the central bureaucracy—in part by coopting members of the intermediary bodies as *officiers* (to use the terminology then current in France), in part by creating new categories of functionaries or *commissaires* to staff schools and government bureaus.[17] These

17. For France see, for example, Roland Mousnier, *Les Institutions de la France sous la monarchie absolue 1598–1789* (Paris: Presses Universitaires de France, 1974), 2 vols. [Published in English as *The Institutions of France Under the Absolute Mon-*

new officials were recruited primarily among the privileged classes (as was quite natural, in view of the social and educational realities of the time), but on an individual basis, in order to weaken any allegiance these newly recruited bureaucrats might feel toward the social class into which they had been born.

It is worth pointing out that the well-ordered police state was most successful where the government was able to harmonize the activities of a centralized bureaucracy with the work of local institutions. This technique worked best in countries of moderate size, where the bureaucracy was able to extend its control down to the village level and local bodies found it to their advantage to collaborate with the central government in joint exploitation of scarce resources. The weakened position of the privileged "orders" after the Wars of Religion and the Thirty Years' War was of major importance in permitting the new type of political culture to spread and ultimately to triumph. In the great European countries, however, particularly those least shaken by the crises of the sixteenth and seventeenth centuries (such as France and to some extent Spain, to say nothing of England, which was really a special case), highly complex social structures dominated by various special interests survived, thus preventing effective use of *dirigiste* policies—despite the joint efforts of Louis XIV and Colbert in France, for example.

It is worth pausing a moment to draw an explicit parallel between the cameralist administrative practices of the well-ordered police state and the modern science that grew out of the work of Galileo, Descartes, and Newton. Both are systems of action based on principles derived from abstract reasoning and systematic empirical observation. Both systems depend on "laws"—that is, on hypothetical regularities in observable phenomena—on the basis of which one can either

archy by the University of Chicago Press; volume 1, translated by Brian Pearce, was published in 1980; volume 2, translated by the translator of the present work, will appear in 1983—trans.]

predict what will happen under specified initial conditions or, alternatively, arrange the initial conditions so as to produce specified results, making use, when necessary, of the principle of reversibility, that is, of the possibility of correcting the initial conditions and repeating the experiment until the desired result is obtained. Finally, both are internally consistent systems that constantly develop under the impetus of their own intrinsic dynamic. In fact, constant change is a consequence of the requirement of internal consistency, which in turn requires each system to develop a language of its own. Natural science found the language it needed in mathematics. Like natural science, "administrative science" also needed a language to express the way in which individuals in society relate to one another and to the material world on which they act. Cameralists accordingly tried to develop such a language. But, since human and social phenomena cannot be described in the exact terms used to describe physical phenomena, the language the cameralists developed was nothing but a parody of the mathematical formulas of natural science. This language was that of law, systematically embodied in legal codes. Whether actually completed or merely conceived as projects, these legal codes set themselves the task of stating the relations between individuals and objects in a consistent and methodical fashion. The coherent, stable relations defined by the codes could in turn, with suitable interpretation, be applied to many different situations and, it was thought, adapt dynamically to the needs of a developing society. In other words, law ceased to describe the qualitative relations between persons, based on their membership of a particular "estate" or "order." The new law codes transformed the law into a consistent, uniform framework for interpreting individual relations in a quantitative manner and established rules and procedures for the regular and mechanical application of the statutes.

Taken together, the phenomena we have been describing amount to nothing less than a revolution in the political culture of Europe. No longer is the sovereign merely a judge or ultimate arbiter, a passive instrument for the defense and preservation of society. He has become the active proponent of a deliberate, methodical policy, the purpose of which is to maximize his country's productive potential, increase its wealth and power, and promote its material well-being. Since there is in principle no limit to such an objective, the dynamic impulse, once unleashed, remains an intrinsic element of the system and becomes an end in itself. Once this happens, of course, the character and image of the sovereign must change accordingly. Regardless of whether the sovereign power is an individual or, as in Holland or the city-states, a collectivity, it must act as a dynamic leader ready to take the initiative and establish active policy objectives. The "gods in uniform"[18] did not merely symbolize the secularization of sovereignty but played the combined role of captain, helmsman, and navigator. The sovereign power imposed system and method on the practices of the well-ordered state, thanks to which the new type of government could be exported from one country to another. Energetic and efficient, sovereign states became imperialistic in both senses of the word: they assumed control over all areas of public life (and by the end of the eighteenth century over private life as well), and they annexed new territories. Such was the nature of the commodity that Peter the Great imported from Central and Western Europe to replace the dying culture of Muscovy.

The Receptiveness of Muscovite Society

The reader may at this point be wondering to what extent Muscovite society was ready to welcome and assimilate this new culture. Didn't all these foreign innovations run counter

---

18. Ernst H. Kantorowicz, "Gods in Uniform," *Selected Studies* (New York: Augustin, 1965), pp. 7–24.

to native ideas, values, and practices? For the majority this was certainly the case, and most Russians found themselves increasingly isolated within the walls of their native culture and shut out of public life. But there were also groups, particularly within the energetic and dynamic social elites where the ground had been thoroughly prepared, that proved ready to accommodate the new. Remember the dissemination of new ideas by the Kiev Academy and its graduates, who brought neoscholastic logic and rhetoric to their colleagues at the Greek–Latin–Slavic Academy and other Moscow institutions. These men were widely imitated by the collaborators of Feofan Prokopovitch and Stefan Iavorski, who introduced western political literature, both in the original and in translation, to Moscow. Foreigners residing in Moscow either temporarily or permanently also played an important role in bringing western political ideas and administrative methods to the Russian capital. Having studied cameralist writings in the universities and academies of Protestant northern Europe, where they observed cameralism in practice before coming to Russia, these men were intimately familiar with the new political culture.[19] Under Peter the Great foreigners played a still greater role in the Russian government, which systematically recruited experts trained at the University of Halle (one of the major centers of cameralism).

Russians also acquired familiarity with other political systems while traveling abroad. Before Peter's accession foreign travel was relatively rare. Still, Muscovite diplomats assiduously collected information about cameralist methods. Current research on the *kuranty* or foreign news bulletins, as well as other sources of information about other countries, shows that Moscow, or at any rate the Kremlin elite, was neither totally isolated nor ignorant of what was going on beyond the

---

19. See E. Winter, *Halle als Ausgangspunkt der deutschen Russlandkunde im 18.Jahrhundert* (East Berlin: Akademie Verlag, 1953); for a bibliography, see Marc Raeff, "Les Slaves, les Allemands et les lumières," *Revue canadienne d'études slaves* (1967) 1(4):521–51.

empire's borders. In Peter's day, of course, it is well known that young Russians were specially selected to go abroad and study not only military science and navigation but also commerce and administration. Their curiosity and attentiveness is illustrated by Fedor Saltykov's *Propozitsii*, for example. The emperor instructed his diplomats to acquire legal and administrative documents and send them back to Russia. Finally, the war with Sweden also helped to spread cameralist ideas and practices. The war was a lengthy one, with many prisoners taken on both sides, which made for prolonged and intensive contacts between the two countries. Swedish prisoners were frequently pressed into service as translators and technical advisers, while certain Russian prisoners in Sweden (like Prince Trubetskoy) made use of their captivity to study Swedish administrative practices and customs in detail. Elsewhere, tsarist diplomats worked diligently to learn as much as they could about Russia's most powerful and implacable enemy. As a recent study of Peter the Great's reforms has shown, all this information was systematically collated and put to use by the tsar and his advisers when it came time to reorganize the imperial institutions.[20]

To sum up, Moscow in the late seventeenth century was ready to accept and to copy the new cameralist political culture that came to it from Western and Central Europe. The ground was prepared in part by the education of the elites, in part by the disintegration of Russia's own culture in the second half of the seventeenth century. The lesson of this collapse was not lost on Peter the Great, who set out to accomplish a radical transformation of his country's government and political institutions based on the West European model.

---

20. Claes Peterson, *Peter the Great's Administrative and Judiciary Reforms. Swedish Antecedents and the Process of Reception* (Stockholm: A.–B. Nordiska Bokhandeln, 1979).

2
PETER THE GREAT'S REVOLUTION

W HEN Peter I assumed personal power in 1694, the need to reform, indeed to reshape, the Muscovite polity happily coincided with the availability of imported western "tools" for carrying out the needed transformation. Peter's personality must also be mentioned: his creative energy (drive or *Tatkraft*) and his determination to breathe into Russian society a vitality comparable to that of the West strongly marked *his* revolution. Like a force of nature, he was able to overcome every obstacle that stood between him and his objectives. Avid for knowledge and always on the lookout for whatever was new, he imparted to his reform program his own intensity and feverish energy. Yet his loudly proclaimed desire for change and his determination to achieve tangible results whatever the cost and in spite of stubborn resistance yielded many superficial changes and reforms that hung suspended in midair and eventually proved to be ephemeral; his helterskelter activity concealed a lack of rigor. The effect of Peter the Great's reign was to tear Russian society apart, leaving behind a legacy of uncertainty and insecurity that ultimately led to an identity crisis among the Russian elite.

More positively, however, Peter's personality and energetic reform program attracted precisely those members of the elite (as well as some more modest subjects) who were hungry for action and eager to use their energies to enhance their country's, wealth and power, as well as their own. Peter found plenty of willing collaborators in his work, which shows that in late-seventeenth-century Russia many people—groups as well as individuals—were eager to throw off the bonds of traditional Muscovite culture, with its static and isolationist outlook. Peter's misfortune, as we shall discover, was his failure to involve large numbers of common people in his efforts—partly because he could not, partly because he would not do so. To mention just one example, the Old Believers, many of whom were determined, tireless, energetic men, eager for action, rejected the very foundations of the Petrine state.

After returning from his first trip abroad in 1698, Peter deliberately set out to transform public life in Russia and to reorganize the administrative apparatus of his government. He shrewdly adopted cameralist theory and practice to give his policies system and coherence. At the same time a fundamental pragmatism governed the choice of means and opportunity; Peter never hesitated to abandon failed experiments in favor of new solutions. The long war with Sweden naturally imposed certain priorities and drained resources that might otherwise have been available for other purposes. But, contrary to the opinion of Kliuchevsky and Miliukov, Peter's policies do not appear to have been dictated solely by the needs of war, a mere series of *ad hoc* measures designed to meet the needs of the moment. Even before 1709–12 (hence before he could have counted on the ultimate victory of Russia over Sweden), Peter pursued a methodical program of reforms based on the model of the well-ordered state, as is shown by documents relating to the preparation of major items of legislation.[1] What is more, it seems highly unlikely that the needs of war, narrowly interpreted, would have required such energetic reforms and such radical innovations. Despite its obsolete army and economic backwardness, Russia had been

1. N. A. Voskresenski, *Zakonodatel'nye akty Petra I*, vol. 1: *Akty o Vysshikh gosudarstvennykh ustanovleniiakh* (Moscow-Leningrad, 1945); Peterson, *Peter the Great's Administrative and Judiciary Reforms.*

successful in a number of lengthy wars against Poland and Sweden in the seventeenth century. The empire's vast human and natural resources (its population far exceeded not only that of Sweden but also that of every other European country except France), together with the military advantages to be derived from its sheer immensity and harsh climate, combined to make ultimate victory by Sweden highly unlikely, at least as long as Russia remained unwilling to accept temporary defeats. Further evidence that this view is correct is provided by the fact that, to build the new capital and undertake needed political and cultural reforms, colossal efforts—colossal in a social as well as an economic sense—were demanded by Peter and made by his subjects while the war was still raging and Russian armies were suffering defeat after defeat.

The success of Peter's program to build a well-ordered state in Russia—a state, that is, that would make optimal use of the country's natural and cultural resources to create a dynamic, progressive society—was due not merely to his own efforts (though he was, beyond all doubt, the *spiritus rector*) but also to the efforts of others, individuals and groups, who eventually formed the new ruling and cultural elite of Russia. Peter's program attracted all who shared a thirst for action and a desire to raise their social status and acquire new wealth—the ambitious as well as the greedy. By assisting the reforming tsar they helped to create a modern Russian culture and a way of life incorporating western values: hunger for knowledge, intellectual and artistic curiosity, and a rational, constructive spirit. Thus a cultivated elite began to take shape around modern European literature, music, art, and thought. In the long run this was perhaps the most important and innovative of Peter the Great's achievements.

The tsar's collaborators included not only "new" men (in a social and cultural sense) but also representatives of traditional social groups and strata. Among them we find many members of the Muscovite "aristocratic" elite—*boyar* fami-

lies—such as the Sheremetevs, the Golitsyns, and the Ro-
madanovskys, as well as many service nobles, such as Ne-
pluyev, Krekshin, Tatishchev, and Saltykov. An important,
though as yet little studied, role was also played by the clerks
(diaki) of the Moscow chanceries *(prikazy)* and above all by
the sons of these men, like Alexis Makarov, Peter's secretary. First- and second-generation descendants of foreign im-
migrants also contributed much to the success of Peter's reign,
particularly in certain specific areas of public life: among these
were Shafirov, Iaguzhinski, Gordon, Bruce, Lefort, Fick, and
Ostermann. All of this is well known. Not to be forgotten,
however, are the many individuals of more humble extrac-
tion who also played a part, though their names have not been
preserved in any document. Peter's projects required enormous amounts of material: the army needed food, clothing,
and munitions; the civilian administration needed paper, ink,
transportation, printing services, and a postal service. From
published documents we know that many of the suppliers of
these necessary services were humble folk who either worked
under contract or farmed the taxes they collected. Military
provisioners and other state suppliers signed contracts involving thousands of rubles, huge amounts for the period. We
know some of their names: sometimes because they were involved in new and remarkable activities (like the Demidovs),
sometimes because they also took part in the cultural life and
"ideological propaganda" of Peter's reign (like T. Pososhkov).
But the documents also refer to many nameless suppliers of
food, equipment, and other goods, sometimes in very large
quantities; these men also played an active role in the transformation of Russian life. Some of them certainly rose to the
upper strata of social and political life, while others remained in the shadows. While the whole area is one that calls
for further research, the main features of the changes in progress are clear.

What about local governing bodies and institutions, the
"intermediary bodies" which were so important to Montes-

quieu and so useful in the administration of European states? As we noted earlier, without the cooperation (whether voluntary or coerced) of these various corporations and "orders" many a sovereign would have found it difficult to impose discipline on his people or achieve the needed investment in the future. But Muscovy, as we have seen, had relatively few such intermediary bodies to call upon. At the local level, particularly among the Old Believers, there were organized groups that exhibited a certain *esprit de corps* and played a role in settling minor disputes and organizing daily activities. Furthermore, during the second half of the seventeenth century, at least in the north, peasants and minor service nobles apparently did organize corporations of some sort to discharge their obligations to the state and maintain order at the local level. According to H.-J. Torke, moreover, some urban groups took tentative steps toward corporate organization.[2] Finally, the Cossacks and *streltsy* were organized into autonomous communities, as were some alien populations in frontier areas. But even if we assume that these various associations and institutions still existed in the late seventeenth and early eighteenth century, it would have been quite impossible to use them for the purpose of introducing cameralist methods of government. Indeed, by the end of the century these local allegiances served an essentially defensive purpose: to protect traditional customs, patterns of thinking, and ways of life against the new ideals of productivity and optimal utilization of resources that were the essence of the new political culture.

Muscovy's traditional institutionalized groups were too passive and backward to adapt to the new culture. What is more, their resistance to change and the nature of their organization, especially in the case of the Cossacks and, to a

2. Torke, *Die staatsbedingte Gesellschaft.* See also P. Bushkovitch, *The Merchants of Moscow, 1580–1650* (Cambridge, England: Cambridge University Press, 1980); J. Michael Hittle, *The Service City. State and Townsmen in Russia. 1600–1800* (Cambridge, Mass.: Harvard University Press, 1979).

lesser degree, in the case of the *streltsy* as well, posed a danger to the state so great that Peter's government was reluctant to make use of them. Peter's distrust and hatred of the *streltsy* are well known: he saw them as powerful allies of the regent Sophia and as a threat to his power. Their rebellion while he was traveling abroad gave him the opportunity to get rid of them once and for all. The Cossacks, for their part, had been instigators and leaders of every popular uprising, including those of Bulavin and at Astrakhan, which were put down brutally with large numbers of troops. Finally, such "corporatist" loyalties as developed toward the end of the century among peasants and in the cities involved mainly Old Believers, who refused even to acknowledge the legitimacy of the post-Nikonian government in Moscow. Cruelly persecuted because of their resistance to the new state, the Old Believers, whose ranks included a significant minority of the peasant and artisan populations led by a fraction of the monks and parish clergy, could not be enlisted in or even associated with the work of modernization undertaken by Peter's regime. Furthermore, legally and socially, these embryonic corporative institutions were an odd assortment indeed, and they would have had to undergo considerable development before they could have hoped to play an active political role in late-seventeenth-century Russia. They lacked sufficient time to develop into true intermediary bodies. The same factors that brought about the collapse of Muscovite political culture also led to the virtual disappearance of autonomous local organizations.

Peter's government therefore had an easy time delivering the final blow. This took the form of a strict reimposition of state service obligations, which were manipulated in such a way as to break down local and familial bonds of allegiance. Recruits to state service were no longer summoned by regional corps, in which kinship ties could be maintained and men could serve under the command of their own ancestors. Instead, recruits from the provinces were called individually, reassigned, and transferred at the discretion of the central administration, and required to remain permanently on duty. Similarly, ties of allegiance among peasants and townsmen, weak to begin with, were completely eradicated by the heavy burden of taxes and payments in kind as well as by conscription into a modernized army, whose soldiers were forced to travel great distances to remote garrisons and work sites (as for the building of the Ladoga Canal or the new capital on the Gulf of Finland).

Under Peter, state service was the only avenue of social advancement. Admission into the service class constituted a social and material advantage as well as a psychological boon, since only members of the state service enjoyed even a modicum of security and legal protection for their property and persons. Wealth in itself counted for little compared with service, and a man's social background was relatively insignificant compared with his position and opportunities for advancement within the privileged service class. The service criterion was institutionalized as the basis of the social structure with the introduction of the Table of Ranks in 1722. With few exceptions, and despite certain internal ambiguities, the Table of Ranks established the framework of social and legal relations in imperial Russia from the time it was introduced until the latter part of the nineteenth century. As a result, the state and the sovereign gained absolute control over the social hierarchy and hence over the members of the service class, the elite of imperial society. Though the meaning of the Table was often bent and twisted over the years, it remained in force because it gave the sovereign ultimate effective control over the elite while allowing a certain flexibility in the social structure which made it possible for active and energetic individuals who identified wholeheartedly with the values and objectives of the well-ordered state to gain access to the economic, political, and cultural elite of the nation.

This being the case, the chief tool of Peter the Great and

his collaborators for achieving their objectives was to make use of the tradition of state service. Specifically, this meant setting up "bureaucratic" institutions, mainly centralized, since the necessary personnel were not available locally. The administration's main function was to take the lead in the transformation of Russia and to lay down specific social goals. As in other European countries at the time, the central administrative institutions, above all the military, took an active part in carrying out the Europeanization policies of Peter and his successors. The task of the imperial government was first and foremost to recruit (and retain) state servants. In the absence of intermediary bodies it was the service class that became the ruling elite and agent of social change.

At the beginning of the eighteenth century the number of people qualified to assume administrative responsibilities was small relative to the vastness of the territory, the number of inhabitants, and the magnitude of the task. Let us add at once, moreover, that the available pool of qualified personnel remained limited and inadequate down to the end of the imperial regime. At every level of the hierarchy the state service needed people possessing a minimum of education and experience. The peasantry, by far the largest social class in Russia, did not measure up (and would not have measured up even if the vast majority of peasants had not been disqualified by serfdom). In this respect Russia was no exception, for nowhere in Europe was the peasantry prepared to supply needed administrative personnel. Furthermore, Russia, unlike England, France, and to some extent Germany, possessed no village "notables" or the like who might have been tapped as local administrators and economic and cultural leaders.[3] The army was the peasant's only avenue of access to the elite. Few traveled the whole way themselves, but moved only a few steps closer, paving the way in turn for sons

---

3. Just compare the situation in Russia with the descriptions of village notables in the works of Restif de La Bretonne or in Jung-Stilling's autobiography.

and grandsons. Military service was, in practical terms, life-long (25–30 years in theory) and freed the peasant conscript from all obligations to his lord (or to the state in the case of state peasants). Children born to conscripts after recruitment were considered to be free men, and the state tried to give them some education as preparation for productive work or low-level jobs in the administration. Thus the children or grandchildren of a conscripted serf could become officers, acquire nobility, and join the ruling elite. Rare as such cases were, there were enough of them to constitute a subclass of the population and to foster the myth of a service nobility open to talent drawn from the lower strata of the populace.[4]

By contrast, for nobles, state service became not just compulsory but permanent, from the time a man was fifteen until he became incapacitated. Peter standardized personnel policies in the service to the point that anyone could be sent anywhere to fill any job at the discretion of the central authorities. Service lists and personnel files containing records of nominations, transfers, promotions, pay rates, and disciplinary measures were kept up to date by the Senate Department of the Herald's Chancery, which was directly supervised by the tsar. The man in service, whether noble or commoner, military or civilian (the boundary between the two was quite vague in the eighteenth century), was in fact nothing more than a pawn of the administration, who could be moved about at will and assigned any task, in keeping with the needs of the moment and without regard to the man's personal preferences, native region, or family ties. In addition, a reasonably broad cultural background was expected of the service noble, and acquiring this was an additional burden on young nobles. Thus service obligations imposed a new discipline—education, lifelong service, and standardized personnel policies—which in turn provoked the opposition of

4. See Elise Kimerling's study of soldiers' children, in *Forschungen zur Osteuropäischen Geschichte*, vol. 30 (Berlin, 1982).

which so much has been made in the historical literature. But once the new system had taken hold (which, it is worth stressing, took no more than one or two generations), it shaped the working life and culture of the ruling elite and even established the standards that in large part determined admission to that elite. The nature of state service and its attendant cultural requirements ultimately determined the ethos and social function of the Russian imperial elite.

For our purposes the most important point to note is that the traditional military service nobility was transformed into an officialdom, the principal instrument of the well-ordered state. Nobles became functionaries responsible for carrying out tasks assigned by the state or its ruler and intended to ensure optimal exploitation of all available resources. The conduct of public affairs was governed by general rules covering every conceivable administrative requirement and contingency. The new "bureaucracy" created its own language, which was couched in such general terms as "needs of state" and "state interests" even when what was meant was really the personal interests of the sovereign.

The General Regulations of 1720

On February 28, 1720, Peter the Great published his General Regulations, which from then on constituted the bible of the imperial bureaucracy. Though directly modeled on the Swedish *Cantselie Ordnung* of 1661, the General Regulations embodied the administrative precepts and notions of modern politics that had been elaborated by cameralist theorists and German rulers since the first half of the seventeenth century. The regulations guided Russian bureaucratic practice and in so doing established a new concept of the relationship between state and people. Nine "administrative colleges" were set up to replace the numerous *prikazy*, only to be supplanted themselves at the beginning of the ninetenth century by ministries. Thus the new administration was organized on functional rather than geographic or historical lines (as the *prikazy* and other Muscovite institutions had been). The purview and jurisdiction of each college was more sharply defined than before, and private influence over administrative activities was eliminated, at least in theory. The General Regulations did not prevent one man from holding a number of different posts, but this was not supposed to be allowed to blur jurisdictional boundaries, as had often occurred in administrations before Peter I. A distinction was to be made between the institution and the individuals who staffed it: the functions of the institution were supposed to continue even in the absence of top officials. Administrative business was to be transacted only in government offices: nothing was to be decided elsewhere, particularly not by a single official, even if he happened to be the minister in charge. Last but not least, a literal and figurative barrier was erected between government and governed. The effect of all these regulations was to emphasize the generalized and abstract character of government and to enhance the role of the government as the planner and guide of society's productive activities, a role that legitimated and justified the exercise of sovereign power.

In addition, the new system established by the General Regulations was designed first to weaken and ultimately to eliminate the personal allegiances and connections that had formed the basis of political life in the Muscovite regime before Peter. In practice, however, it proved impossible to rid the Russian administration of personalized authority and personal influence. It is not difficult to explain why: the government recruited its officials from a necessarily limited circle, given the educational requirements for holding office and the disqualification of most of the population. Family ties and personal allegiances within the service nobility therefore continued to play a major role. Families and clans that had been prominent in Muscovite politics before Peter continued to supply the majority of top administrators and officers throughout the eighteenth century (and even into the nineteenth century, if allowance is made for marriages and adoptions). Despite efforts to "rationalize" recruitment and promotion on the basis of experience and merit, nepotism continued in large part to govern nominations to key posts.[5]

In addition to family ties, personal contacts with influential figures launched a number of important careers. Count Rumiantsev's chancery in the Ukraine, for example, produced many of the top civil servants of Catherine II's reign.[6] Potemkin's entourage (and earlier the entourages of the Shuvalovs and the Orlovs) played a similar role. This is hardly surprising, since there was no other way to recruit qualified officials in the eighteenth century. Still, the Table of Ranks did make it possible not only to increase the number of candidates but also to consolidate personal gains, while at the same time providing opportunities for advancement to ambitious newcomers. The system was obviously riddled with ambiguities: the Table of Ranks and the General Regulations enabled families that had been eminent in the past to consolidate and improve their status, while opening the door to exceptional *homines novi*, provided they were willing to marry into or be adopted by the established "clans." In eighteenth-century Russia, political life—if the term makes any sense at all—was a ballet of favor and disgrace, a carrousel of cliques, personal connections, and family alliances all whirling around the central figure of the emperor.

The sovereign's role consequently took on new importance. Peter the Great seems to have entertained thoughts of depersonalizing sovereign power and authority. But he did not

5. Brenda Meehan-Waters, "Social and Career Characteristics of the Administrative Elite: 1689–1761," in W. Mc K. Pintner and D. K. Rowney, eds., *Russian Officaldom: The Bureaucratization of Russian Society from the Seventeenth to the Twentieth Century* (Chapel Hill, N.C.: The University of North Carolina Press, 1980), pp. 77–105.

6. J.-P. Le Donne, "Appointments to the Russian Senate, 1762–1796," *Cahiers du monde russe et soviétique*, 1 (1975) 16(1):27–56.

do so, and even if he had tried he would not have succeeded. For it was the tsar's strength of character, his powerful personality, that enabled him to play so well the role he had taken upon himself, to be the instigator and promoter of a European-style modernization of Russia. Yet despite the insignificance of his colorless successors, sovereign authority remained just as personal as it had been in the time of Peter, even when it was exercised in the sovereign's name by favorites and their cliques. In the absence of intermediary bodies and formal government institutions, and given the fluid political situation, the autocratic sovereign (or his personal delegate, his favorite acting in his name) was the only person in a position to settle the disputes that arose between clans, coteries, favorites, and administrative bureaus. In this respect there was continuity between the Muscovite and imperial styles.

By contrast, the religious character of the supreme power was totally transformed. The emperor (or empress) was still the head of the Russian Church, just as the tsars had been. This can be seen particularly clearly in the church administration: the patriarchate was abolished and replaced by the Holy Synod, within which the layman representing the sovereign ultimately came to play the decisive role. The sovereign continued to participate in important religious ceremonies and public rituals, to which he came in person. But the number of such occasions was reduced to a bare minimum, and apart from them the government made few references to religion. The administration ceased to play a religious role, whereas the church was required to take an active part in temporal life. In the place of the most pious tsar we find the sovereign emperor, wearing a European-style military uniform, residing at the western extremity of his empire, and isolated from the spiritual and religious life of his people.

In these circumstances the question of the emperor's legitimacy could not fail to arise. Peter's legitimacy had already been challenged by the Old Believers. New doubts arose in the popular mind in the wake of *coups d'état* that brought to the throne a parade of women and children whose claims to kinship with the previous sovereign were often vague and whose conduct frequently ran counter to traditional religious precepts. Decrees, based on Western models, prohibited individuals and groups from petitioning the emperor directly, thus accentuating the feeling that he had become isolated from his people and raising doubts in some quarters of society as to his legitimacy. To be sure, the question of legitimacy did not arise among the upper classes—the service nobility, and specifically those employed by the administration and the army—precisely because the personalization of ultimate authority ensured that members of these groups would remain in personal contact with the sovereign, either directly at court, to which all service nobles had access, or indirectly through their protectors and relations.

This situation also helps to explain why the Petrine state had such a hard time formulating a code of laws. The technical and material problems, real as they were, were not the principal source of difficulty. The real problem was the need to preserve the integrity of personalized autocratic power. In theory as well as practice, every disputed judgment of the courts was brought before the emperor, who decided as he saw fit. The tsar's power to sit as judge and final arbiter and to decide—whether in the name of the law or by his own lights—any case brought before him by any subject entitled to approach him directly was an essential element of his legitimacy. Having dispensed with the sacred and hieratic underpinnings of legitimacy, absolute power needed to justify itself in other terms. This was the task undertaken by Feofan Prokopovich in the treatise entitled *The Justice Is the Monarch's Will (Pravda voli monarshei)*, which he either wrote himself or had written under his direction by his foreign and Russian subordinates who constituted a sort of office of propaganda and information.

In this treatise Prokopovich gave rational arguments for

absolute obedience to the orders of the sovereign. He cites no empirical grounds for his conclusions, declaring simply that (sovereign) absolute political power was "created by man in the state of nature" (in the Hobbesian sense) when he found himself confronted with the presence of other men. This type of power, we are told, is validated by God's commandments and ratified by the Bible. Biblical and historical examples are then cited, not as rational justification for absolute power but merely as illustrations of its use and of the importance of absolute obedience by those subject to it. To round out these examples he turns to seventeenth-century Western philosophers, jurists, and writers. He also points out that the duty to obey derives from the natural duty of children to obey their parents. Thus, even in this political treatise, widely cited in Russian public law, the sovereign is identified with the father. The emperor's authority is said to be moral and personal, like the authority of a father over his children; the emperor stands in relation to his subjects as the father stands in relation to his children. The function of the sovereign, according to Prokopovich, is not hieratic but pragmatic and material. The sovereign's authority is justified by the protection he offers to his subjects: he makes sure that they provide for their needs of food, shelter, and clothing—purely material needs, it should be noted. If society is secure in its economic activities (in an extended sense), well-being, wealth, and power are assured. Progress in this direction is not only desirable in itself, it is also an index of the degree to which society has risen above the state of nature.

This is not the place to go into detail about the policies of Peter the Great. His reign has been intensively studied, though there is as yet no magisterial biography of Peter comparable to those of Alexander I, Nicholas I, and Catherine II.[7] The first task Peter assigned himself (which became a necessity once

7. See, in particular, recent work by R. Wittram, *Peter I. Czar und Kaiser (Peter der Grosse in seiner Zeit)* (Gottingen: Vandenhoeck und Ruprecht, 1964), 2. vols.; N. Pavlenko, *Petr pervyi* (Moscow: Molodaia Gvardiia, 1975).

he had committed himself to it) was to force Sweden to re-
linquish its conquests along the Baltic (in the region of St.
Petersburg, Livonia, and Estonia) and, secondarily, to secure
the southern borders of the empire by waging war against
Turkey and Persia. In order to wage war he had to recruit soldiers and raise money to finance his armies. Here, Peter did
not depart from tradition but merely followed the example of
his father. Of course the technology of warfare and military
organization had evolved in the meantime, so that Peter's
modernized army required far more money and materiel than
had the army of his father's time. To meet these expenses
Peter was forced to pressure his subjects more systematically
and energetically than the Muscovite tsars had done.

THE TRANSFORMATION OF SOCIETY

The most important step taken by Peter's government,
which had considerable impact on the future of Russia, was
its thorough and methodical effort to establish a modern system of education and to bring European culture and technology, military as well as industrial, to the Russian people. The
government's carefully planned and diligently executed policy was designed to shape a new, technologically advanced
and highly productive society (in the short term, of course,
these initial expectations were not entirely fulfilled). This new
society, based on the exploitation of the material and intellectual wealth of the nation, did not call on the services of
all its citizens but mainly on the ruling elite. The institutes,
academies, and schools that Peter established were reserved
for service nobles, clergy, and the children of certain commoners engaged in commerce, manufacturing, or the military. The elite that was tapped to rule Russia was supposed
to be a new class based not on genealogy but on ideals, values, and manners. There is no denying the fact that, despite
strong initial resistance, Peter and his immediate successors,

systematically pursuing a common goal, eventually succeeded in changing the ethos of the Muscovite service class.
After Peter died there was no talk of turning back, of giving
up on efforts to educate the children of the service nobility
in European science, technology, arts, and letters. European
culture henceforth became a prerequisite for membership in
the ruling elite. First court life and later public and social life
changed dramatically, offering a striking contrast with the
situation that prevailed in the Kremlin before Peter's accession.

Beyond that, Peter and his administration took steps to
systematically exploit the material resources of the empire,
doing the best they could with the existing state of the economy and the men and equipment at their disposal. Explora-
tions were made to scout out new mineral resources, timber,
and arable land. Factories, roads, and canals were built, commerce was encouraged, new cities begun—among them the
capital—and old ones restored. The ideal Petrine administrator was also a scholar: he was supposed to be competent in
economics, science, and politics. One such man was Vasily
Tatishchev, an exemplary representative of Peter's generation, whose career and ideas offer the best possible illustration of what Peter was trying to accomplish with the resources at his disposal.[8]

The emperor tried to organize Russian society so as to encourage active and productive work in all areas, including the
private sector of the economy and intellectual activity. To that
end he used the traditional tool: his command of the state
service. His attempt to involve the nobility in economic enterprises proved unsuccessful. It is reasonable to ask why the
nobility resisted involvement in activities that would have

8. See Simone Blanc, *Un disciple de Pierre le Grand dans la Russie du XVIIIe siècle: V. N. Tatischev (1686–1750)* (Lille, 1972), 2 vols.; Conrad Grau, *Der Wirtschaftsorganisator, Staatsmann und Wissenschaftler Vasilij N. Tatiscev (1686–1750)* (East Berlin, 1963); and Herbert Leventer, "Tatishchev: Science and Service in Eighteenth Century Russia," (dissertation, Columbia University, 1971).

made it more prosperous while continuing to squander resources in conspicuous consumption. Peter's attempt to
change all this, his 1714 legislation to enforce single inheritance, proved a fiasco.[9]

Peter also enlisted the aid of other social classes by means
of state service. The *Glavnyi magistrat* or central municipal-
ity provided institutional support for members of the urban
classes who wished to set up commercial businesses and factories. But once again state interests took precedence over all
other considerations: members of the *Glavnyi magistrat* had
to participate actively in the collection of taxes and the
maintenance of security in the towns, and their talents and
resources had to be placed at the disposal of the state. Much
time and energy were wasted as a result, and members of the
Glavnyi magistrat ran serious risks since they were legally
responsible for any losses incurred by the state treasury. The
protection and encouragement offered to private initiative and
individual creative energy were insufficient to yield the results that Peter's observations of West European methods had
led him to expect.[10]

Finally, society—or at any rate high society—was modernized and Europeanized by the importation of court styles from
the West. This proved to be a complete success. Within two
generations the court at St. Petersburg could rival any in
Western Europe for splendor and liveliness. By contrast, the
persistent efforts of Peter and his collaborators to induce his
people to shed the religious customs and prejudices that were

9. The decree of March 23, 1714 *(Polnoe sobranie zakonov rossiiskoi imperii*, vol.
5, no. 2789), authorized the designation of a single person as heir of all real property;
other heirs (brothers and sisters) had to be compensated in cash. Peter hoped in this
way to insure an adequate supply of personnel to fill state service positions (sons
who did not inherit their father's property), while at the same time preserving the
material basis of the nobility by not allowing estates to be so divided up that their
productivity would suffer.

10. Regulation of the *Glavnyi magistrat*, January 16, 1721 *(Polnoe sobranie zakonov*, vol. 6, no. 3708). See also A. Kizevetter, *Posadskaia obschchina v Rossii XVIII
st.* (Moscow, 1903), reprinted in 1978 by Oriental Research Partners, Newtonville,
Mass.

inhibiting the development of a productive *vita activa* ended in almost total failure. In fact, Peter's persistence had the opposite of the desired effect, for it convinced the common people that the emperor and his acolytes were doing the work of the devil and that the sovereign was the embodiment of the Antichrist.

To sum up: in Russia it was the state that took the lead in efforts to create a more dynamic society, better equipped to exploit available resources in a rational way. Broadly speaking, the state achieved its objectives in regard to the service nobility and the intellectual elite. But with the common people the government's failure was virtually complete, at least until the middle of the eighteenth century.

As a result, Peter's reforms never penetrated to the heart of Russian society or the Russian nation. By intervening here and there agencies of the central government achieved limited short-term results that ultimately changed little. One sometimes has the impression that innovations remained suspended in midair: somehow they always seemed temporary. For Russians of the time, and even more for foreign observers, instability was the most impressive characteristic of the new Russia. The service elites, on the other hand, responded enthusiastically to the cultural challenge and adapted so well to imported Western innovations that within two generations they were making contributions of their own to the new culture of modern Russia. Why did they fail to show similar enthusiasm and creative energy in the economic realm? The question is worth coming back to later on. For now, let us observe simply that they were overwhelmed by the burdens of state service, which, during the long years of war with Sweden and Turkey, was onerous, difficult, and highly unpredictable, a strain on a man's health and sometimes even a threat to his life. Given prevailing customs, recreational fashions, and the paucity of available resources, it was therefore impossible for a man to pursue economic objectives while also discharging the professional obligation to keep up with the latest cultural fashions, something that could be done while serving in the army or at court.

Accordingly, the elite showed (and would continue to show) a sincere interest in intellectual imports from the West and wholeheartedly adopted the new Russian cultural values. Cultivated Russians were soon able to deal as equals with cultivated Westerners. But popular culture, largely untouched by Peter's revolution, stagnated with the traditions of the seventeenth century. This not only opened an ever widening gulf between high culture and popular culture but left the latter frozen and dull so that ultimately it withered. The popular mind fell out of step with the mind of the elite and those who identified with the elite. The consequences of this situation made themselves felt with great force in the nineteenth century, when the popular masses returned to the mainstream of imperial life and culture.

To borrow a phrase from Maurice Hauriou, "administration is the foundation of [a structured] society"—but only on condition that the administration is actually involved with the life of society at the grass roots and shares in the crucial activities of the people and the nation. This was not the case in Russia at the beginning of the eighteenth century, and because of this the evolution of Russian society after the reign of Peter I followed a peculiar, "distorted" course. Hence the decades that followed the death of the "transforming tsar" were problematic and paradoxical. Could the personal authority of the sovereign, which had set the stage for social change, be institutionalized and made a regular, permanent force? Could social institutions be established in an autocratic regime? These were the key problems confronting Russian society. Personal rule seemed to be justified by Peter's successes, particularly in the military and diplomatic areas but also in opening a window on Europe for the Russian elite. As a result, the ranks of the elite had been replenished by an influx of new men with a new intellectual and political outlook. Was it not likely that the leading role played by the service elite would sap the strength and impair the creativity of autonomous social formations? And without the development of such autonomous forces, was it not likely that the work of Peter the Great would ultimately come to nought? These were the questions that the generations following Peter asked themselves, and they are questions that we in turn must consider in the light of events that took place between 1725 and 1762.

3
PETER'S SYSTEM IN DIFFICULTY

HE system of government instituted by Peter the Great behaved very differently from the Muscovite system, despite certain similarities between the new institutions and those of Peter's father's day (the Senate became the equivalent of the *boiar duma,* the colleges replaced the *prikazy,* etc.). The reasons for the differences in behavior have to do with a new conception of the tasks of government. The imperial government, unlike the old tsarist governments, was for better or worse involved in organizing new areas of cultural and economic activity. Admittedly, it became involved in these areas out of concern to protect its own interests and for reasons of political and military necessity. Nevertheless, the effect of this involvement was to expand the scope of administrative activities, even if much of the work of the administration, now as in the past, pertained to matters of taxation, military supplies, and personnel recruitment.

One important difference between past governments and the governments of Peter and his successors was that the latter, no longer satisfied merely to collect traditional taxes and dues and to levy troops, laid down new standards of service and demanded specific new payments in money and kind. As a result, the administration took a more active role in daily life, drawing up precise, detailed rules and instructions and interfering constantly in the activities of the tsar's subjects.

Broadly speaking, Peter's successors maintained his system of government, with some improvements. Although government departments were sometimes called upon to decide cases within the jurisdiction of lower authorities or to attend to the interests of private individuals, in general the authority of the officials in the capital increased—and of course, in keeping with Peter's own principles, the sovereign personally intervened in many cases. In sum, the role of the administration greatly expanded during the first half of the eighteenth century.

The theory and practice of the Russian imperial government were based on cameralist theories of the well-ordered police state. Although Russia was primarily an agricultural country, the state attempted to establish cities for economic and commercial as well as military and administrative reasons (garrisons were stationed in the new urban centers). New ways of doing things were borrowed wholesale from the West, including food policies, health and sanitation measures, and methods of "city planning" (spectacularly illustrated in the building of the new capital on the Gulf of Finland) which included building inspection, enforcement of safety standards, and design of city centers with an eye to esthetic and health requirements. These first steps were modest and of limited practical effect. But, the point to notice is that the government diligently continued on its new course and carved out its own field of activity, in which it achieved notable success later in the eighteenth century with the building of new cities in the south and improvement of older cities in central Russia. So far as we are able to judge from available documents, no effort was made to establish proper food and public health policies in the countryside; in this respect the government did not depart from its European model. From time to time isolated attempts were made to improve conditions in a few villages, but generally these were state-owned and contained factories or other activities of "national" interest (harbors, saltpeter mines, etc.).

State initiatives in the areas of education and culture were particularly far-reaching and influential. The major effort was of course to set up training institutions for the service nobility. Eventually, however, the growing personnel requirements of the army and bureaucracy made it necessary to pay some attention to religious schools as well. Let us note in passing that in the Ukraine, where there was a longer tradition of secondary education than in Russia and where it was common for children of the nobility to be sent to secondary schools, the state had no reason to intervene. But in Russia proper matters stood quite differently. Peter inaugurated his program of education by setting up primary schools, literally called "schools for figures" *(tsyfirnye shkoly)* along with the Mathematics (later the Naval) Academy. These primary schools, which were affiliated with the church-run school system, were not particularly successful, but they did point up the need for a well-planned educational system to train civil servants and military officers. Following the advice of Leibniz and the example of the Western monarchies, Peter the Great established an Academy of Sciences as both a research institute and an institution of "higher" education, open to the cultural elite of the empire. Actually, the Academy did not open its doors until after the death of its founder, but its inception was accompanied by the establishment of a school for advanced studies. The first Russian university, the University of Moscow, was founded in 1755 and within two generations had become a Mecca for knowledge-starved noble youths and a center of artistic and literary life for the newborn intelligentsia.

Even more important than the University of Moscow was the Corps of Cadets, if the number of people involved and the importance of its social role are reliable indices. The Corps was established in 1731 (and opened in 1732) at the behest of the service nobility, or at any rate by certain nobles active in the administration, the military, and the cultural life of the capital, who wanted their children to receive an education that would be advantageous in their careers.

As the century progressed the Corps was expanded, and

other institutions in Moscow, St. Petersburg, and the provinces were modeled after it. Private schools sprang up to prepare young nobles for entry into the Corps and to take care of those who were not admitted. Two points are worthy of note. First, the Corps was designed to meet the needs of the service elite. This shows that the service nobility accepted the need for education and viewed it as desirable and that the elite had internalized Peter's desire for Westernization, for Europeanization of Russian culture. Second, the creation of the Corps of Cadets and similar institutions enabled ever greater numbers of people to receive a European-style education and thus to take an active part in cultural life. Hence the Corps and the various private as well as public institutions that came after it helped to spread the new civic culture. Theaters were opened in the capital by former members of the Corps, who were also responsible for the translation of many works of European literature and for the launching of literary reviews, discussion circles, and so forth, which eventually produced a native Russian literature. On a more modest scale these activities were imitated by pupils of other schools and by students at the University of Moscow, one of whose curators (M. Kheraskov), himself a product of the Corps of Cadets, encouraged the formation of literary discussion circles and the publication of literary annuals.

The state played an even more active role in extending the educational system, setting up schools attached to military regiments and special corps for sailors, engineers, and others in provincial cities and metropolitan centers. Even the creation of private boarding schools resulted from a state initiative. Private schools were first needed to prepare children of the nobility who could not receive sufficient instruction at home for entry into the Corps of Cadets, as well as to educate youths who lived too far from the capital to be sent off to the Corps while still very young. Once private schools came into being, the state watched them very closely to make sure that they served the public interest as intended. The state's energetic educational policy was not aimed exclusively at the service nobility. Schools were set up to "Russify" the children of the non-Russian elite and bring them within the orbit of the imperial military and administrative system.

Similarly, the state attempted to modernize the instruction dispensed by the religious schools, a policy that did not necessarily prove wise in the long run. Religious subjects were neglected, as was instruction essential to the pastoral work of the clergy in the parishes. The very fact that Latin became the language of instruction in the theological seminaries shows that the authorities cared nothing for the spiritual needs of the people. Priority was given instead to subjects useful for chancery work, such as rhetoric and logic (which were taught with the help of Western manuals). Thus the religious schools eventually became training grounds for the "bureaucracy" and aided considerably in the Europeanization of Russian culture. Western works of philosophy, literature, mathematics, and rhetoric used in the religious schools became available not only to students but to others outside, particularly civil servants who worked alongside graduates of the religious schools and young nobles who learned the rudiments of Western culture from tutors trained in the seminaries.

It is worth pausing a moment to recall what has often been said about the history of education in Russia. Under Peter, education was primarily utilitarian and pragmatic. Chief among the first emperor's aims was to train a professional elite (still rather vaguely defined) of military experts, engineers, sailors, diplomats, and financial administrators. Now, the striking thing about both nobles and commoners in the service elite was that they showed interest only in the broader cultural aspects of Peter's program; these made the program attractive and won it welcome from some segments of Russian society. Young civil servants showed no interest in technology or finance—indeed, they showed a positive lack of interest. The vast majority avoided these subjects as much as possible. But cultural attainments far in excess of the minimum requirements of the military and civil service (the ability to read, write, and do arithmetic) quickly came to be seen as desirable in themselves and essential for anyone who wished to belong to the elite. As early as 1730, the service nobility demanded the creation of a school that would afford their children privileged access to service positions and help them to advance in their careers. The Corps of Cadets was established in response to this demand. Its program, modeled after that of the *Ritterakademien*, was shaped partly by Peter's utilitarian faith in technology, partly by the elite's desire to gain access to Western culture and literature.

The curriculum adopted by the Corps of Cadets influenced teaching in Russia down to the end of the eighteenth century. Almost all public and private schools founded in this period took it as part of their mission to introduce their pupils to a broad range of European culture, at first primarily German, and later French. The future state administrator was, by the time he took up his duties, fully prepared to live in a Western style. Normally, he would spend his working life in a military or civilian agency under the direct supervision of the court and the central government, but his job would bring him into contact with a milieu in which intellectual life (however rudimentary) was prized and enthusiastically cultivated. Thanks to this experience he would come to feel at ease in the presence of Western visitors to Russia and ready, if need be, to travel to the West. Finally, it is worth mentioning that Russian schools and universities, both public and private, frequently invited foreign intellectuals and specialists in a variety of subjects to teach in Russia, and many of these foreign visitors made significant contributions to the development of Russian art as well as the Russian economy.

The government also used the Russian Orthodox Church as an agency for intervening in the life of the nation. The harmony between spiritual and temporal powers that had prevailed in the seventeenth century had broken down, however. Now it was the government that issued specific directives to ecclesiastical institutions. Thus, as we saw earlier, clerical schools were supposed to meet the temporal needs of the service class (it was to this end that the "arithmetic schools" were created). Things did not work out this way, however, except in the Ukraine, where the number of lay students attending church schools rose steadily. The monasteries were assigned thc job of caring for disabled veterans and of serving as hospitals and hospices for soldiers and their families as well as workers. The seminaries and theological academies set up an alternative system of higher education. Finally, the clergy was forced to resign itself to an auxiliary role, that of providing information about the common people and monitoring their activities—a police function which was not apt to make the clergy popular with its flock and which effectively prevented the church from carrying out its educational mission and from offering moral and spiritual guidance.

Paradoxical as this situation may have been, it was probably inevitable. The subordination of the clergy to the state and the use of clergymen as administrators only encouraged religious initiatives by individuals outside the church and led to an intensification of private forms of religion and to a search for mystical and pietistic forms of religiosity—all of which left deep marks on the cultural life of the elite. Doubtless this inward religious turn should be regarded as the source of ethical populism—of the feeling, common in the Russian intelligentsia in the first half of the nineteenth century, that a moral and spiritual debt was owed to the Russian people.

These attempts by the Petrine state to influence the organization of Russian society had still other consequences. For one thing, the number of state functionaries rose sharply. For another, the influence of the administration over economic life was gradually extended to every sector of the economy and every region of the empire. An extensive system of tax collection was established, and individuals and groups were chosen to serve as tax farmers and state suppliers. The government turned to previously untouched segments of society for help in carrying out its policies—but it bears emphasizing that these agents acted as private entrepreneurs, not as official government agents. The results of this system were paradoxical. Establishing a well-ordered police state required central direction, effectively provided by Peter the Great. Yet no one man can coordinate and control the entire political and economic life of a country as vast as Russia. For this, Russia needed a governmental apparatus, an institutional hierarchy like those found in the monarchies of Central and Western Europe. If, moreover, the transformation of Russian society was to have the desired results, it was important to establish definite objectives, and this required consistent, logical, well-coordinated policies. The job was too big for one man, however powerful, however great a genius he may have been.

Aware of what needed to be done, Peter the Great created the Senate to act as central planning agency and development coordinator—in short, as the concrete embodiment of his imperial policy's systematic logic. Even while Peter was alive, however, the Senate did not function as planned, largely on account of Peter's strong and impetuous personality. When he died matters only became worse. The Senate ceased to play any coordinating role whatsoever. Each of the Colleges pursued its own ends, sowing confusion and disorder at the very center of government. The Secret Privy Council (established in 1727) might have supplanted—and to some extent did supplant—the Petrine Senate. But as a planning and coordinating agency it worked badly. It was overwhelmed by routine matters requiring immediate decisions and never was able to develop a consistent program of long-range goals. What is more, it quickly became a battleground fought over by rival political factions. This led ultimately to its demise during the crisis of succession of 1730.

With the Secret Privy Council out of the picture, a Cabinet of Ministers was set up as a replacement (but not until 1734, after some delay). The cabinet was unable to establish its supremacy, however: if there was ever such a thing as a long-term policy under Empress Anna, it was formulated by her personal advisers (nicknamed the "German favorites"), the most influential of whom was Gustav Biron, the Duke of Courland. After Anna no Russian ruler seems to have been much concerned with the need for a coordinating and planning body. Under Elizabeth not even the Senate was granted the role, despite promises made when she took power. Not until the final decades of Catherine II's reign do we see the first steps toward establishing the Senate chancery as the central coordinator of government activity, thanks to the energetic efforts of the sovereign working in concert with her talented senior advisor, A. A. Viazemski. But Catherine II's policy was entirely pragmatic; if she ever harbored glimmerings of a comprehensive long-range view, she abandoned them. Admittedly, this did not prevent her from pursuing certain vague and far-off goals and from applying various general notions about which we shall have more to say later on.

It may be unnecessary to point out that the very nature of autocratic power, with its implicit need for the autocrat to preserve his or her sovereign and personal authority, played a large part in preventing the emergence of a centralized supervisory body. The members of the imperial entourage, official as well as unofficial, and the various coteries around the sovereign found it advantageous to encourage the preservation of personal authority and to hamper the development of any regular institution with enough power to bring order to—i.e., to "bureaucratize"—the administration of the empire. Only in the absence of such an institution could the sovereign's favorites hope to maintain their own power through their influence over the monarch.

Hence it is not surprising to find that the authority of the sovereign and of the colleges was limited to the capital and broke down outside its limits. Within the administration there was no supervisory hierarchy, no effective way of coordinating policy and settling the jurisdictional disputes that inevitably arose. This had two effects. First, there was a breakdown of administration at the local level, where it proved impossible to establish rules governing the relations between individuals and collectivities. A deep sense of personal and material insecurity affected those who were direct subjects of the emperor (the qualification "direct" excluded peasants), particularly those who had property to administer and a social status to maintain. Second, the influence of the administration and the courts was diffuse, which left plenty of room for private initiative and for such unofficial corporate bodies as found it possible to exist on a local level. In particular, the serfs who worked the estates of the service nobility escaped the control of the central administration almost entirely (except in times of serious upheaval). Thus landowners were able to turn their serfs into virtual slaves, while rural communes paradoxically enjoyed considerable autonomy owing to the more or less permanent absence of the lord, called away on state service.

To avoid any possible misunderstanding, however, I am bound to point out that the administrative apparatus was strong enough, and its presence palpable enough, to prevent the formation of corps, corporations, or legal entities possessing definite rights and privileges and capable of contesting the authority of the sovereign and his government. Thus, we find in Russia, none of those autonomous intermediary bodies that were the chief auxiliaries of the well-ordered police state in Central and Western Europe. Russian society therefore remained fragmented, which in practice left considerable room for individual enterprise in certain areas of economic and cultural life.

To sum up, then, the Petrine system was concentrated in the central government, which monopolized all power. But the central government proved incapable of delegating its authority and of coordinating the activity of subordinate institutions, whose opportunities for action remained diffuse and limited. The resulting system was a very loose patchwork structure in control of a highly fragmented society in which a few individuals, thanks to their wealth, their influence at court or in the administration, or their private activities (which were somehow tolerated), could play a preeminent role, though they enjoyed none of the security that a system based on law and on regular institutions and autonomous corporate bodies might have provided.

This brings us to a fundamental paradox, the importance of which grew steadily during the eighteenth and proved decisive in the nineteenth century. The government, eager to encourage and organize production under its own control, continually encouraged private initiative on the part of certain individuals. State policy in fact required the cooperation of energetic and enterprising individuals, without whom the army would have had no supplies, the schools no teachers, the treasury no taxes, and commerce and industry no possibility of existing. The creative energy came first of all from the service nobility, under the impetus of the state. We know what steps were taken by Peter the Great (and by some of his successors, such as Elizabeth in response to proposals made by P. Shuvalov) to involve nobles in commercial and industrial enterprises, ultimately to no avail.[1] There were, as we saw earlier, two main reasons for this failure: the nobility lacked the necessary resources (in capital and manpower), and it was unprepared to assume an entrepreneurial role, given the total involvement of most nobles in state service and the need, imposed by official duties, to remain for extended periods away from their estates and from the centers of mining and industry. Given the circumstances, it should come as no surprise that nobles never developed much of an interest in long-term investment, since their one overriding concern was the immediate profit to be gained by winning the sovereign's

1. W. R. Augustine, "Notes toward a Portrait of the Eighteenth-Century Russian Nobility," *Canadian-American Slavic Studies* (1970) 5(4):373–425.

favor and thereby securing bonuses for meritorious service.

Most individual enterprise was therefore left to persons not belonging to the nobility, to "declassed" individuals and foreigners who cooperated in state-inspired or state-organized projects intended to develop Russia's natural and cultural resources. Unfortunately, this phenomenon has not been systematically studied, though there is no dearth of useful sources. From bits and pieces of information and allusions contained in published documents, however, we can gain some idea of the nature of entrepreneurial activity on the local level. Merchants, town dwellers not belonging to the urban elites (the so-called *meshchane*), and even peasants supplied food and equipment to the military and to the court as well as materials for urban construction and major public works projects. Circuits of exchange (but not necessarily a "market," as the Marxists would have it) developed and expanded throughout the empire. Some of these circuits included non-Russian alien populations. The Armenians had always played an important role in trade between the people of the Caucasus region (and beyond) and Muscovy proper. This trade not only survived but increased many times over in the wars waged by Peter and his successors against Persia and Turkey as well as the campaigns against the rebellious Cossacks of Bulavin and Astrakhan and against the Kirghiz in the steppes. An increasingly active part in this trade was taken by the Ukrainians, who found themselves astride the route of the Russian army and in the midst of the staging area for the campaigns against the Ottoman Empire and Poland. When the Ukraine was effectively absorbed into Russia, Ukrainian entrepreneurs, merchants, and suppliers were drawn into the economic orbit of central Russia and of the Russian Empire. Finally, merchants, artisans, and military suppliers in the Baltic provinces traded with the empire, and this trade was particularly intense because Riga remained the principal Russian port almost until the end of the eighteenth century.

Social Mobility

The effect of all these activities was to increase mobility, in several ways. In the first place, increased mobility of goods resulted from an intensification of commercial exchange: trade, more voluminous and active than it had been, and involving a wide range of manufactured products and raw materials, was carried on over an ever broader area. The intensification of commerce affected foreign as well as domestic trade. Imports included not only "industrial" products needed by the army and navy but also increasing quantities of luxury goods, for which there was growing demand both at court and among members of the elite eager to furnish their sumptuous homes in the capital as well as their provincial estates. The abolition of internal tariffs under Empress Elizabeth in 1754, ratified in 1762 by Catherine II, gave official recognition and encouragement to the growing volume of trade within the empire.

The expansion of trade and acceleration of the economy that took place throughout the empire in the first half of the eighteenth century are well known phenomena and have been studied fairly thoroughly. By contrast, the increase in the mobility of individuals that took place at the same time has gone almost unnoticed. Before we can hope to paint an accurate picture of this new development, a full and detailed study needs to be done. For now, a rough sketch will have to suffice. What we see is paradoxical: rising social mobility coupled with a hardening of serfdom. It is worth emphasizing that, while serfs accounted for the overwhelming majority of the population, not all of them lived in abject slavery or frightful poverty. Not all serfs were tied to an estate and subjected to the cruel whims of their masters. The serf "system" (that it was a system is our first—erroneous—article of faith about serfdom) was sufficiently incoherent and poorly codified to have left a rather large gray area of informal arrangements; vague laws and statutes left a fair amount of room for maneuver, to say nothing of the possibilities that existed for corruption and illegal activities. Individuals were moved about within Russia in response to the needs of the state and the requirements of landowners belonging to the service nobility; increased trade also encouraged mobility. Among those caught up in these large-scale population movements were serfs, state peasants, and townspeople.

The upper classes were the first to be affected. Not only were growing numbers of merchants engaged in foreign trade, some of them former peasants or rural artisans (who became involved, for instance, in the supply and transport of grain and other foodstuffs needed in the new capital, which had no agricultural hinterland to draw on). Then, too, steadily increasing numbers of service nobles were transferred from regiment to regiment and garrison to garrison or were sent on special missions all over the empire. State servants were also required to move about when transferring from the military to the civilian administration and vice versa, as well as when they took leave or retired to their country estates. Finally, growing numbers of service nobles established residences in the city (or in garrison towns) in order to take a more active part in cultural life, at least during the long winter months.

Of course, the very fact that members of the service nobility did move about so much helped to open a breach between them and the country folk, the common people of the Russian countryside; service nobles felt rootless and alienated and, as Chaadaev noted, had the sense of standing with "one foot always in the air." But by the same token increased mobility broadened the intellectual horizons of the service elite. Its members came into contact with many segments of society and discovered the variety of Russian life and culture. They acquired a new social ease and flexibility and formed rewarding new relationships with people in all walks of life. The mobility of men in service helped to establish the cultural homogeneity of the service elite. State servants were everywhere in their element, in familiar company. All of them shared the same cultural background and the same range of experience; they were at ease with one another. Finally—to mention a point of the utmost importance that is all too often neglected—the Russian service elite could easily accommodate foreigners (or assimilated members of alien elites), provided only that these outsiders were willing to acquire the education and culture and learn to speak the language (in the figurative as well as the literal sense of the term) of their Russian counterparts.

Increased mobility was not limited to members of the upper classes but affected many individuals in less exalted walks of life. Serfs were often required to travel (quite frequently long distances and for long periods of time) in order to transport winter provisions from the master's estate to the capital or garrison town where the master was stationed. Besides provisions the serfs often carried products of local artisans, either for the master's use or for sale in the town's marketplace. Mixed in with all these goods were no doubt items whose sale earned profits that went either to the transporter himself or to people in neighboring villages. Household serfs were brought to town to manufacture domestic items and luxury goods for the master's residence. This group also included the domestic staff proper, in some cases quite large, whose members were drawn from the master's country estates and villages. Great lords and court nobles had very large staffs indeed, necessitating a constant traffic between town and country. This brought domestic servants and artisans into contact with the upper classes, and they learned new techniques (many of foreign origin) for making and using both common items and luxury goods. While in town some serfs were able to do business on their own behalf (competition from this quarter explains why a genuine town-based petty bourgeoisie of merchants and craftsmen did not develop more fully). These complex demographic shifts affected the development of modern Russian culture and helped spread the culture of the elite to lower levels of society, in ways that still need to be examined more closely and in proper historical context. Large-scale troop movements should also be mentioned, though we lack the information needed to form a detailed picture of what went on in this regard. Troops moved both on military campaigns and on domestic maneuvers for internal security and police reasons. Troop movements involved more than just the shift of soldiers and officers from one part of the empire to another. They required large-scale shipments of goods and a whole host of wagoneers and freightmen who were recruited—if need be by force—from the peasantry and compelled to travel long distances and stay away from their native villages for long periods of time.

Mention should also be made, finally, of the movement of non-Russians from the periphery of the empire to its center (which almost always took place one at a time rather than in groups) and of the less common reverse movement, the colonization of frontier areas by people recruited in the central provinces. Large numbers of Ukrainians, for example, came to settle in central Russia, usually in the provincial capitals, where they successfully pursued careers in the administration or in the cultural sphere. The number of Ukrainians employed in the imperial "bureaucracy" in second-level positions is remarkable, particularly under the reign of Elizabeth, during which (thanks to the protection of the brothers Razumovsky, great favorites of the empress) Ukrainian civil servants rose rapidly through the ranks. The trend was not reversed under Catherine II: Rumiantsev's chancery in the Ukraine produced a large number of high-ranking civil servants, among whom Ukrainians like Bezborodko and Zavadovsky attracted particular notice. These men in turn helped many of their compatriots to rise. The Ukrainians of course enjoyed certain advantages over other aliens, since their language is close to Russian and their church Orthodox; furthermore, many of them had attended private or religious

schools that offered a better education than that received by
most Russian nobles. This interregional, interethnic mobility calls for further study.

Under the head of population movements from the periphery to the center, mention should also be made of the Baltic
Germans, another contingent of foreigners who brought their
language and culture to Russia and thus helped broaden the
intellectual horizons of their Russian colleagues. In addition
to the German contingent, which consisted entirely of nobles and members of the bourgeois elite, other foreigners came
in the late eighteenth century to seek their fortunes in the
Russian Empire. Attempts were made to attract German academics (particularly scientists and engineers), who filled almost all the posts in the Academy of Sciences and at the
University of Moscow. The end of the century saw the ranks
of foreigners residing in Russia swelled by French *émigrés* and
others driven from their country by the Revolution. Their influence on and contribution to Russian life were temporary,
even though a fair number decided to stay on in Russia: the
reason they did not exert greater influence was that, by this
time, Russian culture was sufficiently established, and its
character sufficiently defined, to stand on its own. The newcomers were able to make some contributions but not to play
a direct role, as their German predecessors had done in the
eighteenth century, in shaping the culture of their host country.

To round out our survey, let us add to the list the state-
supported efforts to colonize certain areas of the empire using foreign labor, including so-called Serbs (i.e., Slavs from the
regions bordering on the Habsburg Empire) who settled in the
Ukraine under Elizabeth, Germans who settled on the banks
of the Volga under Catherine II, and various other groups
(Greeks, Georgians, Jews, and "Polish" Old Believers) that
Potemkin caused to be sent to the southern Ukraine and the
shores of the Black Sea when he was viceroy of New Russia.

The renewed demographic mobility that we have been describing affected only specific individuals and groups, and then only for a limited period of time. Apart from the peasant colonists, the only segments of society involved were those in a position to absorb the new Westernized elite culture imposed by the state; these consisted of people who had honorific functions at court or in the garrison towns or who belonged to the military or administrative elite of the provincial centers and great estates. This produced tension within both the service nobility and Russian popular culture.

The nobles' mobility, a result of the new system of state service, severed or at least weakened the ties that bound members of the nobility in state service to their estates, native provinces, and provincial relatives and neighbors. The noble in service usually resided in a city or garrison town, where he came into direct contact with the new culture. Inevitably he became Westernized and personally involved with the culture of Europe. At the same time he neglected his properties and hence his economic interests, insofar as these depended upon close management of his estates. Most nobles therefore ceased to acquire new wealth and property, except in a few cases, which usually involved the ability to capitalize on one's position in the state service. The nobility became impoverished; the situation was made worse by the practice of distributing an estate equally among all heirs, which was not abandoned despite Peter the Great's efforts to scrap it in favor of single inheritance. Taken as a whole, the class of noble landowners entered upon a period of economic stagnation.

Since the publication of Michael Confino's magisterial works, there has been nothing more to say on this score.[2] Here I should add that those studies, mostly by Soviet scholars, that have made a great deal of the proliferation of the serf system, emphasizing its increasing profitability, have concentrated

2. Michael Confino, *Domaines et seigneurs en Russie vers la fin du XVIIIe siècle* (Paris: Institut d'études slaves de l'université de Paris, 1963); and *Systèmes agraires et progrès agricole* (Paris-The Hague: Mouton, 1969).

mainly on the second half or even the last quarter of the eighteenth century, alluding to the change in economic conditions that resulted from the intensive exploitation of the southern Ukraine. In any case, the service nobility—the *pomeshchiki* class—whether because of absenteeism, adoption of a foreign culture, or poverty, became increasingly isolated from popular culture and allowed itself to be cut off from the ancient traditions that had shaped Russian life, material as well as spiritual. Those who did not divorce themselves from these traditions were denounced for their crudeness *(grubost')* and backwardness *(otstalost')* and called "wild and woolly bears." They became the butt of jokes and the target of satire in the new Russian literature that was just emerging. They stood as symbols of all that was barbaric and backward compared with the civilization of Europe, to which the cultivated ruling elite of the empire aspired to relate on a footing of equality.

The other side of the coin, so to speak, was the isolation of popular culture. Though popular culture did not disappear, a breach developed between it and the active, dynamic, and creative forces in Russian society. Hostile to all foreign innovation, Russian popular culture quickly petrified. The Old Believers were primarily responsible for this, for it was they who conferred upon popular traditions their static and conservative character. The Old Believers were in fact the best educated segment of the masses (best educated, that is, in Muscovite religious traditions), besides which their devotion to and respect for ancient church tradition gave them the strength to withstand efforts by the official church to convert them to the new religion. Old Believers preserved and passed on seventeenth-century styles and techniques in icon painting, manuscript illumination, and church decoration. In their isolation they conserved much popular music, imagery, language, and poetry (or, if need be, created new works in the spirit of the traditional ones). Preindustrial cultures need not be conservative or unwilling to change and accept innovations; in the case of Russia it was in large part the Old Believers who, by championing traditional Russian culture, made it conservative and kept it static in form and content into the latter half of the nineteenth century. As V. Teteriatnikov has shown, moreover, when the Old Believers and peasants did finally begin to share in the culture of the Russian Empire (especially through their work as artisans and industrial laborers) in order to satisfy rising mass demand for consumer goods, and when members of the elite began to take an interest in Russian "national" traditions, it was mainly to the world of the Old Believers that people turned for inspiration.[3]

The conscious, deliberate, and steadfast determination of the Old Believers to keep popular culture separate from the new elite culture gave rise to "two nations," two cultural universes, between which there was little if any exchange, even though residents of both worlds met daily and maintained constant communication.

Having said that, I must hasten to issue an important caveat, though the subject has not yet been sufficiently studied. Bear in mind that the gulf between the people and the elite was a relative one, and that it gradually diminished as modern Russian culture filtered down into provincial society over the course of the eighteenth century. Even in the first half of the century breaches had been opened in the "great wall" that separated the elites, then in the process of Westernization, from the masses. As paradoxical as it may seem at first, these breaches were opened mainly by the existence of serfdom. The need, increasingly felt by the provincial nobility, to live in a European style, surrounded by objects of a Western type, led nobles to put their serfs—who provided reserves of free manpower—to work creating the European-style setting in which they now wished to live. The serfs had to be

3. V. Teteriatnikov, "Staroobriadtsy—sozdateli russkogo nardnogo iskusstva," *Novyi Zhurnal* (1977) 126:128–45.

trained in the requisite methods. The wealthiest and most enterprising nobles had their serfs taught by foreigners or by Europeanized Russian artisans. Young serfs were taken from their families and villages and sent to apprentice with skilled craftsmen and artists before being put to work in great aristocratic households. Some showed considerable talent in various crafts and even in the arts. A few proved to be exceptionally talented painters, decorators, musicians, actors, or dancers; these artists, born serfs, acquired a national reputation, and their works not only redounded to the glory of their masters but also embellished the life of the elite in the capital cities and provinces of the empire.

That this kind of experience could be humiliating or even traumatic for the artist hardly needs to be pointed out; ample attention was paid to this theme in "abolitionist" literature and in populist and liberal novels, stories, and poems of the late eighteenth and early nineteenth century. The literary accounts are corroborated by autobiographical memoirs that tell of the horrifying lives led by these poor serfs, plucked from their native surroundings and exposed to a "liberated, modern" milieu, only to be again cast out, in many cases, and subjected to the psychological and physical privation of serfdom. Unable to withstand the wrench, many committed suicide.

As deserving of our indignation and pity as the lives of these talented people may be, this is not the point I want to stress here. What matters for our purposes is that the training of serfs as craftsmen and artists meant involving common people directly in the new culture and Westernized way of life. Through these craftsmen and artists the new customs and tastes of the elite filtered their way down to the villages, and the new norms became models for many peasants to imitate in the hope of attracting favorable notice by their masters and peers. Thus, indirectly, and all too often involuntarily, a segment of the peasant population became involved with modern culture, particularly in the Moscow region, where most of the residences and country estates *(usad'by)* of the court and service nobility were located.

Another aspect of the same phenomenon, also much neglected by historians, is the cultural influence exerted by demobilized soldiers and their families. The number of these in the eighteenth century was admittedly not very large: service was for all practical purposes life-long, and few soldiers returned to their native villages when discharged. Most no doubt had little desire to return, having lost all contact with village life during their long years of service. Still, cases are known of veterans returning to live in the villages where they were born, and the number of such cases rose steadily in the second half of the eighteenth and early years of the nineteenth century. It would be interesting to know whether the experiences these men had while stationed in large cities or serving in a "modernized" army, sometimes including campaigns in foreign countries, left deep impressions on them and changed their ways of doing things and, if so, whether they passed on what they had learned to friends and relatives who had stayed behind in the village. We cannot, *a priori*, rule out the possibility that this occurred, but until we have a study of the Russian army as detailed as A. Corvisier's study of the French army, the suggestion can only be put forward as a hypothesis. A hypothesis not without foundation, however: various documents, still quite fragmentary, suggest that disabled veterans and retired soldiers did indeed bring to the villages in which they spent their final years the fruit of direct experience with the cultural world of the elite and familiarity with Western techniques and methods acquired in the course of military service.

To sum up, then, the effects of contact between popular culture and elite culture do not become clearly visible before the end of the eighteenth century. But such contact was an essential prerequisite to what happened to Russian culture in the nineteenth century, which saw a renewal of contact between the elite and the masses. Without these grass-roots cultural exchanges, ethical and political (or social) populism would never have seen the light of day. It is hard to believe that the elite would have shown so much concern for the masses had there not been sustained relations and contacts between the two. After all, Russian serfs and peasants were not like black slaves in the South: the gap between lord and serf was never as wide as that between master and slave in the southern United States before the Civil War. Proof of this assertion may be seen in the fact that, in 1861, when certain peasants gained limited rights to take part in civic life, elite culture, especially literary culture, was immediately accessible to them. Once peasants learned to read and write, they were prepared to appreciate the classics of modern Russian literature. This explains the relatively high level of literary culture among Russian workers and peasants, not only before 1917 (as is attested by the experiences of revolutionary propagandists just before the outbreak of World War I) but also in Soviet Russia today.

The Feeling of Insecurity

It should come as no surprise that the period from the death of Peter the Great to the consolidation of power by Catherine II was dominated by powerful feelings of insecurity, which took different forms in different strata of Russian society. At the head of the list came economic insecurity. The poverty of most state servants—*szlachta* or *dvorianstvo*—was a corollary of their inertia and inability to satisfy the growing need for culture, education, and a European way of life. Small estates offered only modest yields, and the small surplus crop, mainly grains, produced by the serfs of the typical state servant proved inadequate to meet the increasing requirements of the new life style. Arcadius Kahan has calculated that at least one hundred "souls" (male serfs) were needed to meet the costs of educating a nobleman and leading a modest "European-style" life.[4] Scarcely ten to fifteen percent of state servants (counting the very wealthy) fell into this category. Most nobles were forced to spend their lives in the service of the state, even after conditions were relaxed in the reigns of Elizabeth and Anna; official duties made it impossible for state servants to attend to their financial interests or closely supervise the management of their estates. Thus state service requirements, coupled with the high cost of living, prevented members of the service class from seizing economic opportunities or leading the kind of life, based on Western examples, to which many aspired. The inevitable result was discontent, malaise, and a sense of insecurity.

Most landowners were either absentee landlords or in state service and thus prevented from managing their property, which left them vulnerable to greedy neighbors, better off than themselves, who enjoyed the protection of local or central authorities. Traditional inheritance practices demanded that property be divided equally among all heirs, adding further grounds of conflict. Absent landowners were represented by their wives or by peasant stewards, and disputed inheritances gave rise to bitter lawsuits, which often ended with one party or the other taking the law into his own hands, sure of his superior strength or of protection from patrons and officials won over by bribes or other forms of corruption. The legal system offered no real protection: there was no civil code, since the code of Tsar Alexis, theoretically still in force, had been rendered largely obsolete by the changes wrought by Peter the Great. The court system, particularly at the local and provincial level, was the weakest and least developed part of the imperial system of government.

Furthermore, the tradition of personalized authority would have prevented the equitable application of fixed legal norms (or rules of common law), had any existed. The personaliza-

---

4. Arcadius Kahan, "The Costs of 'Westernization' in Russia: The Gentry and the Economy in the Eighteenth Century," *Slavic Review* (1966) 25(1):40–66.

tion of authority was incompatible with regular legal procedure, because the parties to a case preferred to bypass the official judicial hierarchy and appeal directly to the official or officials in charge. This kind of system naturally favored those who had contacts and relations in high places in the "establishment" or at court. Most important of all, any claim or litigation could be taken directly to the sovereign for final judgment. The emperor or empress had the last word in all cases, regardless of the written or common law and legal interpretation. In any litigation there was always one great imponderable—the whim or disposition (not to say the mood) of various government officials and, finally, of the emperor or empress (subject to manipulation by courtiers and favorites). All of this could not help but contribute to the deep feelings of insecurity and vulnerability that the elite felt before the law.

Physical insecurity was of equally great concern. It was for all practical purposes impossible to take precautions against assaults by powerful neighbors disdainful of the law or even to take legal action to recover damages.[5] No one was safe from arbitrary decisions and actions of the administrative and political authorities, who without fear of retribution could take away a man's liberty or property. This threat naturally weighed more heavily on relatively unimportant people, such as provincial civil servants, minor or impoverished nobles, or wealthy commoners living in town, than it did on court officials or members of the government. But not even the most important officials were entirely secure. As in the Soviet Union, any person whose political or social position brought him into the public eye ran a greater risk of getting into trouble than did most lesser officials.

Mutatis mutandis, these remarks hold true for less wealthy

---

5. Good illustrations of this may be found in the memoirs in the form of a novel of S. T. Aksakov, *A Russian Schoolboy* (Hyperion, Conn.: Classics of Russian Literature, 1977; reprint of 1917 edition).

townspeople *(posadskie)*, merchants *(kuptsy)*, and industrious peasants. These groups did not even enjoy the appearance of legal or administrative protection, however ineffective that protection may have proved in reality. Bribery and corruption were their only hope of winning a lawsuit or a claim for damages against a jealous rival or powerful enemy. More than anyone else, merchants who were Old Believers were subject to this sort of persecution, especially during the reign of the bigoted Empress Elizabeth, who attempted to have all Old Believers forcibly converted to Orthodoxy. Since the Old Believers were the most energetic and most enterprising merchants in Russia (especially in the sale of agricultural produce, products from Siberia, and craftwork), the insecurity they felt had serious repercussions on Russia's economic development.

Added to all of this was insecurity resulting from the arbitrariness of administrative decisions. The central institutions established by Peter I were run more or less strictly in keeping with the General Regulation. But the same cannot be said of local administrative agencies, of which the number was insufficient for the size of the country and which operated essentially unfettered owing to a lack of supervisory bodies. This left people at the mercy of tyrannical local officials who had to kowtow to their superiors in the capital and who trembled before wealthy and influential local luminaries. Rules of administrative procedure and legal guarantees rarely filtered down to the local level, and even if they did were subject to arbitrary and fantastic interpretation. The whim of local administrators and the personal authority of influential figures in the region took precedence over rules and laws. Ultimately, individuals were subject to a government not of institutions but of men—men who ruled as they saw fit. The farther one was from Moscow and St. Petersburg, the less the authority of the central government was felt: that authority was practically nonexistent in Siberia and the border areas.

Even at the center the system was not stable and administrative bodies were, as we saw earlier, a long way from achieving institutionalization. The monarch did as he or she saw fit, as did the favorites. The "reign of the favorites," mainly during the time of Anna and Elizabeth, not to mention the minority of Peter II and Ioann Antonovich, helped to perpetuate personal power as the sole source of authority in the empire. As a result, cliques based on kinship and mutual services and modeled on the clans (rody) of another era seized control of the administrative apparatus. A country ruled by cliques and favorites is an unstable country, where insecurity is the general rule and all decisions are subject to imponderable influences. In any monarchy the fall of a favorite always leads to the disgrace of his protégés and clan and all their associates. But in eighteenth-century Russia the fall of a favorite also meant the confiscation of his and his protégés' property, which was then distributed to others. Disgrace jeopardized the life and liberty of the former favorite: consider the cases of Menshikov, Biron, Münnich, and Volynski. If, despite the different nature of the two regimes and the different sizes of their respective elites, we may compare tsarist Russia in the eighteenth century with Stalinist Russia in the twentieth, the fall of a favorite might be likened to the Stalinist purges: as Brenda Meechan-Waters has observed, the psychological effects of the confiscation procedure and of the political trials were rather similar to the psychological effects of the Soviet experience.[6]

The crisis of 1730 threw into relief the central paradox of the political system inherited from Peter and pointed up the difficulties that the ruling elite faced in trying to remedy its defects. The facts are well known, though certain points have yet to be elucidated, as is shown by recent work, some of it

6. Brenda Meehan-Waters, "Elite Politics and Autocratic Power," in A. G. Cross, ed., Anglo-Russian Relations in the Eighteenth Century (Newtonville, Mass.: Oriental Research Partners, 1979), pp. 229–46.

based on fruitful trips to the archives. Let us recall what was the major event in the 1730 crisis of succession: the opposition of a majority of state servants to the proposal put forward by D. M. Golitsyn in the name of the Secret Privy Council to limit the monarch's prerogatives. The state servants, large numbers of whom had come to Moscow for the marriage of Peter II (which did not take place owing to Peter's death) and stayed on for the coronation of his successor, preferred personal autocratic rule to an institutionalized but limited bureaucracy, even if the latter would, in the long run, guarantee greater security to the bulk of state servants. The empress-elect, Anna of Courland, niece of Peter the Great, was thus able to preserve her autocratic power intact and then to delegate it to foreign-born favorites, whose capricious tyranny was turned against the Russian service elite.

The crisis pointed up the rivalry between two contradictory notions of the source of supreme power in Russia: some believed in the absolute personal authority of the sovereign and his or her agents, while others believed in a well-ordered police state based on autonomous institutions and a stable system of rules and regulations. A similar conflict arose during the reign of Peter III, preparing the way for Catherine II's *coup d'état.* Peter III tried to impose personal rule with the aid of a coterie of favorites and their protégés (most of whom were foreigners, either Germans or natives of Holstein, of which Peter III was duke). This government promised to be particularly volatile and repressive. Catherine II was able to overthrow it because she feigned concern to preserve (or restore) the institutional authority of the Senate, that creation of Peter the Great's around which opposition to the rule of cliques and favorites invariably crystallized. In a stroke of political genius, Catherine II never renounced the avowed aim of her coup and worked hard to keep up the appearance of regularly functioning state institutions. With few exceptions her many favorites played no role outside her private life. Only Orlov and Potemkin (if we neglect Plato Zubov, Catherine's lover in her old age) played political roles, but even these men only occupied institutionalized positions in agencies they were appointed to head. As we shall see later on, Catherine planned to place the administration under the authority of the Senate and to create a parallel system of corporate institutions for the nobility and the urban elite.

Let us conclude this chapter by taking a broad view of the problem of psychological insecurity, various aspects of which have already been examined. For the elite—that is, for the court and service nobility—psychological insecurity stemmed from the problem of cultural identity: Should the culture of the elite be Russian (i.e., Muscovite) or European? Until this question was resolved, members of the ruling elite wavered between two worlds and two systems of value and hence felt psychologically insecure and intellectually in disarray. The ravages of this situation proved traumatic for many intelligent, cultivated, and enlightened individuals who saw clearly enough that Muscovite culture was done for and yet, even though they took on Western ways, ideas, and values, continued to feel different from other Europeans—to feel, in a word, Russian, if only by dint of their religion. Prince M. M. Shcherbatov gave voice to this typical feeling in his writings and polemical speeches, as did the older V. N. Tatishchev and Shcherbatov's contemporary, the historian I. Boltin. This psychological split, this idea of a cleavage between two cultures recurs frequently in the debates that dominated intellectual life under Catherine II. The problem found literary expression in the satirical journals published by N. I. Novikov and in the comedies of D. I. Fonvizin.

Faced with a government that decked itself out with imported trappings, the people, deprived of the security afforded by tradition, felt the uneasiness that comes from cultural disorientation. Ruled by foreign values (and even by foreign lieutenants), values which were in no way rooted in the Muscovite traditions to which the masses still adhered, the Russian people felt that they had been forced to wear a particularly heavy yoke, that their government was unusually arbitrary and hostile. In all probability their feeling of insecurity was due not so much to the burdens of serfdom, taxes, and conscription (heavy as these were for so primitive an economic system) but to the psychological discomfort they felt as subjects of an "alien" government. These feelings gave rise to popular uprisings, the most serious of which was led by Pugachev. These uprisings grew out of the demands of the Cossacks, traditionally autonomous social groups such as the *odnodvortsy*,[7] and the alien populations of the frontier areas. They were revolts against the St. Petersburg-dominated order, against the methods and the form of the central government, against centralization, institutionalization, and standardization based on foreign models. Pugachev's rebellion, though it came at the end of the period considered here (1773–75), was a dramatic illustration of this. It was the crystallization of a whole range of social tensions, of the ambivalence and insecurity that had beset the masses since the time of Peter the Great. The fact that Cossack Old Believers played a leading role in the uprising suggests that this was a rebellion against Europeanization and modernization and not against serfdom. This would also explain why the attitude of the elites toward the "Pugachev phenomenon" was so ambiguous, as was so acutely noted by two great Russian poets, Pushkin and Tsvetaieva, both of whom were inspired to write poems about this last great peasant uprising.[8]

The level of tension due to psychological and cultural insecurity can be gauged by looking at the disappearance of such

7. The *odnodvortsy* or "one-homesteaders" were originally men who had served in the army on the southern frontier and been granted a small estate (a single "homestead") by the tsar. In response to pressure from noble landowners in the eighteenth century, the *odnodvortsy* suffered a decline in status to the rank of taxable peasants and therefore faced the threat of enserfment.

8. R. Portal, "Pugačev: une révolution manquée," *Etudes d'histoire moderne et contemporaine* (1947) 1:68–98; Marc Raeff, "Pugachev's Rebellion," in R. Forster and Jack P. Greene, eds., *Preconditions of Revolution in Early Modern Europe* (Baltimore: Johns Hopkins University Press, 1970), pp. 161–202.

ritual forms as the *mestnichestvo* system that Muscovy had developed to resolve personal, social, and political conflicts by externalizing them. Such things were eliminated or vanished when Peter introduced Western norms and practices. The peasantry had one last opportunity to mount an old-fashioned rebellion. As for the elites, it now became difficult for them to externalize personal conflict, for want of accepted or acceptable ways of doing so. Tensions were bottled up or hidden and overt conflict was suppressed, so that internal pressures became increasingly difficult to control. Conflict therefore burst suddenly into the open in a violent form. The state, which should have quelled the sudden blaze, lacked the physical resources to do so and had lost its traditional moral authority and influence. Thus we see a new development in the second half of the eighteenth century, a curious mixture of violence and brutality (especially in the provinces) and no-holds-barred satire in the critical literature. The ambiguous nature of the Muscovite legacy and of the influence of Enlightenment philosophy was reflected in debates within the Academy of Sciences, in Sumarokov's satires, Fonvizin's plays, and in the moral preaching of the Freemasons. While Catherine II unequivocally typified the official triumph of European values, her most famous favorite, Potemkin, exhibited in his personality and behavior all the ambiguities and paradoxes of the Russian elite, an elite that had yet to discover or even describe its new identity. Is there anything surprising in this? New national and cultural identities are not built in a day, and in the case of Russia a place had to be found for persistent Muscovite tradition, even as the lion's share was being handed over to the culture of modern Europe.

4
THE SYSTEM OF
PETER THE GREAT
To Reform or Not To Reform?

HE ruling elites were perfectly aware of the imperfections
in Peter's system, which they saw as a source of conflict and
blamed for their feelings of uneasiness and insecurity. Oddly
enough, it was the "establishment" that gave the leading
segments of society, above all the cultivated elite, the means
to express their concerns and describe the nature of their insecurity. In this way people became aware of their identity
in circumstances quite different from those of the seventeenth century. What happened was that, in 1767, the government called elections for an assembly, which turned out
to be reasonably representative and which was charged with
the responsibility of working out a new legal code.

Since the time when Peter the Great first realized that his
legislative program had introduced confusion into the Muscovite legal system embodied in the *Ulozhenie* or law code
promulgated by Tsar Alexis in 1649, many commissions had
been established for the same purpose. These commissions
had called on the services of various administrative departments and social groups, primarily merchants, with experience in legal matters. The men representing these departments and groups were not elected but appointed to serve on
the commissions. But when Catherine II decided in 1767 to
set up a supreme legislative commission, she commanded that

its members be elected by the free "orders" and classes of the empire.

François-Xavier Coquin has written an invaluable monograph showing that the very way in which the electoral procedures were applied caused an awakening of consciousness among certain "orders" of society.[1] Such an awakening was, in Russia, unprecedented. Since the beginning of the seventeenth century, no Russian had been given an opportunity to perform any act as the member of an "order" (the term being used in Russia to mean something quite close to what it meant in France under the *ancien régime*). Consciousness of belonging to a specific order or class implied a newfound sense of identity, a perception that one shared a community of interests, education, and way of life with other members of the group. This feeling of belonging to a more or less coherent group was able to develop even though, since each "social formation" was in fact a congeries of highly disparate elements, members of a given group might still differ in many respects. Within the nobility, for example, there was a great range of wealth and social rank; yet a sense of belonging to the traditional service nobility did develop and take hold, admittedly in opposition to the *esprit de corps* that bound together newer members of the service class, who were regarded as inferiors by members of the traditional elite. Of even greater significance was the fact that the service class as a whole felt a sense of solidarity in opposition to free peasants and merchants. Finally, members of the urban classes felt, despite wide differences of social and legal status, that they formed a unified urban community and were not merely members of different social groups without connection to the place in which they lived and worked. So that, whereas the legislative commission of 1767 did, in one sense, by revealing divergences over issues of economic interest, lay bare the deepseated conflicts and lack of structure and cohesion in

1. F.-X. Coquin, *La Grande Commission législative (1767–1768). Les Cahiers de doléances urbains* (Paris-Louvain: Nauwelaerts, 1972).

Russian society, in another sense the procedures for choosing the members of that commission pointed up social and psychological bonds based on shared life styles, regional identification, or similar social functions, the full importance of which had not previously been grasped.

The petitions *(nakazy)* submitted to the high commission in 1767 reveal the thinking of commission representatives (and probably also of their constitutents) on social questions, about which we are also informed by reports of debates within that body, which unfortunately Catherine abruptly halted when the discussions took what seemed to her an overly liberal and critical turn. Bear in mind that the commission's members and their electors represented only a small fraction of the various orders of Russian society and made up only one segment of the social elite, those most directly involved in public affairs. What did this embryonic "electorate" want? It is worthy of note that the first thing the members of the electorate wanted was a precise definition of the legal and functional status of the varius "orders" of society.

The nobility wanted a clear demarcation of its boundaries, about which there was controversy among nobles themselves. Some insisted that priority be given to birthright, while others wanted to continue, or even expand the practice of giving priority to state service. The issue was whether the nobility would remain a relatively open class, as it had been under the Table of Ranks, or become an almost closed "caste." The very fact that such a debate took place points up the confusion and ambiguity surrounding the social position of members of the service nobility. To a lesser extent a similar confusion surrounded the position of members of the urban classes, the free peasantry, and certain specific groups, such as the Cossacks, alien populations, etc.

The petitions of the nobility also raised the issues of individual rights and the security of property and demanded for their children educational assistance and preferential access to government posts. The other classes emphasized rights and security just as much if not more than the nobility, but they made their case less emphatically, so far as we are able to judge from published documents.[2] In any case, representatives of all social "orders" and groups demanded assurances of their rights and protections against arbitrary imprisonment and confiscation of their property either by force or by rudimentary judicial proceedings. The principle that these guarantees might vary from one social group or "order" to another was not challenged. However different the legal safeguards might be, the point was that they should, at the very least, be clearly defined and firmly enforced. It should be noted that these demands were not aimed primarily at acts of the sovereign, even those acts seen as despotic. What was at issue was the arbitrariness of state administrators, against which the judicial system offered no adequate protection. Yet there was no demand for a code of laws or "charter" like those in force in the Baltic provinces, whereby the rights and privileges of each individual might be spelled out. The Russian deputies even spoke out indignantly against a proposal by representatives of the Baltic nobility that such a code be drawn up and submitted to the empress. Here again we encounter the same paradox as before: the ruling elite seems to have preferred relations based on a personalized form of ultimate authority to a system based on a legal code and impersonal regulations.

The Commission debates also show that representatives of all social groups backed a division of society into classes and "orders" in accordance with the specific socioeconomic functions performed by each. Accordingly, the nobility would brook no interference by merchants and peasants in the agrarian system, and merchants refused to allow nobles to participate in commerce and manufacturing. As for serfdom, noble and other landowners claimed a monopoly on the ownership of serfs and "populated" lands, while conceding to the

2. Most of the published documents pertain to the nobility and the cities, moreover.

merchant class the right to employ hired labor. Merchants, for their part, protested against nobles who used serfs as agents in commercial activities, and against commercial activities by peasants (often with the protection and on behalf of their noble masters). On the whole, the members of Catherine II's legislative commission had a quite "medieval" conception of society as an "organic" structure based on a hereditary division of functions, a vision of a stable, harmonious society in which, by its very nature, conflict had no place.

The commission of 1767 revealed that Russian society, as envisioned by its elites, had started off in a direction opposite to that of the well-ordered police state as it had been conceived by Peter the Great. The social elite took its distance from the bureaucratic state that had set itself the task of changing the social structure and developing the country's long-term productive potential. To put it another way, the representatives of the upper strata of society preferred a passive political stance to a program of "rational constructivism" (to borrow von Hayek's phrase); they favored a harmonious society in which social and economic functions were carried out by "orders" and "estates" in keeping with tradition and respecting hereditary privileges. Is there anything surprising in this? Most societies are fundamentally conservative. Radical change is usually favored by at most a minority of the elite; the prospect becomes real only when change is thought to be absolutely necessary (as in a time of revolution). In mid-eighteenth-century Russia there was no group or social institution outside the administration itself that was concerned with recasting the Russian state. The radicals and "revolutionaries" were found in the service elite, not in the society at large. What is more, Western Europe had not yet provided the model of a secular ideology advocating radical transformation from below. The only model the West had provided by this date was that of enlightened absolutism, the product and direct heir of the cameralists' well-ordered police state, which Peter I had transplanted to Russian soil.

Catherine II appears to have been rather surprised by what the petitions submitted to her Commission and debates within the Commission revealed about Russian society. At this point she still harbored illusions and showed little awareness of the true desires of the society over which she had reigned for the past five years. Doubtless this was a result of her having limited her contacts, from the time of her arrival in Russia, to the "bureaucracy," the court, and the army. She believed that cameralist methods coupled with an active, dynamic, and productive social program had won the approval of all cultivated Russians. Once in power, she probably felt that her job was simply to improve the existing system by developing administrative procedures for dealing with problems that had arisen since the death of the first emperor so as to place the country squarely on the path of progress. However that may be, it seems that Catherine took very much to heart the lessons gleaned from the commission of 1767. As a result, she developed two tactical approaches to domestic policy, from which she never wavered in any essential respect from that time forth. In retrospect these two approaches might seem to have been contradictory, but neither Catherine nor her collaborators seem to have noticed this.

Catherine II's Administrative Policies

In the area of administration, Catherine II steadfastly and skillfully pursued a policy, first adopted by Peter the Great, that aimed at systematically expanding Russia's resources and productive potential in every possible way.[3] To that end, she attempted to reorganize the government to make it more rational and hence more effective in the long run. It is enough

3. For a recent survey and excellent interpretation, see Isabel de Madariaga, *Russia in the Age of Catherine the Great* (New Haven: Yale University Press; London: Weidenfeld, 1981).

to leaf through the pages of the Complete Collection of Russian Laws to note an impressive change, compared with earlier periods, in the aims and language of legislation adopted under Catherine II. This impression is corroborated by other sources, such as Catherine's letters and memoranda, minutes of committee meetings and investigative reports, and the correspondence of Catherine's collaborators. In the area of economic policy, Catherine encouraged and even set up trading companies and allowed greater freedom to private enterprise. The government did all it could to colonize underpopulated regions in order to increase agricultural production. It stimulated trade by mandating special tariffs and privileges, offered direct encouragement to manufacturers, searched for new sources of raw materials and helped to exploit them when found. It offered new protection to the owners of private property and allowed landowners to dispose freely of minerals taken from their property. Inhabitants of the countryside, including serfs, were confirmed in a limited freedom of movement, provided they obtained authorization from their master or his steward. The code of order *(Ustav blagochiniia)* was shaped by similar considerations. It put the finishing touches on the government's work by sanctioning a series of measures intended to provide Russian cities with a sembance of security, order, and modern amenities. When it came to carrying out these measures, however, the empress found herself at an impasse: Russian society was not sufficiently well organized to bear the brunt of improvement and enforcement on its own. Catherine therefore had to involve the bureaucracy and officially mobilize her subjects to assist the authorities. Therein lay a paradox.

In reorganizing her administration, Catherine attempted to coordinate local and central institutions in a systematic and rational manner. The Provincial Statute of 1775 decreed that the local administration was to be modeled after the central one. The governor was to be assisted by a council, each of whose members was charged with a specific function. Each councillor was to report to the appropriate "college" of the central administration, whose activities were supervised and coordinated by the Senate. The latter, under the leadership of the Procurator General, A. A. Viazemski, was transformed into a sort of council of ministers, which advised the sovereign. The result of these changes was to accelerate the evolution toward monocracy in the departments of the administration, thus leading in the direction of a ministerial system, which by the beginning of the nineteenth century was firmly established. This reorganization of the government also enabled the empress, her cabinet, and the Procurator General of the Senate to exert a more direct and effective control over all the operations of the administration, at both the local and the central level. Under the new system the government began to intervene directly in local affairs, which it treated peremptorily. Additional responsibilities were entrusted to provincial agencies and functionaries, some of whom were elected by the nobility and the urban elites. By shifting a part of its burden onto the shoulders of these local officials, the central administration gave itself greater latitude to promote its cultural and economic policy, while entrusting implementation of that policy to local elites.

In the realm of foreign affairs, Catherine II pursued an expansionist imperial policy based on military force and requiring the imposition of new taxes. Expansion enabled the state to extend its administration into almost virgin territory. This was the most tangible result of Catherine's policy of conquest, colonization, and social integration, which was carried out on behalf of the sovereign by Potemkin, her all-powerful viceroy in the provinces of New Russia on the northern shore of the Black Sea. The military glory won by the imperial army and navy also helped to foster feelings of national pride and cohesiveness, at least within the ruling elites, and these feelings in turn helped to weld together the energies of the various segments of society. New administrative methods were tested out in the newly acquired territories in the South. In addition, following the Pugachev rebellion, the traditional organization of the Cossacks was scrapped in favor of a new approach.

Although Catherine shared with Peter the Great the goal of creating in Russia a well-ordered police state, she took an approach opposite to his. Where Peter had delegated authority to a centralized bureaucracy which he headed, Catherine attempted to establish in Russia "orders" modeled on the *Stände* of her native Germany, which were supposed to help the government to carry out its policy. Her ambition seems to have been to lay the foundations of a system that would shape the development of a dynamic and productive, yet peaceful and harmonious, society, which would proceed to acquire power, prosperity, and happiness under the guidance of the autocratic sovereign. In so doing she may have anticipated desires that came to light in the elections of members to the Commission she formed to write a new code of law and in debates that took place within that body. What is certain is that the initiative came from her and that she acted before the wishes of her subjects became known, as is clear from the legislation involved, which had been in preparation before the commission met and even before the Pugachev rebellion, which provided the pretext for speeding things up. In this work Catherine was aided by an able administrator, Count Sievers, a German from the region of the Baltic, who hoped to reform Russian society to resemble that of his native province.

The first concrete step was taken by Catherine in 1775, with the promulgation of the statute on the provinces, which set up local police departments and charity services administered by elected officials belonging to the local elite. The real keystone of the whole effort was laid in 1785, when charters were drawn up for the nobility and the cities.[4] A third charter,

---

4. Paul Dukes, *Catherine the Great and the Russian Nobility* (Cambridge, England: Cambridge University Press, 1967); R. E. Jones, *The Emancipation of the Russian Nobility, 1762–1785* (Princeton: Princeton University Press, 1973); J. Michael Hittle, *The Service City. State and Town in Russia. 1600–1800* (Cambridge, Mass.: Harvard University Press, 1979).

dealing with state peasants, was also drawn up but never put into effect for reasons that are still not entirely clear (opposition from the elites may have been responsible, or perhaps fear of the spread of liberal and revolutionary ideas from the West—we cannot be certain). If the elections of 1767 helped to shape a corporate spirit among the various components of the imperial elite, the charters helped to establish an institutional framework within which that spirit could flourish.

The charters actually served two functions, one official, the other unofficial. The official function was straightforward in its effects, the other more indirect, working over the long run through the private sector. The charters set up an official mechanism whereby elected representatives of the urban and noble "estates" could assist in the implementation of imperial legislation at the local level. As representatives of autonomous corporate bodies, those elected were also authorized to defend the material and social interests of those of their peers who were not in a position to defend their own interests as individuals (orphans, widows, invalids, the insane, etc.). The representatives of the nobility, who enjoyed some degree of autonomy, played a considerable role on the local level: among other things, they were responsible for policing the countryside and by proxy judged, in lieu of the masters, peasants charged with minor offenses. They also arbitrated in conflicts between nobles. The city charters were more limited in scope, owing mainly to the isolation of the provincial towns. City representatives, elected by the members of the commericial and manufacturing elites, worked under the direct supervision of the local bureaucracy, of which they were merely deputies. Still, by taking a direct part in the administration of the country, elected representatives of the towns, like those of the nobility, helped not only to broaden the base of the administration but also to involve the elite in the work of the government, something that needed to be done if the plan of restructuring Russian society to develop its productive potential was to have any hope of success. This kind of

participation enhanced the effectiveness of government action at the local level and made possible a more extensive exploitation of the available resources. Striking confirmation of
the value of this participation came during the long and difficult war with Napoleon, particularly during the invasion of
1812. In addition, even limited participation of this kind offered an alternative to reliance on the traditional service elite
and stimulated the interest of those involved in the development of their region. This led, ultimately, to a situation as
paradoxical, perhaps, as that of the intelligentsia: the autocratic establishment itself helped to create a number of social groups which, because they wanted more independence
than the bureaucracy was willing to allow, later became centers of opposition.[5]

The second function of the 1785 charters, this one unack-
nowledged and "unofficial," did not produce tangible results
until well after the death of Catherine II, but, since these
reinforced the effects just described, their importance should
not be underestimated. The need (or obligation) to elect representatives at periodic intervals, and the attraction that local office held for many individuals, meant that the members
of district, town, and provincial corps and "estates" had to
meet regularly, and this helped to maintain a social life within
the elite. At the same time, the fact that, during these meetings, public as well as private business was transacted helped
to foster within the elite a sense of belonging to a definite
social group, and the resulting feelings of solidarity heightened awareness of the common interests that members of the
group might wish to defend or pursue. To an elite which had
been a prisoner of Muscovite tradition and which had been
fragmented by Peter's reforms, the charters opened up new
possibilities, new ways of escaping from a situation in which
the individual was a plaything of fate, dependent on the un-

---

5. The events surrounding the *zemstvo* reforms of 1864 unfolded almost identi-
cally.

predictable fortunes of imperial favorites and on arbitrary and impersonal decisions made by agencies of the imperial bureaucracy. We see signs of new feelings of security, strengthened by new guarantees of individual rights and property contained in legislation promulgated by Catherine though still ignored by her underlings. The newly acquired *esprit de corps* helped to check the arbitrariness and brutality of tyrannical local officials, at least when it came to dealing with titled luminaries and wealthy merchants. Psychologically more secure, members of the elite now felt freer to embark on new ventures. Above all, they were able to form their own judgments, develop their own attitudes, and live in a way that was not dictated by the sovereign or imposed by fiat.

In the late eighteenth century we see a decentralization of elite social life and culture. The capitals lost their monopoly, and members of the elite embraced a broader range of ideas. Some were nonconformist. New reserves of creative energy were tapped. By the nineteenth century, the local elites, having withstood the Napoleonic invasions, were ready to contribute to the development of critical thinking that came in response to the conformism and uniformity imposed by the sovereign and the court: the "thick journals," as they were known, found an enthusiastic audience in the countryside and helped to expand the intelligentsia.

Until the beginning of Alexander I's reign, however, these tentative gropings by local elites in the direction of greater autonomy were held in check by the sovereigns Catherine II and Paul I and their agents, whose outlook was paternalistic and suspicious of local initiatives. It should be noted, too, that the charters themselves were paternalistic documents, and the way they were put into effect was even more so. This paternalism affected the attitudes of governors, garrison commanders, and police chiefs, who left noble assemblies and urban *dumas* very little latitude. The "societies" or corporations of the provincial nobility were placed under the control of the governors, who did their best to make sure that the men elected marshals of the nobility would be loyal and pliable. Elected administrators responsible for such things as charitable assistance and local police wielded very limited authority, and their field of action was restricted by the fact that the bureaucracy controlled their budgets.

Finally, it should be noted that the state, by setting up these local "corporations," that is, by restructuring Russian society on the basis of "estates" (or "orders"), reserved for itself the right to play the role of arbitrator or mediator among them. This merely accentuated the traditional role of the autocrat. Since the initiative for reform came from the sovereign, the feeling that only the sovereign could improve conditions and make fundamental changes in Russian society was reinforced. Of course, this only meant that, ultimately, the sovereign would also be held responsible for the system's defects.

Catherine II thus attempted to reshape Russian society. And it must be admitted that she was quite successful in expanding the administration and in moving toward greater local autonomy. Local elites were allowed to take the lead in organizing cultural life and charitable assistance and guaranteed certain basic rights as individuals and property owners. But, when measured against their ambitious aims, Catherine's efforts fell far short of complete success: paternalism degenerated into bureaucratic arbitrariness, and the primacy granted to the will of the autocrat infringed upon individual liberties. In my view, however, the major factor responsible for the failure to consolidate a system of "orders" or autonomous intermediary bodies was the absence of a stable and coherent system of law. Admittedly, personal and property rights were more assured after 1785 than before. Capricious and arbitrary measures by the government or private parties against individuals and their property were, in theory at any rate, no longer tolerated. Landowners could dispose of the produce of their land and of the minerals beneath it as they saw fit. But there was no code of law to enforce respect for these ostensible rights. The autocrat and his or her agents were not required to respect private rights when these conflicted with state interests: witness the resurgence of arbitrary arrests and seizures of property from nobles and merchants by agents of Paul I. Nor were such procedures entirely eliminated during the reign of his son. The fact is that, beyond the formal rights, there loomed the slavery-like system of serfdom, which left its stamp on personal relations and shaped the character of authority throughout Russia.

The lack of a comprehensive and systematic code of law was increasingly felt in both the public and private spheres and made the corporate structures that Catherine had tried to establish quite fragile. The important thing to notice is that the lack of a legal code also precluded the development of a strong, independent judiciary to enforce respect for the law: there was no possibility of establishing a *Rechtsstaat.* Russia did, of course, have a judicial system, and Catherine's legislation helped to improve its quality, in particular by limiting inquisitorial proceedings. But the whole judiciary was part and parcel of the imperial administrative system: with no independent status or standards, it was subject to the whim and caprice of state functionaries.

Unofficial publicists of the time as well as liberal historians have made much of the "tribunals of conscience" *(sovestnyi sud)* established under the provisions of the charters granted to the nobility and the towns. These tribunals were supposed to hear private lawsuits of minor importance, especially those having to do with inheritances and property damages (up to a certain amount). But those who argue for the importance of these tribunals forget that the proceedings were merely arbitration hearings, normally presided over by the marshal of the nobility alone. Both parties had to accept the judge's verdict, which was based on grounds of equity; otherwise, the case was brought before the state tribunals, where it followed the usual channels (going first to the court of appeals, then to the Senate, and finally to the tsar). The sovereign was not bound by any prior judgment and in fact decided cases without regard for edicts and legislative acts that were supposed to carry the force of law. Hence the judges in these courts *(sovestnyi sud'ia)* were a far cry from English justices of the peace, to whom they have often been compared in the historical literature. Indeed, one might even argue that their function was to issue judgments without regard to existing laws (in the sense of previously promulgated edicts and decrees), just as the sovereign did in the last resort. To allow such tribunals was to acknowledge that there was in fact no coherent system of laws and that, in many cases, it was preferable for the parties to reach an agreement outside the legal system, based on a concept of equity different from that embodied in imperial legislation; the mechanism for reaching such an agreement was a kind of arbitration and really amounted to little more than a private accommodation between the parties. The *sovestnyi sud'ia* cannot be compared to English judges in equity or justices of the peace. Rather, they embodied power at the local level and wielded a moral authority similar to that wielded by the sovereign at the imperial level. This accounts for the opinion of at least one Russian jurist that the *sovestnyi sud* delayed the establishment of a *Rechtsstaat* in Russia.[6]

Such was the paradoxical, not to say wholly unanticipated, result of Catherine's efforts to create a society of "estates" in Russia. The seeming paradox is in fact the logical consequence of a mistaken notion of how civil society develops and of the preference for a state-mandated recasting of society from top to bottom. By taking this course Catherine ensured that Russian civil society would not enjoy the benefits of a fixed, stable, and coherent system of law enforced by an independent judiciary.

6. G. Barats, "Ocherk proiskhozhdeniia i postepennogo zatem uprazdneniia v Rossii sovestnykh sudov i suda po sovesti," *Zhurnal grazhdanskogo i ugolovnogo prava,* vol. 23, no. 3 (1893), pp. 1–40.

It is reasonable to ask whether a society of "orders" can in fact be created by fiat. If Russian society, or at any rate its elites, already had a sense of identity deriving from its division into "orders" or other intermediary groupings, should not the government have been content to foster the slow and steady growth of this natural social identity? It could have done this by granting individuals and groups far greater freedoms than Catherine II and her successors were prepared to do. Serfdom, in my view, was not necessarily the reason for the reluctance to grant these freedoms. Admittedly, the existence of serfdom did limit the state's room to maneuver. But the government could have shifted much of the burden of the serfdom issue to the landed nobility, as was done in Prussia (even in Russia many of the practical problems of the serf system were handled by the nobility). But the Russian nobility, fearful of the peasantry, was unprepared to accept full responsbility for maintaining the serf system: it needed the state as a shield. Without this shield the provincial nobility, tradition-bound, distracted by state service obligations, impoverished, and culturally backward, would not have been able to survive. Hence it accepted its subordination to the state and its lack of corporate autonomy.

What is more, a society of orders was becoming more and more of an anachronism, as is evident from developments in Central and Western Europe. By the end of the eighteenth century, such a model was no longer appropriate for a country that saw itself as a great power engaged in a process of modernization. The society of orders ran counter to the growing force of individualism, especially in the areas of economic and cultural activity. Catherine's contributions to Russian culture were considerable. It is fair to say that, during her reign, deliberate and systematic progress was almost entirely confined to the social and cultural spheres. Yet the results of Catherine's cultural policy ultimately proved paradoxical, and this had a major impact on the relations between state and society in the decades following her death and beyond.

Cultural Life

Catherine II was passionate about intellectual life in all its forms. As she recounts in her *Memoirs*, during the long years of insecurity when she was kept away from the court of her predecessor, Elizabeth, and lived married to a child who did not love her and for whom she could feel only contempt and disgust, books were her refuge and consolation; romantic adventures had almost no influence on her thinking or politics. Hence it is hardly surprising that, when she finally came to occupy the throne, she energetically supported and encouraged the cultural life of her country, not only within her court entourage but also in the provinces. Sometimes she sounded the keynote herself, sometimes she offered subsidies and financial support either directly or through functionaries and favorites. Mention has already been made of the proliferation of public and private schools. Catherine also encouraged systematic use of new teaching methods based on the writings of Locke as well as those of Wieland, Basedow, and also, without acknowledgment, Jean-Jacques Rousseau. New academies and boarding schools were set up for children of the nobility, and the corps of cadets was extended to the provinces. The Smolny Institute accepted young girls from good families. The University of Moscow was revitalized by the appointment of Russian professors; nobles were encouraged, by the creation of a special *gymnasium* and by the prospect of special career preferment upon graduation, to attend courses. The Academy of Sciences was reformed and essentially converted into a research center. The brilliant success of Catherine's educational and cultural policies may be judged by the names of those who added to the luster of Russian culture in the early nineteenth century. I hardly need remind the reader that the objective of the new teaching methods was to produce a new kind of man: the enlightened subject of the Russian Empire, a man (or woman) equipped to play an active and useful role in the development of the country's economy as well as its culture.

Literature and the theater were also encouraged by Catherine II. Literature (mainly in the form of periodicals and plays) followed contemporary Western models in taking a didactic, moralizing tone intended to develop a cultivated elite whose highest ideal would be one of social utility and service. Satirical magazines, some of which included polemical articles by the empress herself, were only one facet of this didactic literature. In 1783 Catherine abolished the state monopoly on publishing and authorized the establishment of private presses and publishing houses. Her censorship policy was relatively mild.[7] The number of books printed rose sharply. Publishers sprang up in the provinces, and literary magazines appeared to make room for the first fruits of a new regional literature. Encouraged by the organizing talent of N. I. Novikov, publishing in Russia experienced an unprecedented period of growth, and for the first time books became available in Russian for specific groups of readers, such as children, estate managers, religious devotees, and so on. Novikov's work in publishing provided the background for the establishment (avant la lettre) of "societies of thought" and for the encouragement of translations from Western literature; it also helped to spread Western philosophical and religious ideas and practices (the publications of the Free Economics Society are a case in point).

Masonic lodges and societies also became quite popular, partly as a new center of social life, partly in response to deepseated social and spiritual aspirations. The church had

7. See the recent study by K. A. Papmehl, *Freedom of Expression in Eighteenth-Century Russia* (The Hague: Nijhoff, 1971).

fallen under the administrative tutelage of the government, as a result of which its cultural life withered and its importance as a spiritual and moral guide diminished. Many cultivated people found that the official church no longer fulfilled their religious needs and so looked elsewhere to satisfy their moral cravings and assuage their spiritual thirst. Influenced by the European Protestant revival (Methodism and Pietism), many Russians sought satisfaction in individualistic forms of spirituality and religious experience or in social activism illuminated by religious fervor. The Masonic lodges, various mystical and spiritualist sects, and the teachings of people like Skovoroda and Tikhon Zadonski all contributed to a revival of private religious life; devotees communicated with one another through a network of lodges, charitable organizations, and religious publications. Many of the leading ideas of the Enlightenment were popularized in Russia by spiritualist circles, but the emphasis was on enlightenment of the heart as much as enlightenment of the mind and veered in the direction of pre-Romanticism and sentimentalism.

Intellectual life changed as it became possible for cultivated people living in the provinces to maintain contact with another. There is still no proof that nobles returned in large numbers to the land and to their country estates once state service ceased to be obligatory in 1762. It is clear, however, that the acts of 1775 and 1785 encouraged the landed nobility to make more frequent and extended visits to their residences in the countryside. Time in the country became easier to bear as cultural life in the leading provincial cities advanced and it became possible to obtain reviews and other reading matter. A provincial society began to develop. This society saw itself as independent of the state, and its members developed a new sense of identity and solidarity no longer based on state service. The needs of this developing provincial society were anticipated by legislation sponsored by Catherine II, whose intention was to create a society based on "orders" and intermediary bodies. But the new society lacked a solid institutional base and hence could not assume the functional role for which the empress had intended it. The contradiction, or rather the disparity, between, on the one hand, Catherine's intention to assign to the social "orders" and corporate groupings an economic and administrative role designed to serve the needs of the state and, on the other hand, the individualistic and centrifugal tendencies of cultural and intellectual life was the underlying cause of the conflict between state and society that began to develop at the end of the enlightened empress's reign.

The efforts of the empress and of the other leading proponents of the enlightenment in Russia—most notably Novikov, Fonvizin, Krylov, Radishchev, and Karamzin—all aimed at the same objective: to educate active individuals, loyal and patriotic subjects, who would have an acute sense of their moral obligations not only to the sovereign and the empire but to all of Russian society, including the peasantry.[8] Here we must pause and look back to an earlier period. As was mentioned previously, the new forms of state service imposed by Peter I played an important part in shaping a cultivated elite that adopted a European style of living. Service obligations engendered an ethos of loyalty toward the government, a sense of commitment to the state for which members of the reorganized state service corps labored in the public interest. Western education, especially the new teaching methods that gave priority to the moral and cultural responsibility of the individual, helped shape the ideals of the new elite: devotion to the life of the mind and the service of the people.

Yet nobles in state service were rootless and alienated men who saw themselves as anonymous cogs in an enormous machine. They were cut off from the people, who did not share

8. Isabel de Madariaga, "Catherine II and the Serfs: A Reconsideration of Some Problems", *Slavonic and East European Review*, 1974; Jean-Louis Van Regemorter, "Deux images de la paysannerie russe à la fin du XVIIIe siècle, *Cahiers du monde russe et soviétique*, vol. 9, no. 1 (1968), pp. 5–19.

their culture and who, literally as well as figuratively, spoke a different language. The decree of February 18, 1762, whereby Peter II freed the nobility from the obligation to serve the state, enabled nobles who had once bestowed their loyalty upon the state to turn instead to the people. As was mentioned a moment ago, nobles began spending longer periods of time in the countryside, and they now had greater freedom to pursue their own course culturally as well as economically. The upshot of these changes was that the cultivated elite, or at any rate its most advanced and liberal members, began to focus their efforts on a new task: that of serving the people as moral guides and spiritual and cultural teachers. People were at first barely conscious of the change. Yet the first tentative steps in this direction presaged the growth of a new critical attitude toward the imperial establishment and particularly the government. Thus, within the elite of Russian society, there began to develop the seeds of future dissidence and even subversion.

Change cut two ways. Individualism in intellectual and ethical life was the result of changes in Russian society that had been encouraged (not to say triggered) by Peter's reforms and Catherine's legislative program. But was not this individualism in contradiction with the standards of behavior implicit in the system of "orders" that the government attempted to foster? The activism of Masons like Novikov in the areas of culture, religion, and social life—an activism wholly in keeping with Western ideals of spiritual and intellectual individualism—ran counter to the material interests of much of society and, in particular, to the limited objectives that the empress had laid down. This explains why Catherine opposed the establishment of community-based charitable organizations and efforts to assist the hungry and sick or to educate the poor. She viewed with suspicion any group that took it upon itself to provide needed public services, independent of government supervision. Her suspicion was only reinforced by her belief that such activities were a potential source of subversion, like that responsible for the recent revolutions in France and the Low Countries. Here we see one of the first signs of the mutual misunderstanding that marked relations between the autocratic government and the intellectual elite. Russian rulers were not averse to the development of growing numbers of cultivated individuals with a sense of moral responsibility, devoted to improving the general welfare and contributing to the progress, material as well as spiritual, of the nation. But they did not like the idea of individual social, cultural, and moral commitments leading to the development of independent institutions not subject to government control. Accordingly, some of the most outstanding representatives of the cultural elite were dealt with severely: witness Catherine II's treatment of Novikov and Radishchev.

Thus a new problem came to the fore: Could the moral teachings and intellectual standards of the European Enlightenment (whether in the rational-philosophical form these took in France and England or in the spiritual-sentimental form they took in Germany) be reconciled with autocracy and with the arbitrary, personalized authority wielded by the agents of the tsar? The negative answer given to this question constitutes the "birth certificate" of the intelligentsia, the avant-garde of the cultivated elite that was the first to perceive the contradiction between, on the one hand, the elite's conception of its moral mission and responsibility to work for the good of the people and, on the other hand, its commitment to the state and to its supreme embodiment in the person of the autocrat.

By the end of Catherine II's reign, the blueprint for a civil society in Russia was ready, but none of the necessary social institutions had yet been erected, and none would be erected, for the reasons we have seen. The intelligentsia, the critical fringe of the ruling class and cultural elite and a fertile ground for the growth of ideology, was almost fully constituted, thanks to state policies first instituted by Peter the Great and continued, with new methods, by Catherine II.

A void opened up between, on the one side, civil society and the intelligentsia and, on the other side, the autocratic state, which worked hard to circumscribe the area of permissible independent activities. How was this void to be filled, and by whom? This was the challenge that Russia faced as the nineteenth century began.

5
THE DAWN OF
THE NINETEENTH CENTURY

THE reign of Paul I, despite its brevity, had a strong influence on the policies of Paul's successor, Alexander I, and on the thinking of the intellectual elite. Paul's regime was repressive and capricious, though there were some tentative steps toward social reform (including a limit of three days per week on labor owed by tenants to their lord) and probably also a plan to reorganize the government, which was apparently designed to lay the foundations of a regular legal system and possibly a constitutional monarchy.[1] The period of Paul's rule was a nightmare for the cultural elite of the nation, and particularly for those who lived in St. Petersburg, under the eyes of the emperor. Paul's peculiar behavior left officials and ministers afraid for themselves and their careers. No one felt safe when a change in the sovereign's mood might mean exile from the capital, loss of office and rank, or even imprisonment for an indefinite length of time. Social and cultural life in the provinces, which had begun to blossom toward the end of Catherine II's reign, was jeopardized by Paul's determination to recall nobles to active state service. Many who had been ranking officials under Catherine took refuge in Moscow after being disgraced by her son, and there they lived

1. C. Scharf, "Staatsauffassung und Regierungsprogramm eines aufgeklärten Seslbstherrschers. Die Instruktion des Grossfürsten Paul von 1788," *Studien zur europäischen Geschichte*, 1968.

a sumptuous, if seditious, existence that gave fresh luster to cultural and social life in the old capital. But most nobles living in the provinces knew that at any moment they might be called to St. Petersburg and lose the fruits of their efforts to create a cultivated and carefree life in the country.

Intellectuals saw the reign of Paul I as especially tyrannical. After the execution of Louis XVI, Catherine had inaugurated a kind of *cordon sanitaire* to protect Russia against contagion by the germs of Revolution; Paul instituted still more Draconian measures in this regard, with a pettiness at times bordering on the ridiculous. He forbade not only French books and ideas but also fashions alleged to be "revolutionary" in origin and, like his father Peter III before him, attempted to induce the Russian elite to adopt the Prussian style of dress by forcing people to wear the same uniforms, as grotesque as they were uncomfortable, in which he dressed his own guards. Censorship was fierce: even books of mathematics and music were outlawed, on the pretext that mathematical symbols and musical notes might be used as codes whereby subversive ideas might be introduced surreptitiously. The government again clamped down on Russian literature, which had just begun to come into its own: presses were closed or subjected to intolerable controls. Militarism set the tone for all public events, particularly in the capital: Paul's mania for parades was proverbial. Education suffered greatly, above all the institutions of higher education and private schools that offered a broad, humanistic training. Young graduates had almost no choice but to pursue a sterile career in the military or accept a post in the administration, which at this time was run in the most regimented manner possible.

The repression was far worse than it had been in the final years of Catherine's reign, and literary and artistic life (especially the theater) suffered greatly under oppressive government control. Arts that had just begun to flourish were threatened with extinction. Given the circumstances, it is hardly surprising that news of the assassination of the emperor by a group of quite prominent, hence quite vulnerable, officers and dignitaries was received with indecent glee by the cultivated elite and most of officialdom. Paul's reign had demonstrated how fragile Russia's social and cultural progress was. The lesson was clear: the political and cultural gains of the past would have to be consolidated. Paul's capricious rule exposed the vulnerability of all that had been achieved since Peter the Great and thus helped to trigger a positive reaction on the part of both government and society (or at any rate by the cultural elite). The changed atmosphere was apparent from the moment Alexander I took the throne.

To begin with, the government made a series of administrative and political changes that helped to shape further social and intellectual developments. The objective was to reorganize the government in such a way as to continue, in the spirit of Catherine II, the work of Peter the Great. Peter had labored in haste to meet the needs of the moment and had never established a coherent and stable structure of government. Catherine II had worked to shore up the social underpinnings of the cultural and administrative changes introduced by Peter. The policy of Alexander I was designed to establish an administrative system that would draw its personnel from elite groups within the society, groups that would be allowed to act independently of the government in the cultural sphere and other areas.

The Reforms of Alexander I

What Alexander's contemporaries referred to as programs of "constitutional" reform were in fact plans to rationalize the structure of the bureaucracy and increase its efficiency. Alexander (and indeed his successors) achieved far less than he had hoped in this regard. Nevertheless, the first steps were taken toward creating a stable, rational, and reasonably efficient bureaucracy; the durability of this system is attested by the fact that it survived, almost intact, until the revolutionary upheavals of the early twentieth century. As in the time of Peter I, the government's main concern was with the central administration. Alexander's reforms, which included the creation of ministries and a Council of State, merely culminated an evolution that began in the second half of the eighteenth century. By the end of Catherine II's reign, A. A. Viazemski, the Procurator General of the Senate, was acting almost as a prime minister, coordinating the activities of the several executive departments, which were headed by officials with virtually ministerial responsibilities.

But Alexander's reform program, begun in 1802 with the creation of ministries and completed in 1811, when the internal structure of the leading ministries was fixed, went much further than his predecessors' efforts in this direction. Alexander believed firmly in a policy of making one man responsible for the work of each ministry. Ministerial responsibilities were divided up in a rational way, so as to avoid jurisdictional conflicts between ministers. Internally, the hierarchy of each ministry (modeled on that of Napoleon's army) resembled a pyramid. The minister could call upon the assistance of his staff, made up of the heads of the major departments within the ministry. Each of these departments had distinct functional responsibilities. Each department head wielded considerable authority in his own domain, within which he enjoyed a good deal of autonomy. Coordination of the ministry's functions was accomplished by a council of department heads, which met regularly and referred all conflicts to the minister. The minister in turn reported to the commander-in-chief: the tsar.

In theory, the tsar, too, had a staff, consisting of the ministers of all the various ministries. But Alexander I refused to consolidate the system by taking this final step. Although a Council of Ministers did exist, not all ministers were invited to its meetings, which were held only when the monarch deemed it necessary to deal with matters involving a number of different ministries. The Council of Ministers was never a truly indispensable tool of long-range imperial policy. Alexander I preferred to work with individual ministers, one at a time, while reserving to himself the right to decide in case of conflict between ministers, thereby preserving his autocratic power intact. His successors followed the same course. Nevertheless, the reforms, which were carried out with great skill by competent men, greatly enhanced the efficiency of the central government in many areas of economic, social, and political life. In particular, legislation was more thoroughly prepared thanks to preliminary study and discussion of technical aspects of the issues involved.

The main architect of the ministerial reform and especially of the internal organization of the ministries was M. M. Speransky. He was also responsible for the creation of the Council of State, whose main tasks were to supervise the activities of the various ministries and to plan major legislation. This council was first established in 1811 and, though it never functioned as Speransky envisioned, subsequently became one of the most important bodies in the imperial government. It was divided into three sections (dealing with economics, justice, and the military). The economic and military sections were very effective, thanks to the talents of their respective chiefs, Admiral Mordvinov and General Arakcheev, who developed their sections into centers of information and legislative committees. In plenary sessions, however, the Council acted as a mere drafting committee, which thrashed out the language of legislation without exerting any real influence over its content; this was particularly true after the disgrace of Speransky, who served as the Council's first secretary of state. Once again, an attempt to find an effective institutional means to coordinate and plan state actions came to nought, stymied by rivalries among high officials, personal jealousy, and the monarch's desire to preserve his autocratic authority intact. In this the emperor was abetted by seg-

ments of the ruling elite, which divined greater influence, security, and privilege for themselves in this form of power.
Under this system there was no need for political parties to
seek a broad base of support; indeed, parties were prevented
even from forming. Many influential people had no use for a
powerful and increasingly professionalized bureaucracy
standing between them and the sovereign.

Alexander's reforms were doubly important because they
affected the local as well as the central government bureaucracy. The institutional reorganization of the central government was therefore not, as it had been in the time of Peter I,
left suspended in midair, unconnected to what was going on
at the local level and unrelated to the country's real needs.
Admittedly, under Alexander I the link between the capital
and the provinces was not as close or as reciprocal as it needed
to be in order for government to be really efficient. But a new
and more effective system of communication had at least been
begun. Although this system was allowed to fall into disre-
pair under Nicholas I, it proved to be an essential tool for the
reform of the local administration that was carried out under
Alexander II.

Alexander I's major innovation in regional government was
to link the provincial councils (gubernatorskie pravleniia)
created by Catherine II to the ministries rather than to the
Senate. The provincial council served the governor of the
province as an advisory body. Members of the council were
usually career civil servants with fairly specialized knowledge of some area of government. Each one was assigned to a
particular area of local administration (tax collection, justice,
commerce, police, etc.). Obviously, such an organizational
structure was not exempt from jurisdictional conflicts. Since
the governor could communicate directly with the monarch,
moreover, the authority of the various department heads (in
charge of taxes, disbursement, and so on) was diminished. If
the governor was an energetic man who wielded considerable
influence in St. Petersburg, his subordinates were little more

than clerks. But the new system also meant that he could govern his province with the aid of experienced men and call upon the assistance of ministries with specialized knowledge and skills. Some measure of administrative decentralization became possible. Local officials could be afforded somewhat more latitude and allowed to take greater initiatives than before. This helped to lubricate the whole administrative machine, which ran more smoothly as a result. The regional policy that these changes made possible was essentially maintained throughout the first half of the nineteenth century, at least in outlying areas such as Finland, Siberia, and the Caucasus.

In the economic and social spheres, the government of Alexander I followed the course first set by Catherine II and attempted to create conditions favorable to economic growth. On the one hand, the administration encouraged private enterprise, offering aid to a variety of entrepreneurs. In this it was responding to the influence of Adam Smith's ideas and of *laissez-faire* liberalism, an economic and social ideology just then coming to prominence in the West. In the same vein the government helped to promote the formation of private groups and associations with common economic interests in the hope of encouraging enterprise and stimulating economic growth. On the other hand, however, the government was aware of some of the causes of Russia's economic backwardness (lack of capital and lack of managerial talent, for example). It therefore tried to subsidize industrial and commercial development throughout the empire. One of the tools for doing this was protectionism, on which the government relied increasingly after 1815. Such a pragmatic compromise between the statist ideology of cameralism and the *laissez-faire* ideology of liberalism may indeed have been the best way to hasten the modernization of Russian society.

In any case, the policy bore fruit. The rapid expansion of the textile industry is one illustration; another is increased exploitation of raw materials. Machinery manufacturing ad-

vanced only slightly, however, in part because the importation of English machinery impeded the development of domestic manufacturing (overall demand was still low). The
relatively liberal economic policy that made this possible also
helped the country to recover rapidly from the damages it
suffered in 1812; recovery was also aided by peasant entrepreneurs, who provided transportation, raw materials, and
much of the needed manpower. The situation enabled the
more dynamic segments of the popular classes, particularly
the Old Believers, to establish networks of communication
and sources of credit which in turn contributed to the rapid
growth of mass-consumption industries such as the manufacture of cotton goods and household articles, thus creating
the conditions for an industrial takeoff a generation or two
later. The essential point for our purposes is that these developments in the economy helped to enlarge the sphere of
action open to individuals. Common activities helped to develop new forms of solidarity, and new groups arose to meet
new needs. Thus a civil society developed around material
interests, complementing the society that had formed around
shared cultural and intellectual interests. But the seeds sown
in the early part of the nineteenth century did not bear fruit
until the end of that century and the beginning of the next.

It is important to keep in mind that serfdom constituted a
major, if not quite unsurmountable, obstacle to social and
economic modernization. As was mentioned earlier, Catherine II had seriously considered allowing serfs, or at any rate
state peasants, to take an active part in the economic development of the nation. Recent research has shown that this
was one of her constant preoccupations but that social and
political considerations prevented her from acting. Paul I set
limits to the amount of labor owed by a peasant to his lord
out of a similar concern that the state must do something to
improve the peasant's lot, for economic and social rather than
philanthropic reasons (though philanthropy, too, may have
played some part, encouraged by Radishchev's diatribe against

serfdom and by the moralistic writings of Fonvizin, Novikov, and Krylov). In any case, after Alexander I came to the throne, the question was reexamined by the new tsar and his "young friends," who formed a sort of unofficial advisory committee. The desired solution would have to reconcile two objectives. First, something had to be done to improve the economic and administrative status of the state peasants and to prevent them from falling under the sway of private landowners (as gifts of the sovereign). Second, a way had to be found to allow land-owners to free their serfs on terms that would guarantee the former serfs both personal liberty and enough resources to earn their living. With respect to the first point, Alexander I stopped making gifts to nobles of "populated" lands. To compensate his loyal servants and favorites in the future, the monarch would give away only the usufruct *(arenda)* of certain popu-lated lands; in other words, the recipients of these gifts would own only the income produced by the land and not the land itself or its inhabitants, which would remain the property of the state. Published announcements of serf sales were made illegal, though the law in this regard was never really obeyed. Improvements in the administration of state peasants—a pre-requisite to improvement of their physical and social condi-tion—were barely begun under Alexander I; what was done was due mainly to the initiative of Speransky. The definitive legislation was completed and put into effect only two de-cades later, under Nicholas I, when the Ministry of State Do-mains was created with the responsibility to take steps to improve the standard of living of the peasantry.

Private arrangements between serfs and their masters were legalized in some circumstances, such as those envisaged by the "free farmers" decree of 1803, but this remained a largely symbolic gesture of no real benefit to anyone. Between 1816 and 1819, landowners in the Baltic region, mostly German nobles, were allowed to emancipate their serfs but without land. What emerged in the Baltic provinces then was the spectacle of a peasantry that was legally free but in fact subject to harsher exploitation than ever by landlords who were the only prospective employers in the region. The Russian government and elite learned a lesson from this experience. From 1820 on, all proposals to emancipate the serfs agreed on one point: that the serfs could not be freed without also being given enough land to earn a living.

The foregoing brief summary of economic and social policy under Alexander I shows what a pivotal role property relations were destined to play in Russian history from this time forward. Trade and the sale of rights to land and to the labor of others called for clarification of existing laws governing property and persons. The need for a comprehensive code of law began to be felt. People understood that such a code need not concern itself with public or constitutional law but could focus exclusively on the private sphere. The great Prussian, Tuscan, and Austrian codes could be taken as models, along with that supreme example of how to construct a code of laws, the Napoleonic Code. All of these showed, if any demonstration was necessary, that a code of laws could be introduced without changing the social hierarchy or jeopardizing the existing political system.

Thus, in the early decades of the nineteenth century, commissions were appointed on a number of occasions to look into the codification of Russian law. There was nothing new about the idea of appointing such commissions, which harked backed to Catherine II's experiment with her legislative Commission. What was new was the approach to the law. The legislative commissions of the eighteenth century saw their job mainly as a matter of compiling "customary" statutes and perhaps of condensing the existing legal tradition for the purposes of teaching and everyday use in the courts. The commission appointed by Alexander I at the beginning of his reign, like the several other commissions named in later years (the best known, owing to the opposition it aroused, being that headed by Speransky, which sat from 1809 until 1812), took a different approach. It saw its task as one of drafting a comprehensive new code of law based on principles set forth in other countries and not merely on Russian legal tradition and existing laws.

This is not the place to examine critically the methods used. What should be noted is the new spirit in which the attempt at legal reform was made, a spirit of radical, rational constructivism. Rather than assembling existing laws into a handy, practical compendium, the commissions set out to elaborate new legal standards. The method used by these commissions was to copy other modern legal codes, most notably the Civil Code of France. It is perhaps fortunate that no attempt was made to put such a code into effect. But the effort of drafting one taught Russian jurists an important lesson: they saw the need for establishing legal standards, for formulating principles on which a legal system could be based, principles which in turn could serve as guidelines for social and economic modernization. This was the general outlook that governed later attempts to reform the legal system, again led by Speransky, under Nicholas I. This time the results were substantial: in 1832 the Complete Collection of Russian Law *(Polnoe sobranie zakonov)* was published, followed in 1835 by a condensed version (the *Svod*). Still, the logical next step, that of formulating a truly useful and comprehensive legal code, was never taken. No such code was ever promulgated in imperial Russia.

Opposition to Reform

Modest as the policies of reform were, they nevertheless stirred up considerable opposition. There was predictable opposition, to begin with, from conservative circles under the influence of men who had been high-ranking officials under Catherine II and who, ever since the reign of Paul, had been living in semi-exile in Moscow. These men judged Alexander I's reforming zeal to be inopportune and his policies to be inappropriate for Russia. They found support in the Senate, a majority of whose members were men who had been ranking officials in earlier years. Many of them felt that the importance of the Senate was threatened by the reforms, which in any case were based on French rationalist ideas whose dangerous revolutionary tenor had been confirmed by events. Although the conservatives spoke French in their salons, they had been brought up in the intellectual traditions of cameralism and the German *Aufklärung* and were attracted by the manners and political values of the Whig aristocracy in England. Most of the conservative opposition belonged to the Senate and hoped to use that institution to prosecute its own program of reforms.

It is reasonable to ask why, throughout the eighteenth century and again at the beginning of the nineteenth century, was the Senate both the symbol and the rallying point of all those who wished to see administrative and political change without accompanying radical social transformation? And why did the Senate become the center of a conservative *fronde*, which seemed, at least implicitly, to condemn the reforms of Peter the Great and to look back to a more traditional, more autocratic, and less dynamic political style? This is something of a puzzle, since the Senate was, after all, the crowning achievement of Peter himself, and its original members had typically been dynamic innovators rather than retrograde conservatives.

I want to suggest two possible answers to these questions. First, the Senate was, in the eighteenth century, not only the imperial institution in which all real administrative authority was concentrated but also the symbol of the continuity of Peter's system. Even in periods during which the Senate suffered a brief eclipse, it continued to hold the reins of administration in its hands. It was the Senate that made sure the administration ran smoothly, even as sovereign succeeded sovereign and favorite succeeded favorite. One of the most important privileges that Peter's system had to offer, the right to appoint and promote members of the civil service and the military, was bestowed on the Senate. In other words, the Senate controlled the service nobility, whose members' dossiers were kept by one of its subsidiaries, the Herald's Chancery. Finally, the Senate derived considerable political and moral prestige from the fact that it gradually came to act as a supreme court, whose decisions were final unless overruled by the monarch.

The second reason for the Senate's peculiar conservatism is more difficult to pin down. By its composition, the Senate would seem to have been dominated by the "clans" (or great families) that had traditionally presided over Russia's destiny. Recent studies have shown that the majority of Senate members were related by blood or marriage and that a small number of great families dominated the entire body. Many senators, particularly during the reign of Catherine II, were former high officials or dignitaries in semi-retirement, and the Senate was therefore a basically conservative institution that symbolized the continuity of the system over and above day-to-day fluctuations in policy. In short, the Senate was the one administrative organ that carried any political weight, and it carried this weight because it institutionalized and reproduced the basis of the system of government established by Peter the Great.

This observation brings us straight to the political objective of those who opposed the reforms initiated by Alexander I: they wished to institutionalize the central role of the Senate, whose membership was drawn from the most prominent families in the empire, in order to thwart what they saw as the tyrannical, arbitrary, and rationalistic designs of the emperor's youthful advisers—designs that threatened to shift supremacy from the Senate to the bureaucracy, which was staffed by people whose social backgrounds were far more diverse than the senators' and who, as the conservative opposition believed, would likely become the blind agents of imperial despotism. What is paradoxical in this conservative view of the Senate's role is that it was held by traditionalists who had always stressed the importance of personalized power. Yet, by arguing in favor of an institutionalization of the supreme authority, they ultimately undermined the basis of personal rule and helped pave the way for a system of government based on fixed and stable laws guaranteed by an institution.

The details of reform projects proposed by the Senate in the hope of influencing the political evolution of the regime are of little interest for our present purposes. Most of them were aimed at transforming the Senate into a body resembling either the English House of Lords or the Pre-1789 Paris *Parlement* (which was empowered to register the king's decrees and make remonstrances to the king concerning decrees it disapproved). The reformed Senate would have included a limited number of provincial nobles together with representatives of the commercial and cultural elites, whose votes would have been purely formal and not binding. It is impossible to say how a Senate with such a composition would have evolved or to guess what influence it might have exerted in changing the autocratic nature of the imperial regime. Without undue exaggeration it is possible to say that the "senatorial party" (as we shall call it, perhaps misleadingly, given the fact that the group in question was of heterogeneous and shifting composition and represented nothing more than a shared attitude and purpose) stood for an oligarchic constitutionalism like that of the English Whigs under the first of the Hanovers, or again, for a "parliamentary opposition" such as we find in France at the end of the *ancien régime*. By contrast, Alexander I and his young advisers stood for a somewhat modernized form of the well-ordered police state and enlightened absolutism.

Another center of opposition to the policies of the young emperor and his friends (doubtless of less importance in this regard than the Senate, however) was the court. Opposition at court came from several quarters. There was, first of all, the circle around the empress-mother, the widow of Paul I, who never got over the death of her husband and who wielded great influence through the philanthropic institutions over which she presided. There was also the seditious, anti-French, anti-Bonapartist "little court" of Alexander's sister, the Grand Duchess Catherine, whose husband was governor-general of Tver. Finally, there were the parties to the 1801 conspiracy, who had never reaped the expected profits from their sacrifice. (I mention these details only to make clear that it is impossible to talk of a unique and monolithic "establishment.") The different "coteries" at court, each presided over by an influential figure, were centers of cultural life as well as political intrigue and so helped to shape and direct public opinion or, more precisely, the ideas and views of the cultivated elite.

The opposition factions described above flourished mainly in the period before the French invasion. The invasion and the war with France reconciled most of Alexander's surviving enemies to his patriotic military and diplomatic policies. But the war did not put an end to all political opposition, as we shall see later on. For the moment, it is enough to say that, after 1815, opposition to the emperor's policies grew and may also have acquired a broader base as various segments of society realized that the patriotic outpouring that enabled Russia to prevail over Napoleon was not leading to political liberalization.

Complaint at first focused on the apathy of Alexander, who seemed to take less and less interest in domestic affairs as he became more deeply involved in mysticism and bogus, backward forms of religion.[2] Still, the emperor remained, all in all, fairly popular, and the brunt of criticism, discontent, and even hatred was borne by his favorite and principal minister, A. Arakcheev. A childhood friend of the emperor's, Arakcheev

2. One thinks of Pushkin's poem "Skazka" (Christmas): *"Ura! v Rossiiu skachet kochuiushchii despot"*

had been, at the time of Gatchina, the comrade and right-hand man of Grand Duke Alexander, whose martial spirit he had absorbed and made his own. Arakcheev was a talented administrator who had done yeoman service in helping to prepare Russian armies in advance of the French invasion; he was also an opportunist, loyal to an almost fanatical degree to Alexander, whose orders he obeyed without question. His brusque manner and limited vision repelled most cultivated people, indeed everyone who possessed the slightest spark of idealism, patriotism, and concern for the public good. Arakcheev was, moreover, the last imperial "favorite" in the eighteenth-century sense of the term, and cultivated nineteenth-century Russians saw his position as an anachronism, an insult to the political and civic maturity of Russian society. Sovereigns of course continued to have their personal friends, whom they were not, unfortunately, always very careful in selecting. But whatever influence these friends had over the private life of the monarch, none held high position or played a public role comparable with that of an Arakcheev or an eighteenth-century favorite.

After Nicholas I came to the throne and dismissed Arakcheev, it was the monarch alone who had to bear the brunt of public criticism; like it or not, the sovereign was forced to assume responsibility for the actions of his government. Even if the advice of favorites had all too often proved harmful, they had been useful in the past as shields for the sovereign and had helped to keep intact the notion of personalized authority, of paternal (or maternal) power. If a policy proved unsuccessful or disastrous, the favorite could always be blamed without besmirching the sovereign's sacred escutcheon or benevolent image. After Alexander I, however, sovereigns had to face criticism directly and alone. Not all the emperors were adept at learning how to protect their image and authority in this new situation. From this time on, for better or for worse, the autocratic emperor would be personally responsible for whatever happened. He could no longer escape blame by sending a former favorite to prison or into exile as the needs of politics demanded.

The Development of Civil Society

Let us return for a moment to the attitudes and goals of the opposition. The opposition was now stronger and more important than it had been in the eighteenth century thanks to the rapid development of Russian civil society in Alexander's reign. New political ideas, some critical, some supportive of the established order, began to circulate among the elite and to have repercussions on public life. Indeed, it is in the realm of political thought that the period proved most innovative, since all of Alexander's administrative, economic, and even social reforms, as well as his success in foreign policy, turned out to be of only temporary importance. By contrast, the growth of civil society proved to be irreversible and had a decisive impact on Russian history down to the end of the nineteenth century and even beyond.

What happened to Russian cultural life in the first quarter of the nineteenth century was different from what happened in the previous century in one important respect: culture became more and more "professionalized." Intellectual and artistic life ceased to be the exclusive province of a handful of amateurs. Specialization and professionalization are apparent in every area, including state service, the work that occupied most members of the elite. This was a major change. It is difficult to say whether the growth of a civil society distinct from the administrative and military establishment and the court was due mainly to increased specialization in the state service or to increased professionalization of intellectual life. No doubt both processes were important and reinforced one another.

Specialization and professionalization were encouraged by changes in public education. Attending a state school henceforth became an essential part of the education of every cultivated person. Private education, conducted at home by the family, did not entirely disappear, but the importance of the private tutor declined considerably. Even children of wealthy nobles attended public schools (though admission standards were very strict). The change began late in the reign of Catherine II with the establishment of a boarding school for nobles attached to the University of Moscow. Young people from good families who enrolled in this school went directly from there to the university. The curriculum was reasonably structured, and students were required to attend the prescribed courses even if they were not taking a diploma or receiving a certificate. They were taught that the only life worth living, whether in state service or outside it, was a cultured life based on a sound education. New universities were established and old ones refurbished: all repeated the same message. Graduates of the boarding schools enrolled in the University of Moscow or went abroad to specialize in the social sciences and humanities (there was as yet little emphasis on the natural sciences). Most of Russia's leading intellectuals and writers in the early nineteenth century (including Turgenev, Batiushkov, Merzliakov, and Kaisarov) attended courses at the University of Moscow, and some were trained in history or the law at German universities, particularly Göttingen, where they went to study with the elder Schlözer and his son. The universities of Kazan, Kharkov, and Derpt (Iur'ev/Tartu), as well as Vilno (which was completely renovated), followed the example of Moscow and helped to train an intellectual aristocracy in the provinces.

Other new schools, established to provide somewhat more specialized advanced instruction to future civil servants, shared the same philosophy. The famous lyceé at Tsarskoe Selo, originally intended to provide classmates for Alexander I's younger brothers, subsequently became a training ground for high state officials as well as an active center of literary and intellectual life. Yet most of its pupils came from prominent and usually quite wealthy families and had no need to pursue professional careers. The lycée at Tsarskoe Selo is particularly well known because Pushkin was a student there, but it was not the only one of its kind. Other schools may have had more modest facilities but offered even more highly professionalized programs of instruction, such as the Bezborodko Academy at Nezhin (where Gogol studied) and the school founded by Demidov at Iaroslavl, which gave instruction in the law. Somewhat later on, the government established still other schools in special subjects, such as the Army Medical School and the Institute of Jurisprudence.

Mention should also be made of efforts to modernize the curriculum of the theological academies and seminaries. These schools offered good, rigorous teaching that combined traditional subjects (such as the classical languages, logic, and rhetoric) with training in natural science and modern languages; they trained students who would become the leaders of Russian science in the middle of the nineteenth century. In fact, the majority of scientists, scholars, and academics were trained in such schools, as were many civil servants and men of letters.

It is hardly surprising that, given the changes in the educational system, the government should have given consideration to professionalizing the civil service. As the administration grew increasingly complex, the educational and cultural requirements for holding official posts rose accordingly. Well-trained personnel were needed to manage the increasingly complicated affairs of a society undergoing rapid change, whose elites were better educated than ever before. The military bureaucracy also became increasingly specialized as well as increasingly distinct from the civilian bureaucracy. The cultivated amateur and the almost illiterate minor noble of limited vision may have been enough to keep the machinery of state running in the time of Peter the Great, but they no longer sufficed in the time of Alexander I. Surveying the situation, the government, on advice of Speransky (himself the product of specialist training in a church academy), drew the logical conclusions and in 1809 decreed that a certain level of education, certified either by diploma or by examination, would be required for access to the higher ranks of the imperial bureaucracy. These new laws caused a furor and had to be redrafted and toned down in the wake of numerous protests. Despite widespread opposition, however, they were not abrogated but systematically and rigorously enforced.

Within the space of a generation the minimum educational requirement was applied to anyone who wished to rise above the rank of copyist. Older civil servants, who were either too old, too lazy, or too spiritless to meet the new requirements, found their way to promotion blocked. Many became pathetic pencil pushers, described with humor and sadness by Gogol and with greater sympathy by Dostoyevsky.[3] But the vast majority of civil servants were forced to meet the minimum educational requirements (not in fact terribly ambitious) that made the civil service a province of "specialists." The social and political consequences of this development will be discussed later on.

Even more important, in the first few decades of the nineteenth century a professionalized intellectual life began to develop outside the schools and universities. Members of the social elite, along with a few representatives of the "masses," enthusiastically threw themselves into intellectual and "academic" activities. Alongside the universities and academies there grew up various cultural organizations and groups with a passionate interest in culture or scholarship. Many of these were the result of private initiative; having dispensed with state patronage, they also hoped to avoid state control. Libraries, museums, and university teaching chairs were all fi-

3. H. A. McFarlin, " 'The Overcoat' as a Civil Service Episode," *Canadian-American Slavic Studies* (1979)13(3): 235–53.

nanced with private funds. Bezborodko and Demidov have already been mentioned. Another important benefactor was Rumiantsev, the founder of the Moscow Library (now the Lenin Library), which quickly became an important center of bibliography, research, and publishing. University chairs were established with private funds at Moscow, Kazan, and Kharkov. A number of literary and scientific societies, some of which lasted for many years, were also established by private individuals. All this activity shows that Russians took a lively interest in culture, which played an important part in the development of civil society in Russia.

The developments described above owed much to the literary and philosophical circles founded by members of the younger generation, which helped to shape that generation's spiritual and intellectual development. Mention was made earlier of the circles established in the eighteenth century by progressive teachers and curators at the University of Moscow and the academy of the Corps of Cadets. These precursors were not forgotten. Indeed, after the somber years of Paul I's reign, people enthusiastically revived these pioneer efforts, though the impetus for doing so was now private rather than official and the climate quite different from what it had been. By 1800 student "circles" at the university and the academy were not merely "clubs" that made student life more agreeable and amusing. Nor did they regard it as their mission to bring the boons of European civilization to a broader segment of Russian society. Indeed, the cultured youths who founded these circles wanted to keep them entirely closed; their only purpose was to foster the spiritual, artistic (or literary), and intellectual growth of members of the circle. The youthfulness of the participants and their predilection for displays of emotion, borrowed in large part from the sentimentalism and romanticism then fashionable in Western Europe, made the circles centers of intimacy and friendship (possibly homosexual) that played an important part in shaping the personalities of their members. From the circle *(kru-zhok)* came the Russian youths with the most advanced moral and intellectual views.

In the circles young intellectuals first discovered the ethical and intellectual principles from which their social and spiritual ideals later derived. Isolation and self-absorption were the unfortunate byproducts of the privileged environment in which these youths came to maturity. Circle members were cut off and alienated from the rest of Russian society. They rebelled against officialdom and against the material concerns of their compatriots. Some of those who retreated into themselves failed to develop the capabilities necessary for taking an active and constructive part in shaping social progress. In criticizing the system and protesting against the iniquity they saw around them, they displayed high moral standards and at times served as examples for others. But few of them succeeded in joining their own society and lived instead in a closed world of their own making, where they were susceptible to the temptations of ideology—that is, to a verbal substitute for reality which to them seemed the only reality possible.

The circles were also responsible for spreading the latest European ideas and fashions. Thus, by the beginning of the nineteenth century the state was no longer the only or even the major source of Western ideas, concepts, and techniques; it lost a monopoly that it had held since the time of Peter the Great. The circles replaced the government as the sifter of Western influences. In the period 1800–1820, the youthful members of the circles, spiritually isolated from the rest of society, were particularly susceptible to romantic sentiments and ideas, while in the period 1820–30 their interests shifted under the influence of German idealism and *Naturphiloso-phie* to metaphysics, aesthetics, and the philosophy of history. French rationalism and English empiricism were relegated to the second rank by the vogue for German philosophy;

for social and psychological reasons, elite Russian youths also felt attracted, throughout the nineteenth century, to historiography and philosophical anthropology and to *Wissenschaftslehre* of German origin. Until the 1830s, however, the circles had no ideological ambitions. They served merely to enhance the aesthetic and spiritual lives of their members and, in so doing, helped lend fresh vitality to Russian intellectual life, which for the first time moved outside the confines of the state service and the court.

In the crucible of social life Russian intellectuals were fused into a distinctive social group. Society no longer meant high society: social life had freed itself from the ties of etiquette. In the previous century social life had been confined chiefly to the court and the "official" residences of influential members of the government; less commonly, it also extended to the garrison towns and, after 1775, to the elected assemblies of nobles in the provinces. When Alexander I came to the throne, social life became increasingly private, moving from these official settings to private salons and clubs, such as the English Clubs in St. Petersburg and Moscow. For many people clubs were merely for recreations such as dancing and gambling, but they also served as meeting places for those with higher intellectual ambitions. For example, Chaadaev was a mainstay of Moscow's English Club, where he held a regular "salon." In the clubs people exchanged ideas and information about what was going on in literature and the arts. Renowned travelers made appearances. The Masonic Lodges, authorized to reopen by Alexander I, were no longer primarily charitable organizations, as they had been in the eighteenth century, but discreet meeting places that attracted members of the elite who wished to criticize the social and ethical character of the regime. Young officers returning from the battlefield after 1815 followed the example of the *Tugendbund* in attempting to establish fraternal societies in the garrison towns and the capital. These societies, whose spirit is reminiscent of Novikov's fraternal associations of the previous century, were supposed to prepare their members for public service roles.

As the forms of social life grew more various, society and the government establishment went their separate ways. Members of the elite now belonged to many different organizations and played different roles in each. All of these developments helped to create a civil society, distinct from the government and the court. In this changed setting many people realized what common interests and intellectual affinities they shared with others and began to cast about for an active role they might play in public life.

The war against Napoleon was the crucial factor, the seed around which civil society crystallized. A wave of patriotism swept over the nobility, especially in the provinces, and this, coupled with the emperor's appeal to every Russian to lend a hand in turning back the invader, welded the various elites into a single unit dedicated to a common cause, united by a fervent desire to save the fatherland. Many men volunteered for the army and there found that they could play a useful public role. Others tried to make themselves useful by recruiting their peasants and training them as militiamen or by helping out with transportation and depriving the invading armies of supplies.

Even more important than this for cultivated youths was the discovery that they shared common intellectual, artistic, and cultural interests with others of their generation, even if the actual cultural level varied rather widely. If Chicherin's diary can be believed, this was the first time in history that it dawned on Russian youths that they were not alone in wanting to live the life of the mind and devote themselves to their country.[4] The war gave many young people the opportunity to break out of their isolation in provinces and schools and make contact with others of like mind. Friendships formed

4. *Dnevnik Aleksandra Chicherina* (Moscow: Nauka, 1966).

in the army gave those who survived (as Chicherin unfortunately did not) the impetus they needed to form new clubs and organizations and to cast about for ways to serve the public interest. Such activities gave new life to civil society, which after 1815 began to become aware of its own possibilities. It is also worth mentioning that, as von Schubert's memoirs tell us, members of the bilingual and "bicultural" elite associated with Russo-German academic and bureaucratic circles in St. Petersburg made a similar discovery, which helped to tighten their bond to the Russian elites and strengthen their loyalty to the Russian Empire.[5]

An Active Role for Civil Society

Even more significant, perhaps, was another discovery made by members of the ruling elite during the invasion and the subsequent foray into Europe. This was a genuine discovery and not, as it might appear at first glance, a rediscovery: what was discovered was the Russian people—the peasants and the "little people" of the towns, who took part with their betters in the common struggle against the invader. I have no wish to paint an idyllic picture of this discovery and of the "friendly" relationship between the populace and the elite that is supposed to have resulted from it. The reality, as Soviet historians never tire of telling us, was certainly less rosy and relations were certainly far less cordial than contemporaries remember. Nevertheless, the important point is that elite youths felt that they had made such a discovery and that this discovery heralded the dawn of a new era in the relationship between the elite and the people. This attitude is of considerable interest for our purposes, because it had important historical consequences.

5. F. von Schubert, *Unter dem Doppeladler: Erinnerungen eines Deutschen in russischem Offiziersdienst. 1789–1814* (Stuttgart: Koehler, 1962).

What the elite youths discovered was that the peasants were both human beings and patriotic Russians. What is more, they found that these simple, uneducated, even illiterate men were capable of constructive action, ready to take initiatives, and even prepared to sacrifice their own good for the sake of their country and their compatriots. Young members of the elite saw that the peasants could behave in surprising ways when placed in new circumstances far from the daily routine of the country estate and the village commune. They saw, too, that the role of the elite must also change, that, as members of the elite, they must give up their sense of superiority and their paternalistic attitudes, that they must drop the sentimental style of Radishchev and Karamzin and put their education and their knowhow to good use in serving the people, bringing material and technical assistance while at the same time offering spiritual and moral leadership. With the new elite clearing the way, the people would soon be able, and could be trusted, to carry their own weight. The elite must help to make the people's job easier, however, by sharing its ideas about how best to improve Russian society.

The young patriots rejected the traditional condescending and authoritarian paternalism in favor of an approach involving intellectual and moral authority: generously but without ostentation they would distribute their knowledge, their experience, and their familiarity with various economic and social systems and with other ways of life. They saw themselves as older brothers leading the people rather than, as in the past, as strict, authoritarian, yet benevolent fathers. The sentiments that inspired them did not apply exclusively to Russian peasants. Influenced by the new romantic concept of nationalism, the ruling, not to say governing, elites, fervent admirers of national and popular cultures as they were, developed and promoted a less centralized and more flexible policy, one that would show greater respect for the indigenous customs and traditions of the alien populations settled in outlying regions of the Russian Empire. This new attitude harmonized well with diplomatic and military requirements, which forced the imperial government to grant a special, "liberal" status to newly acquired territories in the West, especially in areas taken from Finland and Poland. The same ideas influenced St. Petersburg's policy in regard to the administration of Siberia and the Caucasus, though bureaucratic practice all too often turned out to be in contradiction with progressive thinking and liberal intentions.

Between Alexander I's accession to the throne and the end of the Napoleonic wars, the "reform" government and "civil society" (narrowly construed, by which I mean essentially "informed public opinion") felt, or labored under the illusion, that they were working together for a better future. This feeling of harmony led to real collaboration and a common commitment in the battle for Russia. But the belief in common goals and methods later induced some members of civil society to expect and demand to play an active public role. After the victories of 1815 civil society was no longer willing to make do with Masonic lodges, private clubs, and closed artistic and literary societies. People wanted to work openly in the public interest, to recruit others in the same cause, and to train new leaders. Above all, they wanted the state to recognize and the people to accept a new role for civil society. Many young people had looked enviously at the civic role played by patriotic associations in Germany after the expulsion of the French. They also knew (sometimes from direct experience) that Western and Central European elites were openly participating in political and social life. Young Russians hoped to transplant this type of political participation in Russian soil. For this to happen, the literary societies would have to move beyond discussion of questions of style and aesthetics and undertake a broad program of civic education. Members of these societies became leaders of a movement to spread the new ideas and assisted in the administration of the country as unpaid experts. It is in this light that we should view the projects of Ivan Turgenev,[6] one of the most energetic and cultured men of this generation. In the course of his extensive labors in the public interest Tugenev glimpsed the beginnings of a local reform movement in which society itself would take the lead and carry the burden. This movement, Turgenev believed, would parallel the government's broader reform efforts.

The ideas of Ivan Turgenev and others like him were put into practice in various areas of Russian life. For instance, officers on active duty attempted to raise the cultural level of their troops by setting up schools based on the Lancaster system, which offered a rudimentary education to a fairly large number of soldiers. A society for prison reform was established with government approval. Various charitable societies received imperial patronage, as did the Biblical Society. Young social activists went to work for the administration at the local level in positions concerned with the general welfare. In this way they hoped to exert direct influence over a reform program that would bring Russian society and the Russian economy into harmony with Central and Western Europe. The offices of the military governor of St. Petersburg and of the chief of the capital police were infiltrated by youthful activists from the literary and civic societies. The future Decembrist and poet K. Ryleev held an important position in the Russo-American Company, which he hoped to use to influence Russian commercial and colonial policy. Other well-known men of culture obtained posts in the civil service and the military and openly used these to further the cause of civil society: among them were the brothers Turgenev in the Ministry of the Interior, M. S. Lunin, who served on the staff of the Grand Duke of Mikhail, and others.

One final aspect of the changed political climate should also

6. Not to be confused with the writer of the same name (but different patronymic), who was a distant relative.

be mentioned, since its influence was far from negligible: it was now possible to discuss basic issues of social structure and reorganization in the press and in public lectures. High society flocked to Kunitsyn's lectures on natural law, for example. Dissertations and other academic publications placed the issue of serfdom on the agenda by discussing its economic character and considering the prospect of its abolition. Political systems, legal questions, and issues of political economy were discussed in journals and reviews. Foreign books and newspapers were fairly widely available and found interested readers, ready to listen to what they had to say. It is no misnomer, then, to speak of "Decembrists without December" in referring to cultivated members of civil society who, without going so far as to join secret societies or raise the flag of rebellion, tried to contribute actively to the spiritual and material progress of the nation. Included in this group were some eminent figures, such as Viazemsky, Orlov, and Turgenev, along with innumerable anonymous members of the various organizations and groups that constituted the avant-garde of civil society. To judge by the work of Griboedov and the biographies of Pushkin and other writers of the period, the "Decembrists without December" or active dissidents must have formed a large and brilliant group.

At issue in this movement was not merely the problem of how to involve civil society in public life and enlist the aid of the younger generation in the modernization of Russia. Equally important was the question of how to transform Russian political life by changing the nature of authority and the way authority was conceived. Those activists who took on public roles hoped to establish the basis for a more institutionalized system of government. Rather than a government by the sovereign and his minions—personalized authority which, by its very nature, was capricious and tyrannical—they hoped to give Russia something like a true *Rechtsstaat*, a government of laws not men. Russia would then become a country where people would not only enjoy guar-

antees of personal and career security, property rights, and
freedom of thought but would also play an active part in running the country. Such a system of government would afford
greater autonomy to private as well as public activities, especially those involving the most industrious and forward-
looking individuals. This would help Russia to achieve the
second objective of Peter the Great's revolution: to develop a
nation of energetic, industrious people, ready to take the initiative in developing the country's resources to the full for
the benefit of all.

The paradox or contradiction in all this lay in the emphasis that was placed on individual action by members of the
cultivated elite, which merely reproduced, in slightly modi-
fied form, the tradition of personalized authority. But is this
not the dilemma faced by any cultivated elite or intelligentsia, even an intelligentsia that has yet to be completely in-
doctrinated with an ideology? In this sense, Russian civil
society in the early nineteenth century was simply reinter-
preting, in its own terms, the rationalistic policies first introduced in Russia by Peter the Great.

As in the time of Catherine II and Novikov, however, the
government under Alexander I cut this effort of reinterpre-
tation short. The emperor went back to policies he had condemned while his father was alive and abandoned his grand-
mother's efforts to foster a climate of mutual understanding
between the state and the educated elite. What is usually referred to as the reactionary policy of the post–1815 period involved, apart from Arakcheev's particularly brutal role, the
prohibition and prosecution of worthwhile civic organizations in every sphere: education, literature, welfare, etc. Only
strictly private groups such as literary salons and circles were
tolerated, and even these were subjected to close scrutiny by
the police. Public issues were declared out of bounds for private individuals and made a monopoly of the state.

The government's stubborn refusal to allow the generation
of 1815 to fulfill its dreams of civic action drove some mem-

bers of that generation to organize secret societies modeled after the Italian *carbonari* and conspiratorial groups of officers in Italy and Spain. Of course any secret society worthy of the name must have a political program compounded of theoretical as well as practical tenets. What would be the good of a conspiratorial group without concrete plans, without a vision of what the country lacks and what it needs? Such a program in turn requires a rationale, a more or less comprehensive *Weltanschauung* capable of explaining existing conditions and of showing the best way to meet the future. Hence it is not surprising that the organizers and leaders of the secret societies founded around 1820 or so devoted much energy to working out such a *Weltanschauung*, which was really a sort of "proto-ideology." Equally typical of conditions of Russia in this period, however, is the fact that, but for one exception, no coherent and comprehensive ideology emerged from these efforts. The one exception is associated with the name Pavel Pestel, the founder of the Southern Society, who set forth a systematic, Jacobin-inspired program—a radical ideology. The coherence and radicalism of Pestel's ideas left an indelible mark on Russian intellectual history and political thought. The ideologies produced by the other secret societies remained rudimentary at best, though some of them might, in suitable circumstances, have served as the basis for a program of reforms.

Aided by the confusion created by the death of Alexander I and the still unsettled question of his succession, the secret Northern and Southern Societies attempted, on the Senate Square in St. Petersburg, a *coup d'état* on 14 December 1825 (whence the term *Decembrists* to denote the participants) and later sparked a mutiny in regiments attached to the Second Army in the Ukraine. The government had no difficulty in stamping out these rebellions, arresting the leaders, and bringing them to trial. The Decembrist uprising was nothing less than the first overt sign of an incipient radical, revolutionary movement. The failure of the rebellion and the fate meted out to its leaders created a hiatus in the political and intellectual evolution of the cultivated elite. The Decembrist leaders had been very much involved in the effort to make room for private citizens to play a public role in the years after 1815. The hopes that were aroused in that year, only to be dashed by the reactionary policies of Arakcheev, were responsible for the formation of the secret societies and for the abortive coup attempt in December 1825. Most of the Decembrists were too young to have seen active duty in 1812–15 and came from backgrounds too modest to have afforded them direct personal experience of the West.[7] But their minds had been shaped by the various cultural forces described above, and this experience prepared them to take up the torch from the elite of the previous generation. They were, in a word, Young Turks *avant la lettre*, forerunners of all those junior officers who have, in our own century, provided the leadership for nationalist and anticolonial revolutions in the "underdeveloped" countries of Asia and Africa.

Did the abortive rebellion of 1825 mark a definitive repudiation of the state by educated public opinion? Did it reveal a breach between civil society and the government of the autocratic tsar? Many scholars believe that it did, but I remain skeptical. To the extent that there was a civil society in Russia, it did not break with the state—how could it? Collaboration continued and in a sense became more efficient. We shall have more to say about this later on. The fourteenth of December 1825 did, however, mark the end of attempts by the educated elite to carve out for itself a useful public role. Henceforth, social, economic, and administrative problems would be discussed *in camera*. Solutions to these problems would be worked out and implemented by the bureaucracy alone, without any participation by society at large. But many

---

7. W. B. Lincoln, "A Reexamination of Some Historical Stereotypes: An Analysis of the Career Patterns and Backgrounds of the Decembrists," *Jahrbücher für Geschichte Osteuropas*, (1976)24(3): 357–68.

people had already had a taste of political participation, many were engaged in intellectual life, and public forums did exist: for all these reasons the repression that followed the revolt of December 1825 was experienced as a brutal return to despotism. The seeds of alienation were sown: the harvest would come later, when state efforts fell short of their goals. In the meantime, society had its martyrs: their memory was both a reminder of failure and a source of hope.[8] Society for the time being turned inward. The result was a "privatization" of intellectual and cultural life. The only remaining form of collaboration with the government was in the nature of providing expert advice or services on an individual basis.

8. Five were hanged, and 125 were condemned to forced labor or exile, where they were able to write their memoirs and contribute to their own mythology.

6
THE REGIME OF NICHOLAS I

*A*FTER putting down the Decembrist uprising, the government of the young Emperor, Nicholas I, energetically reasserted its control over the country. Every aspect of life in the empire was subjected to close scrutiny. The government's policy had a positive as well as a negative side. The negative side involved strict repression of any sign of dissidence or independent criticism. The positive side involved the bureaucracy in laying the groundwork for social and economic transformation. The repressive character of the reign is well known, and liberal as well as Soviet historians have invoked this as grounds for issuing an adverse judgment on the regime and for condemning Nicholas I as an enemy of progress and modernization. This negative view is not false; and it is certainly just as a characterization of the last decade of Nicholas's reign. But more subtle judgment is called for, particularly in regard to the first part of the reign and its "organic" aspects, which were not clearly perceived by contemporaries and which bore fruit only after the severe ruler's death.

The tsar's first objective was to put an end to the educated elite's efforts to play an open and active role in the administration and political life of the country. The administration and the police were reorganized; an effective repressive apparatus was created under the Third Section of His Imperial Majesty's Private Chancery. Because of this, some journalists and "historians" have accused Nicholas I of being a forerunner of totalitarianism: this is an anachronistic judgment if ever there was one, not least because Nicholas lacked the one essential ingredient of every totalitarian system, namely, an ideology. Admittedly, the government did make some feeble attempts, none of them very successful, to elaborate a sort of theory or, rather, a legitimating rationale for its rule—think of the notorious "trinity" of Uvarov, the minister of education: orthodoxy, autocracy, and fundamentalist (or populist) nationalism. The formula may have been useful to the censors, but it carried no weight with the educated, or even the governmental, elite. This shows, if any proof is necessary, that it is impossible for a traditionalist, conservative regime to equip itself with an ideology in the modern sense of the term and, further, that the Russian government was incapable of justifying its policy in clear theoretical terms.[1]

Meanwhile, Nicholas's government worked hard to prevent Western liberal ideas from gaining a foothold with the educated public. Censorship was extremely severe: anything suspicious or capable of being interpreted as adverse criticism of the existing state of affairs was proscribed. It became very difficult to import foreign publications, though controls were never carried to the absurd extremes they had reached under Paul I. The authorities did everything possible to prevent Russians from traveling to Europe, and all travelers were closely scrutinized. But students were regularly sent abroad, especially to Germany, for advanced education, and many budding young intellectuals were able to travel to Europe and attend public courses in the universities; among them were Stankevich, Granovsky, Bakunin, and Botkin, to name a few. Even though Herzen had difficulty obtaining permission to go abroad, he was ultimately allowed to do so and even to take part of his fortune with him. Far more serious was the prohibition of new newspapers and periodicals. After 1848 it

1. On censorship, see S. Monas, *The Third Section: Police and Society in Russia under Nicholas I* (Cambridge: Harvard University Press, 1961). On "Uvarov's trinity," see N. V. Riasanovsky, *Nicholas I and Official Nationality in Russia. 1825–1855* (Berkeley: University of California Press, 1959).

became for all practical purposes impossible to establish a review or newspaper, and those that already existed were subjected to increasingly strict and repressive censorship. All writers worked in a climate of suspicion (the case of Pushkin is merely the best known illustration of what was a common plight), and this could not fail to have an impact on all forms of intellectual endeavor. There is no doubt that all intellectuals, all those who took part in literary, artistic, religious, scientific, and academic life, whether inside the establishment or outside, felt that they were being watched, oppressed, and persecuted. Evidence for this may be found in the diary kept by Nikitenko, a censor, a professor of literature , and a conservative whose political loyalty was beyond reproach. Paradoxically, though, these constraints seem to have stimulated creativity and imagination in the arts and did not prevent the golden age of Russian literature from taking place—quite the contrary.

The educated elite did, however, suffer greatly in another area, the universities, which, for it, was of the utmost importance. The revolt of 1825, in which a fair proportion of the educated elite and the nobility had been implicated, caused the government to reinstitute and strengthen repressive measures against the universities first introduced by Alexander I, though now without the regressive, anti-intellectual mysticism attached to them in Alexander's day. The statute of 1835 subjected the universities to close administrative scrutiny and severely limited faculty autonomy. The teaching of philosophy was at first restricted and then banned altogether, though professors continued to give public lectures that touched on philosophical subjects in the guise of methodological issues in the natural sciences. The ban on the teaching of philosophy and the cloud of suspicion that hung over the humanities in general had the predictable result of driving many students to the natural sciences (which were popular in the West and just then experiencing a period of rapid progress). Even more painful for many students was the limitation—admittedly only temporary—on the number of students admitted to the faculty of letters, which was reduced to 300 for the entire empire. Yet in spite of these police measures—and perhaps a sign of their fundamental inadequacy—university amphitheaters became public forums to which people flocked in the hope of hearing lectures of high moral and intellectual content, typified by Granovsky's courses at the University of Moscow.

These repressive measures against the universities are perhaps primarily repsonsible for the idea that Nicholas's reign was particularly repressive and anti-intellectual. But to stop at this is to take a very partial view of what was actually happening to Russian education under Nicholas I. Although the government had little interest in promoting broadly based humanistic studies, it did attempt to stimulate interest in professional education. Since this turned out to be crucial in subsequent years, it is appropriate that we say a few words about this aspect of the question.

The imperial government was prepared to do everything possible to develop technical education. It may be that even its best effort was not enough, or again, it is possible that the government could and should have done more in this regard. However that may be, given conditions in Russia at the time and the limits on what was possible (remember that social policy remained extremely conservative), Nicholas did lay the groundwork for a major social transformation. In this and many other respects, Nicholas completed the work of Peter the Great, and did so in the same spirit as his illustrious predecessor. Like Peter, Nicholas emphasized the importance of training professionals in many specialized fields, medicine and surgery foremost among them. Members of the lower classes (excluding serfs unless they obtained permission or individual manumission from their masters) were readily admitted to these disciplines, moreover. Most military doctors, for example, came from humble or even non-Russian origins (converted Jews, for example). Special institutes for the study of law and technology were established, and additional technical courses were offered in the universities, some of which even had new technical departments established. Many secondary schools were set up to train lower level technical specialists, and some pupils of these schools later moved on to acquire university training in their specialties. It was also during the reign of Nicholas that a system of secondary schools *(gimnaziia)* modeled after the German system was established throughout the empire, creating a need for growing numbers of specialist teachers.[2] Since there were not enough foreign teachers to fill the need, the universities had to assume responsibility for teacher training, with support from the Academy of Sciences.

As a result, the reign of Nicholas I saw the beginnings of a period of very rapid growth in Russian science. Scientific work was carried out in the universities, the Academy of Sciences, and other specialized institutions. The education of scientists and scholars was placed on a firm foundation, Russian science began to make its influence felt in the rest of the world as early as 1860, as is attested by the illustrious names of Lobachevsky and Mendeleev. Scholarship also advanced in fields other than physics and the natural sciences. The 1840s and 1850s saw the first flowering of Russian scholarship in such fields as history, archaeology, and the classics. The methodological inspiration for this scholarly work may have come from Europe, but Russian scholars made quite a name for themselves by using the imported methods to break new ground. They then turned this renown to good account in obtaining material and moral support for their work from the general public.

Paralleling this blossoming of Russian science and scholarship was a broadening of the audience interested in such

2. For an overview of education under Nicholas I, see Alain Besançon, *Education et société en Russie dans le second tiers du XIXe siècle* (Paris-The Hague: Mouton, 1974).

work. This audience kept itself informed in part by reading
the "thick journals" *(tolstye zhurnaly)*, which, despite censorship and restrictions on printing and distribution, managed to establish themselves securely and to expand their influence into the provinces as sources of new ideas and
information about scientific progress.

Given the rigidity of the empire's social structure, not the
least significant aspect of which was the persistence of serfdom, it is reasonable to ask about the social background of
the growing number of young people who pursued careers in
science, technology, and scholarship. Apart from the nobility, for which, as we shall see, opportunities still remained
in the state service, many future scholars came from the urban classes. But the number of town inhabitants was still fairly
small, and most either remained passive or availed themselves of new opportunities not in eduation but in textiles,
construction, railroads, and grain processing and export.

We have still said nothing about one other class or, rather,
"order" or "estate" or *Stand*, namely, the clergy. And in fact
it was from among the numerous progeny of clergymen, whose
prospects of finding clerical employment were drastically
curtailed by demographic pressures in a rigidly stratified society, that many of the students who filled the university
amphitheaters, the scientific laboratories, and the scholarly
libraries were drawn. The professional, scientific, and tech-
nological elite of modern Russia was rooted chiefly in the
clergy, as the names of its members attest. It is not hard to
see how this happened: as was mentioned earlier, the ecclesiastical schools had, ever since the time of Alexander I, offered a course of instruction particularly well suited to the
training of future scientists and scholars. Not that these
schools were without defects: physical conditions were harsh,
discipline was severe, and teaching methods dry and tyrannical. These took a toll on the less gifted and less energetic
pupils. Yet those who had the gifts and the ambition needed
to survive in such an environment received a good prepara-

tion for further training. Thus the church schools helped to enlarge the country's pool of talent. This prepared the way for rapid and thorough modernization and for the introduction of heavy industry. Nicholas may have been guilty of not wanting or not being able to take the first genuine steps in this direction; nevertheless, he should be given the credit for having cleared the way and trained the people who would be needed to venture where he himself did not.

It is time now to say a few words about the indirect effects of increasing professionalization—and of the clergy's involvement in it—on religious life. As growing numbers of clerical children chose careers in science and scholarship, religious life underwent considerable change. Since the middle of the eighteenth century, the harmful effects of state control of religion had become increasingly apparent. Educated Russians had a thirst for religion and spirituality and felt the need of better moral guidance than that dispensed by the official church and clergy. In the late eighteenth century many cultivated Russians had consequently developed an interest in pietistic and mystical sects, partly Protestant, partly native in origin. In the early years of the following century Protestant pietism and mysticism (Arndt, Boehme, etc.) and illuminism (Saint-Martin) came to dominate spiritual life among certain influential segments of the cultural elite. The same appetite for religion also manifested itself in other ways, including, as we saw earlier, spiritualistic and philanthropic forms of Freemasonry.

Spiritual and moral cravings were also felt by the common people, among whom there was renewed interest in the mystical tradition of Russian Orthodoxy (e.g., Hesychasm, philocaly), which had been kept alive in rural areas and in certain groups of Old Believers. Thus, the revival of popular religiosity, which manifested itself in frequent pilgrimages, distribution of religious images and books, popular interest in "holy fools," and so on, paralleled growing interest on the part of the educated in Russian spiritual life and religious traditions. No doubt the war of 1812 also played a part in bridging the gap between elite and populace in the area of religion.

The reform of religious education was intended in part as a response to the feeling that firmer guidance was needed in religious, moral, and intellectual matters. Western influences helped to rekindle interest in metaphysics and in the sources of Western morality and religion. As a result, *Naturphilosophie* and philosophical romanticism were popular in Russia in the period 1830–40. The shock of the Decembrist rebellion, particularly within the educated elite, and the subsequent turning inward on the part of many intellectuals, lent new urgency to questions that bore intimately on both the religious and the historical consciousness of the Russian elite, issues of theological as well as national identity. In their search for identity and growing awareness of historical tradition, educated Russians drew on scholarly work in history, philology, and theology. The theologically curious turned both to secular studies of the Western as well as the Byzantine and native roots of modern Russian civilization and to the writings of clerical scholars trained by the religious academies. The result was a theological renaissance not only within the church but also in the salons of St. Petersburg and Moscow during the reign of Nicholas I. Among the laymen important in this movement were the Slavophile philosophers and theologians Khomiakov, Kireyevsky, and Samarin, along with Gogol. As for the church, Filaret, the metropolitan of Moscow, played a particularly important role, as did the Theological Academy of the Trinity-St. Sergius' which he ruled with an iron hand. Theological reviews, teaching chairs, courses, and publications were also influential. In addition, growing numbers of theologians maintained relations with the educated elite in the capitals and major provincial cities. All of these things helped to bring about the first theological and religious renaissance in modern Russian history. One result of this was of course the study and dissemination of the history and dogma of the Russian Orthodox Church. Another was the establishment of faculties of theology, religious acade mies, and scholarly religious journals. Thus were sown the seeds that would bear abundant fruit later on, in the late nineteenth and early twentieth century, a period of great spiritual, metaphysical, and religious creativity.

These developments impinged on others affecting the service nobility and landowning class. The religious renaissance was related to the "privatization" of certain sectors of the elite, which constituted its social basis. The reign of Nicholas I saw the culmination of a long period of evolution of the Russian ruling class (i.e., the service and landowning nobility); this evolutionary process continued throughout the eighteenth century and into the first quarter of the nineteenth, when Peter the Great's ambition of creating a true professional civil service was finally realized. Following the general policy laid down by Alexander I, Nicholas's government required most civil servants, particularly those in the middle ranks and just above, to meet minimum standards of professional competence. Officials of the highest ranks were not always included, but even at this level the clear tendency was toward increased specialization.

By contrast, at the lowest levels of the bureaucratic hierarchy, the ranks of copyist and clerk, it makes little sense to speak of professionalization, though the poor devils who held these jobs were indeed professionals in the sense that they had no other skill or source of income. During the reign of Nicholas I, the "upper middle" ranks of the bureaucracy were held exclusively by men who had deliberately chosen civil service careers and who lived on what they earned from their positions, having no other resources. These men began training for their posts while still very young, and their education had become increasingly technical.

Official duties became more and more specialized. Provincial officials generally remained in the provinces for their whole careers, as promotions or transfers to the central bureaus became increasingly rare. These officials came to form a distinct subgroup among the career civil servants, whose members had no prospect of any career beyond the local administration. By the same token, those who started out even in relatively low-level positions in the central bureaus of the capital spent their whole careers there. Thus the gap between officials working in the capital and officials working elsewhere grew wider, leading to professional rivalries that added one more obstacle between the government and its objectives. Specialization was even greater in certain ministries, such as Finance and Interior, and in the courts. None of this diminished the shuffling of personnel back and forth between one ministry and another, as the pool of officials with the knowledge and skill required to perform certain complex tasks was not yet very large. The boundary line between military and civilian careers was rather more distinct, however, and could be crossed only at the highest levels (governor general, senator, minister) or by officials attached to the sovereign's entourage (the police and *fligel' ad' iutanty*[3] assigned to carry out special missions or embassies).

This degree of professionalization and specialization called for appropriate kinds of education and/or apprenticeship. The minimum educational requirements for the civil service were laid down by the decrees of 1809. A graduate applying for a higher-level administrative post had to demonstrate familiarity with bureaucratic procedures and exhibit technical competence in his own area of expertise. The institution of these requirements was in large part the result of a carefully planned effort by the emperor and his advisers, who were particularly wary of two social groups: the aristocracy, which they believed had supplied the leaders of the Decembrist revolt and which was in any case suspect because of its economic and cultural independence, and the educated among the common

3. The *fligel' ad'iutanty* were general-grade officers assigned to the emperor's personal staff who served as the emperor's personal representatives on delicate and important missions.

people, who in their eyes were the close kin of the regicide *avocats* who had waged the Reign of Terror and of the radical antimonarchists who had led the European revolutions of the nineteenth century.

Nicholas preferred to rely on nobles whose incomes were too small to enable them to live without the additional sum provided by the state—in other words, on a class of noble (or ennobled), yet paid, professional bureaucrats. His conception of the service nobility was therefore identical to Peter's, with one big difference: at last it seemed possible to attract such men to state service without resorting to coercion.

The economic position of the majority of nobles, which even in the eighteenth century was not particularly brilliant, deteriorated still further in the wake of the Napoleonic invasion and the leveling off of agricultural output in the central provinces of European Russia. The poorest nobles, as well as those lacking in drive and ambition, were "put out to pasture" on their remote country seats. But their children, who were educated to the minimum standards in public schools and whose loyalty (founded as it was on material need as well as class traditions of service) was beyond doubt, provided an easily tapped source of civil service personnel. Those nobles with a modest amount of property, including the "cadets," or younger sons of large families without sufficient resources to set them up properly, provided a pool of talent that could be tapped to fill the "upper-middle" ranks of the bureaucracy. The majority sought military careers; for the time being we shall leave them aside. The rest, who either could not or would not become officers, were ideally suited to service in the administration. This was where the state came in, since only the government was in a position, thanks to the many schools set up during the reign of Nicholas I, to provide free training in many different specialties.

These schools were not reserved exclusively for the nobility, though nobles did receive preferential treatment, particularly in regard to promotions. Still, many students of relatively modest background, whose fathers had served the state in low-ranking positions (such as the sons of noncommissioned officers), were able to obtain the education they needed to qualify for specialized administrative posts and for promotion to higher ranks.

Even more important than the minimum educational requirement for civil service employment was the emergence of a new ethos of service. The ideal of impoverished or relatively impoverished nobles (one thinks first of all of the Miliutin brothers) was to serve not only the sovereign and the state but the nation as a whole. A feeling of moral and professional indebtedness to the nation (and the sovereign) was the predominant trait of the best civil servants educated under Nicholas I, as Richard Wortman has shown in his study of the development of a Russian legal consciousness in the wake of Speransky's work on codification.[4] After learning the fundamentals of the law at the Institute of Jurisprudence or the Demidov school in Iaroslavl or the university, young employees of the Ministry of Justice were sent to the University of Berlin for further training. They thus developed a sense of professional responsibility and of duty to the Russian people. It was these same officials who, in the next reign, prepared the great legal reform and put it into practice. The situation was similar in the other ministries and departments of the imperial government at St. Petersburg.

One striking characteristic of ranking government officials involved in the economic and social administration, beyond their impressive educational background and broad outlook, was their conviction that knowledge of actual conditions in the country was essential for effective and progressive government. As W. Bruce Lincoln has pointed out, this belief was fostered not only by the universities and other schools in

4. Richard S. Wortman, *The Development of a Russian Legal Consciousness* (Chicago: The University of Chicago Press, 1976).

which they had received their training but also by membership in professional scientific organizations.[5] The Imperial Geographic Society, for example, organized efforts to survey the empire's resources and to study the nature of peasant society—work that had to be done before an effective solution to the problem of serfdom could be found. High officials of the interior and finance ministries took an active part in this scientific work, and departments of these ministries provided support for statistical surveys and economic and social analyses conducted by specialists. This work provided training for the administrators and experts who would later draft Alexander II's program of reforms; indeed, the first rudimentary reforms were prepared by departments of the bureaucracy under a regime that historians have traditionally depicted as static and ignorantly reactionary.

Although Nicholas's government curtailed efforts by members of the educated elite to assert for themselves a public role, it did nothing to impede the growth of cultivated society in salons and private circles. On the contrary—possibly as a reaction to the government's actions—cultured society flourished as never before: salons, clubs, and private organizations promoting scientific, scholarly, and philanthropic pursuits sprang up everywhere. The existence of these meeting places vastly increased the influence of the new bureaucratic elite described above. For perhaps the first time in modern Russian history, there was real intellectual exchange between cultivated society and the governmental elite. What contact there had been in this respect in the eighteenth and early nineteenth centuries was primarily a matter of family

---

5. See the works by W. Bruce Lincoln: *Nikolai Miliutin: An Enlightened Russian Bureaucrat of the Nineteenth Century* (Newtonville, Mass.: Oriental Research Partners, 1977); *Petr Petrovich Semenov-Tian-Shanskii: The Life of a Russian Geographer* (Newtonville, Mass.: Oriental Research Partners, 1980); and above all *In the Vanguard of Reform: Russia's Enlightened Bureaucrats, 1825–1861* (De Kalb: Northern Illinois University Press, 1982).

ties or contacts among officials and intellectuals who happened to move in the same social circles. Since these circles were quite small, such contacts were usually based on personal acquaintance. To judge by surviving memoirs and letters, it is doubtful that any real or valuable intellectual exchange took place. Political and cultural affairs do not seem to have been discussed in the salons, at court, or in country houses in this period. This contrasts sharply with the period of Nicholas I. By then, high officials were meeting with eminent writers, journalists, thinkers, and critics in salons presided over by leading dignitaries and aristocratic matrons. One of the most prominent and influential salons was that of Grand Duchess Elena Pavlovna, the sister-in-law of Nicholas I, who brought together leading officials and politicians and well-known writers. Conversation centered on political, social, and religious questions. It was in the Grand Duchess's salon that Nicholas Miliutin first voiced his ideas for legislation that would ultimately lead to the emancipation of the serfs. Another political circle gathered around Grand Duke Constantine. Discussion was more literary and philosophical in the salons of Princes Odoyevsky and Viazemsky, which were frequented by governmental officials, men of letters, and artists.

There was a constant bustle in the salons of important officials and leading figures in literature and the arts. All belonged to a single elite and believed that they had a constructive role to play in building a better society, be it in business, administration, or efforts to better the cultural and social condition of the people. In the salons people exchanged information and opinions, plans and ideas, criticism and enthusiasms. Men of letters, writers, scholars, and thinkers were thus put in direct contact with Russian realities, while top government officials and administrators learned of the latest philosophical and moral ideas, the most recent developments in science and scholarship, from conversation with leading intellectuals.

The conversations and debates that took place in the salons concerning the present and future of Russia had influence in a much wider sphere, not only because the people who frequented the salons and circles saw many others who did not attend them, both in the capitals and in the provinces, but also because men of letters who were privileged to attend them summarized controversial ideas and issues in the "thick journals," which were eagerly read throughout the empire.[6] In short, even though the elite (cultural plus governmental) was officially muzzled in public, it was able to prepare the country for the moment when reform would become possible. Despite the official censorship and controls, the reign of Nicholas I was one of the most dynamic periods in Russian intellectual history, a time when intellectuals did have an impact and played a fundamental educational role.

The coming together of the governmental and cultural elites, like the development of a specialized, professional bureaucracy, was the culmination of a long evolutionary process whose consequences were complex. Starting in 1762, when compulsory state service was officially abolished (though it long remained the main occupation and principal ambition of the nobility), some nobles began to take their distance from the state. Usually this took the form of early retirement from state service rather than a total refusal to serve. As a private individual, the retired noble often adopted a more or less idle and "cultivated" style of life, within the limits of his intellectual capacities. By the end of the eighteenth century we begin to see the typical petty noble, living on his estate, visiting the provincial capital only to vote for the marshal of the nobility, and leading a life circumscribed by changing seasons, hunting and fishing, his daughters' marriages, his sons' departure for school or the service, and his own supervision and disciplining of his serfs.

6. For example, *Vestnik Evropy, Sovremmenik, Biblioteka diia chteniia*, to mention a few of the most widely read.

The Napoleonic wars, and especially the invasion of 1812, forced many of these minor nobles to return to service and thrust them into the cultural and political mainstream in the capitals. After the war they resumed their pre-war life style, however. Many nobles retired to the provinces, there to take up once more their familiar occupations. Still, they retained their awareness of belonging to the service nobility and regarded themselves as members of a class whose traditional values and interests distinguished it from the other classes of Russian society.

It was this sense of solidarity, this feeling of belonging to a unified noble class, that was destroyed by the reign of Nicholas I. There were many reasons for this. In the first place, even though only a few nobles were actually involved in the Decembrist uprising, the revolt alienated a segment of the nobility from the government and raised again the old specter of tyranny and autocracy. Second, thanks to the expansion of grain growing in the South and the intensification of economic life in town and country, many nobles living in dynamic regions of the country found themselves drawn to new occupations and new centers of interest. With greater wealth they were able to live more interesting lives socially and culturally, and their ties to the establishment were weakened.

Most important of all, to my mind, was the emergence of a group of professional bureaucrats of modest means, whose primary interest lay in state service and in a sense of moral commitment to the people, with the result that the members of this group became increasingly alienated from the class into which they had been born. In their eyes the general interest must take precedence over all private interests. As servants of society and the state rather than any special interest, class, or "order," they embodied the ideal of Peter the Great and enlightened absolutism. In fact, they were prepared to sacrifice or neglect the interests of their own class (whose tie to serfdom made them ashamed) for the sake of the general interest as they understood it.

The result was a split in the nobility, which exacerbated the feeling of nobles living on their estates that they were cut off and isolated from the government, bottled up within their families, confined to the provinces. The middling nobles felt more and more acutely that the conflict of interest had become irreconcilable and, worse, that they had been betrayed by their own brothers, who had gone over to the state: by and by, this feeling became a settled conviction. Relations between the governmental apparatus and the provincial nobility that lived by its ownership of land and serfs became increasingly acrimonious; muted conflict occasionally erupted into the open as happened at the beginning of the century in reaction to Speransky's reforms. When at last it came time to carry out further reforms, these had to be made over the opposition of the landed nobility, and this had consequences of which we shall have occasion to speak later on.

The intelligentsia first began to stand out as a group distinct from the nobility at the end of the eighteenth century, and the Decembrists represented a particular tendency within this group. What was its situation as the nineteenth century progressed? All the standard histories stress that the intelligentsia, which by the reign of Nicholas I had become firmly established as a group, played a central role in Russian intellectual history. This accepted view of the intelligentsia's role was first set forth in the *Memoirs* of Alexander Herzen, an influential member of the brilliant generation of intellectuals of the 1830s and 1840s and, like many other Russian intellectuals throughout the nineteenth century, a man much concerned with the debate between Slavophiles and Westernizers. It is high time, however, to set matters straight; the historians have neglected a great many facts in their almost hagiographic admiration for the values proclaimed by the liberal and radical intelligentsia of the nineteenth century.

When we begin to look more closely at what was going on, bearing in mind the ties that existed between the bureaucracy and the world of culture and literature, we want to ask the same question that the hero Chatski asks in Griboedov's play *Gore ot uma* (Woe from Wit): "How many of you were there?" To which we might add, "And who were you?"

To begin with, Herzen's was a very small group, a tiny minority not simply of the population as a whole but even of the cultivated nobility. It consisted of some twenty-odd young people or, if we include friends and relatives, at most thirty or forty. Second, this small minority refused to join the establishment and adapt itself to the usual mold, whether by taking a position in the state service or by retiring to the provinces to lead an active and productive private life. Had members of this group been willing to join the bureaucracy, they would have been forced to acquire specialized skills. This would have gone against the grain, since these were in fact the last vestiges of the cultivated society that had flourished under Alexander I and had attempted, after 1815, to concern itself with public affairs. When this avenue of political involvement was closed off, intellectuals of this bent turned inward, surviving in intellectual and social isolation in youth "circles" *(kruzhki)* that grew up around schools and universities. The romantic *kruzhok* also shaped the intellectual and moral life of the *intelligenty* of Herzen's generation. This was where young intellectuals passionately debated questions related to the uniqueness of Russia's history and character. Their main concern was to define themselves, to find and express their identities as individuals and as members of Russian society: to do so was as necessary for them as it had been for the members of A. Turgenev's circle at the beginning of the century.

They felt this necessity with particular urgency because of their estrangement from the previous generation, the fathers who, in the eyes of their sons, had been incapable of maintaining their ideals or preserving their spiritual freedom in a socially and economically backward country ruled by a capricious administration and sustained by the institution of serfdom. An identity crisis of this sort can be resolved only in a protected environment, such as that offered by the circles, which afforded shelter from any contact with real, active life and provided a setting in which youths felt free to devote themselves to metaphysical speculation and *Schöngeisterei*, influenced by the vague and mystical aestheticism of the Romantic tradition fostered by German *Naturphilosophie*.

The purpose of such speculation was to define—I would almost say to create—a reality capable of confirming the identity that the youths in the circles fashioned for themselves in an atmosphere of emotional and spiritual intimacy. Thus, the search for solid metaphysical foundations and stable ethical principles was a matter of defining not merely the self but Russia as well. Young intellectuals asked and attempted to answer the questions, "What is Russia? Where did it come from? Where is it going? Is it different from the West, and if so, how?" They attempted to define the external world by examining the inner world of members of the intelligentsia. For the intelligentsia the important thing was that this attempt proved valuable and fruitful for the individual; it made no difference whether the world in terms of which individuals defined themselves really existed or not.

The result was that intellectuals created an image of a Russia that never was, a Muscovy (in the case of the Slavophiles) compounded of mystification and their own invention. They were interested in historical development only insofar as this could help them in their quest for an identity. They were, in a sense, in the grip of an ideology: members of the circles fabricated ideologies and tailored reality to fit them solely in order to achieve harmony between their sense of identity and their actual daily lives.

The case of Stankevich, however pure his idealism and moral aspirations may have been, is typical. He did not live long enough to formulate a clear ideology, but he did create one powerful enough to have served as a model for his friends in the Moscow circle, for whom he was both *magister ludi* and a figure of inspiration. The fact that he created this ideology out of bits and pieces of German idealist philosophy, especially the work of Schelling and Hegel, is merely a chronological accident, a matter of secondary importance. The next generation took its inspiration from the materialists of the 1850s: the intellectual baggage was different, but its contents were used in the same way, to create an ideology which served the same purposes as the ideologies current in the Stankevich and Herzen circles.

The imperial government, fearful as it was of a revival of the secret societies, the breeding ground of the Decembrist uprising, reacted to any manifestation of friendship or solidarity among noble youths with suspicion and mistrust. This merely exacerbated the feeling of isolation that existed among circle members and left them even more firmly ensconced in the narrow and restrictive setting of the *kruzhki*. To be sure, there were some young intellectuals who enthusiastically engaged in political discussion whenever the opportunity arose. Herzen is an obvious example: when his circle was closed down and he himself was arrested and sent into administrative exile in the provinces (where he served in the local bureaucracy), he entered upon a period of rebellion that was as much political as it was religious or metaphysical. The experiences of Bakunin and Ogarev were similar. Herzen is a very important figure, because he politicized the aesthetic and philosophical speculations of the intellectual circles. He took the intelligentsia's intellectual concerns and its moral rejection of contemporary standards and turned these into an effective anti-government political ideology. The practical effect of this on Nicholas's Russia was negligible. Herzen was able to achieve real influence only in exile. Looking back on his youth in the *Memoirs*, moreover, he attached ideological and political value to debates and discussions that grew out of efforts by the idealistic younger generation to define its own identity. The Slavophiles followed a similar path, with one important difference: because they interpreted contemporary

Russia as a perversion of the true Russia of yesterday and to-morrow, they were able, after the death of Nicholas I, to regain a place in Russian society and to participate in the reform movement begun by his successor.

Another point to keep in mind about this intelligentsia of a few dozen young men who came of age in the 1830s was that it was disgusted by society's materialistic values and above all by the newcomers to the public stage: entrepreneurs, merchants, and bureaucrats. In part this was an expression of aristocratic disdain for the pettiness of economic life on the part of wealthy scions of the old nobility, which had never attached much value to material concerns. For similar reasons the intelligentsia also withheld its sympathy from and refused to collaborate with the new professionalized bureaucratic elite, which saw its mission primarily as one of promoting economic progress.

Thus the intelligentsia, having turned its back on its aristocratic origins and declared its unwillingness to cooperate with either the government or the business community, chose instead to define its identity in relation to "the people." Alienated from its native class, this tiny minority of the young fervently desired symbiosis with the people, with the Russian peasantry of the past and present (and even the future, as in the case of Bakunin, for example). Such a symbiosis could not be achieved, however, unless the intelligentsia could show what special role it had to play in the future of the peasantry, the class left behind by the advance of modern Russian civilization. The role it hit upon was that of bearer of a radical ideology designed to show the people the path to the future: it was in terms of this role that the intelligentsia defined its identity and justified its function in the contemporary world. The role of the people was to put into practice the ideology propagated by the intelligentsia so as to give that ideology concrete reality. Thus the intelligentsia saw its role as one of preaching the truth, spreading the new revelation; it was obviously difficult to reconcile such a conception with the idea of "organic labor" (to use a phrase that became popular in Poland after 1863) or other actions designed to bring about mere piecemeal reforms in the short term, unless such reform efforts could be related to radical long-range goals. Even if the imperial government had refrained from its clumsy policy of censorship and persecution, the intelligentsia would have been organically incapable of taking part in productive activities under the direction and with the encouragement of the imperial administration. It therefore kept aloof from all reform efforts. Unable to accept change on any terms other than its own, it chose intransigent opposition instead. This was a consequence of its profound nature and not the result of a deliberate choice or a reaction to government persecution.

The framework and methods of Alexander II's reforms, as we have just seen, were in fact developed during the reign of Nicholas I. It is well known that some reforms were also carried out or at least attempted under Nicholas: these included establishment of the Ministry of State Domains, reorganization of the administration dealing with state peasants, changes in educational policy (discussed above), a reform of St. Petersburg's municipal administration (which was to serve as a model for urban government in 1864), "codification" of laws, improvements in finance and budgeting methods, and a progressive industrial policy. Nicholas's government also seems to have been ready to cap these efforts with major changes in the country's social and economic structure, including abolition of serfdom and reorganization of the local courts and administration. The problem was that such reforms were long overdue: they were a belated version of the Stein-Hardenberg reforms in Prussia. To have had a chance of success they would have needed to be carried out without delay. It would have required a titanic effort to bring Russia up to mid-nineteenth-century European standards, to realize the dreams of Peter the Great in a world that no longer resembled his. The reform program that Nicholas I passed on to Alexander II has sometimes been described as Bismarckism *avant la lettre.* Perhaps, but it must be added that it would have been a far more radical form of Bismarckism than anything Bismarck ever conceived. Had such a program been carried out, the state, assisted by a revitalized professional bureaucracy, would have laid the foundations of a modern society and then allowed civil society free enough rein to establish itself on a firm and solid footing.

It was on a project of just such gigantic proportions that Alexander II and his advisers (drawn from the new bureaucracy created by his father) focused their energy and attention once the Crimean War was over. What needed to be done was neither easy nor obvious. The key reform, abolition of serfdom, desired though it was by the great majority of people, nevertheless provoked considerable opposition, and the way it was carried out in practice drew much criticism. This opposition had to be overcome, and the only way to do this was to invoke the autocratic authority of the emperor himself. This in turn meant preserving and even reinforcing the tsar's personal power, harking back to Russia's old political tradition.

To quell the opposition the tsar made use of the weapons of a bureaucratic, if enlightened, police state, with the result that the same contradictions and paradoxes that had always plagued this form of government manifested themselves once again, more acutely than ever, in the middle of the nineteenth century. The issue was not merely to begin the transformation of a traditional society but to establish a modern civil society and an economic system based on industry and international trade. The way reform was carried out under Alexander II was not without similarities to the paternalistic methods of the *ancien régime* and cameralist *Disziplinierung* of the eighteenth century. There was no choice but to rely almost exclusively on the professional bureaucracy, backed up by recent graduates of the universities and scientific in-

stitutes: in other words, reform was carried out by a techno-
cratic elite with didactic and authoritarian tendencies.

The reform establishment had to face opposition of two
kinds. The minority intelligentsia was hostile to both the
program and the methods of the government, because it aspired to lead the people itself. In its view reform would mean
nothing unless it led to a radical transformation of society from
top to bottom, including the government and the economy.
The intelligentsia not only sought to play an active role but
also elaborated a series of radical ideologies, all of which joined
in rejecting or repudiating a reality of which their authors
knew little or nothing. These ideologies stemmed from an almost religious belief in progress defined in strictly material
terms, coupled with populist aspirations, with a will on the
part of intellectuals to submerge themselves in the masses.

Opposition to the policies of the bureaucratic state also came
from another quarter: groups within the educated elite whose
members felt that they were the natural leaders of civil society. Those who were engaged in productive activities demanded as much autonomy as possible to pursue their own
goals and to protect themselves against abuses of power by
the bureaucracy; they wanted a government of laws, not men.
From the government's point of view, to allow intermediary
bodies to develop as representatives of this embryonic civil
society was tantamount to an abdication of authority by the
sovereign that would ultimately lead to the destruction of
autocracy. This was unacceptable, since without autocratic
power the reforms already underway could not be completed.
From the outset, then, the civil elite and the governmental
bureaucracy misunderstood one another.

In fact, neither the intelligentsia nor the bureaucracy wished
to see the country develop without its aid. Neither wished to
see progress and organic development based on rising productivity and increased prosperity. Paradoxically, those two sworn
enemies, the radical intelligentsia and the imperial bureaucracy, were linked together by hostility to the real civil so-

ciety, to pluralism, administrative autonomy, common law, and liberalism in politics and culture. The underlying cause of this unconscious alliance may have been, on both sides, mistrust and even fear of what had long been, in Russia, the great unknown: the people, the peasant masses. Thus we come full circle: the Europeanization of the elites had led to the cultural isolation of the people and thus to mutual incomprehension and lack of communication between the two Russias. After 1861, a constant concern of both the intelligentsia and the government was the need to regiment the Russian people, out of fear for its anarchic and destructive potential. This common fear, born of ignorance, made an objective view based on accurate knowledge of Russian society impossible. As a result, with the coming of the twentieth century, intelligentsia and government alike were swept away by the *stikhiinost'* or elemental force of the people.

7
THE TRANSFORMATION OF IMPERIAL RUSSIA
Continuity or Change?

HE last half-century of imperial Russia's history was marked by changes both rapid and profound. Events seemed to follow one another at an ever accelerating pace leading to the final collapse. Anyone reading contemporary documents, memoirs, and histories would be likely to conclude that a maelstrom had descended upon Russian society and precipitated it headlong into war and revolution. This impression is no doubt reinforced by the fact that the memory of these momentous events, which took place not so very long ago, has perhaps been more effectively preserved than that of earlier events, thanks to the press and to the increasing volume of information collected by the government for administrative purposes. But this storm that grew to hurricane force rose out of an ocean whose depths are uncharted even today. We sense that Russian society and culture underwent earth-shattering changes. Yet all we have to back up this feeling are impressions and intuitions. Scholars are only now beginning to uncover what happened, when, and why.

Various Views of the Revolutions of 1905 and 1917

Since the events in question occurred relatively recently and there is massive documentation available, it is possible to establish their chronology in detail. For the same reasons, many varying interpretations of those events have been put forward. Each interpretation of course reflects a particular way of looking at the underlying tendencies and trends that culminated in the revolutions of 1905 and 1917. Inevitably, therefore, interpretations of the period have been markedly teleological in character, with a positive or negative cast depending on the political or ideological stance of the historian doing the interpreting. In judging the revolution of 1917 and its sequel, the historiography of the prerevolutionary period in Russia resembles French historiography of the revolution of 1789 in its overall intellectual contours.

The monarchist and conservative historiography of the period need not detain us long. Its view of things is very simple: Russia was making rapid progress in all areas because the government and the people had remained faithful to the immutable traditions of monarchy, patriotism, and religiosity. The revolution was an accident, triggered by a conspiracy of Russia's enemies, domestic as well as foreign. This conspiracy undermined the social structure and corrupted the popular mind and soul.

Liberal historiography, for its part, has proposed an "optimistic" interpretation of the period, according to which rapid economic and social change would eventually have transformed Russia into a prosperous, industrialized nation with a democratic and constitutional form of government, if only World War I had not intervened.

By contrast, radical and socialist historians are convinced that the changes going on, no matter how profound, would never have resulted in a liberal and prosperous Russia even if World War I had never taken place or Russia had remained neutral. In their view, the tendencies which they and the liberals agree might have produced these desirable effects had been stymied, partly because of the intrinsic dynamic of capitalism and imperialism, partly because of the failure of the ruling classes to understand what was going on, and partly

too because of the anachronistic survival of an autocratic regime, whose true nature remained unchanged despite apparent concessions to constitutionalism. This last factor is also
invoked by some liberals, who lay the blame for the revolution directly at the feet of the imperial government, which,
they say, was either unwilling or unable to permit the healthy,
progressive elements in Russian society to take an active political role.

Much ground has certainly been cleared by both liberals and
radicals, and solid foundations have been laid for further historical research. Both schools have done much to stimulate
discussion and debate and have shed new light not only on
what happened but also on various aspects of the intellectual
and methodological issues that must be resolved before we
can hope to achieve an adequate understanding of this period. It is clear, however, that neither the "optimists" nor the
"pessimists" have taken a sufficiently comprehensive view
of the subject: to begin with, their research and their analysis
ends with 1917 (just as some schools of French historiography make 1789 the focus of all prior history). This leads to
an overly constricted view of the tendencies uncovered. Nor
do these historians give adequate consideration to other possible avenues of change, with the result that they overem-
phasize the importance of historical accidents such as World
War I and the emperor's influence over his entourage. The issue is not merely whether or not the evolution begun in 1861
could have ended at some place other than the revolution of
1917. Rather, the problem is to understand the process of
change as a whole by considering other possible courses of
events and other possible outcomes.[1]

Soviet historiography, for which the revolution was an ineluctable consequence of inexorable historical laws, a trium-
phant vindication of the Bolshevik analysis, would be of no

---

1. Martin Malia, *Comprendre la révolution russe* (Paris: Editions du Seuil, 1980),
takes this approach.

more interest than monarchist-conservative historiography were it not for the fact that it has aroused the curiosity of Western historians and spurred new research. Led by Americans, these historians, while essentially approving the Bolshevik revolution, have had enough distance on the events, enough perspicacity, and enough intellectual freedom not to settle for the simplistic interpretation imposed by Soviet orthodoxy. In their search for the underlying causes which, as they believe, made the revolution of 1917 inevitable, they have not overlooked the possible importance of political, cultural, and bureaucratic factors. This approach is still in its infancy, and the results of research based on unpublished documents are not yet available in their entirety. To judge by what has been published so far, however, it is clear that the pattern of government intervention in society was complex, as was society's reaction to that intervention (particularly on the part of the nobility and the industrial and commercial bourgeoisie); thus the range of policy alternatives was wider than has been thought.

It would not be surprising—such things have happened before—if, ironically enough, historians who began with the conviction that the Bolshevik revolution was an inevitable consequence of immutable historical laws should eventually be compelled by intellectual honesty and respect for professional standards to admit that many alternative explanations of what happened are possible and many alternative outcomes are conceivable. However things turn out, these historians have done pioneer work in developing the kind of social and political analysis that will some day enable us to understand the nature of the relationship between the state and civil society. Of course, in Russia, civil society was still in the process of formation, and much work remains to be done before we can hope to describe its structure and assess the importance of spiritual and intellectual factors (which also demand further study). The crucial point, finally, is that historical research along these lines demands that we reconsider the period in its proper perspective, starting from contemporary perceptions of events. I am not suggesting that the revolution of 1917 be ignored, quite the contrary: the very fact that it occurred justifies the exploration of certain avenues of research that would be inconceivable without it. But the revolution must not be viewed as a predetermined outcome. In what follows I shall attempt to summarize recent research and begin to analyze the results. I shall begin by reviewing the major events of the period and then move on to distinguish what was variable from what was constant in society, politics, and culture.

The Great Reform Era

The final fifty years of the imperial regime began with the emancipation of the serfs (on February 19, 1861), which inaugurated the great reform era. Freedom was granted to more than twenty million serfs formerly owned by private individuals. Each freed serf was given a small plot of land (to prevent immediate proletarization). At the same time, their former masters, the rural landowners, were relieved of responsibility for maintaining order in the countryside pending establishment of a new system of local administration. This was accomplished in 1864 when the *zemstva* were established as more or less autonomous bodies in the districts and provinces. Elected representatives of the major social groups sat on the *zemstva*, which assumed responsibility for police functions, social services, and public health. In fact the powers of the *zemstva* were limited. Their activities were closely regulated, and they could take few initiatives on their own, since the central government kept control of the budget and delegated tax-apportionment authority to certain local officials (governors, etc.). Some influential nobles attempted to use the *zemstva* to establish political contacts that they hoped would lead to the organization of a national movement for constitutional reform; this triggered a conflict which had grave consequences.

While reorganizing the local administration the imperial government also set up a new court system more liberal and progressive than its West European counterparts. Among the reforms introduced were trial by jury, permanent tenure for judges, and new standards of competence and honesty to be met by those chosen to sit on the bench. Accused persons henceforth had to be treated with respect, provided with attorneys, and allowed to confront their accusers. The provision of defense attorneys raised the standard of judicial proceedings, as did the opening of trials to public scrutiny; social and psychological factors began to be taken into account in penal law. The only thing lacking was a code of laws; efforts to draft one had been made repeatedly since the beginning of the century, but down to 1917 none succeeded. The judicial reform also suffered from another major defect: peasants did not enjoy the same status before the law as other subjects of the emperor. Litigation involving peasants fell within the purview of special courts and could be heard by the regular courts only in specific cases. In the absence of a modern civil code the rural courts enforced customary law, and peasants did not enjoy security of property on a par with other subjects of the realm. This legal discrimination not only limited the scope of the reform but actually accentuated the hostility it provoked on the part of both peasants and intellectuals involved in peasant affairs, including liberals and populists employed as officials by the *zemstva*. A robust legal consciousness was thus able to develop rapidly only among the educated middle classes, leaving the vast majority of the population untouched.

The last major reform of Alexander II's reign was the introduction, in 1874, of universal compulsory military service, of brief duration. This reform put an end to the forced recruitment, which had affected only peasants and led to virtually life—long military service; ultimately, it gave rise to a citizens' army. In the long run the effect of the reform was to democratize and professionalize the officer corps. By the time of World War I, the Russian army could boast of a corps of field officers and noncoms of high quality. Unfortunately, its mediocre high command led it straight to disaster. Though the military reform was no doubt of enormous social importance, it has not yet been the subject of serious study, and I shall therefore limit myself to a few brief remarks. Compulsory military service was an important instrument for integrating the peasantry (Russian as well as alien) into the civil society of the empire and an effective means of transmitting modern culture to the masses. Illiterate soldiers were taught to read and write (with what success we do not yet know). In the army many recruits came into contact with modern equipment and techniques for the first time, and rubbed shoulders with men from every conceivable background. Since service lasted only a few years, veterans were able to return home with the knowledge gained from their military experience. The social and cultural consequences of this form of military service call for thorough investigation from a number of different angles.

The four major reforms carried out during the reign of Alexander II were extraordinarily successful in the short term, which is particularly surprising since they were the work of a conservative government in a relatively poor and backward country. As a result, Russia moved a long way toward catching up with the industrializing West. The reforms undoubtedly did initiate a thoroughgoing transformation of the social structure and did so without upheaval, turmoil, violence, or serious crisis, at least in the short term. Yet if we take a somewhat more detached view and look at what took place some decades later on, it becomes necessary to temper our judgment, for initial success soon gave way to grave difficulties. It is to these delayed difficulties, many of which could not have been foreseen, that radical and Soviet historians point, I think without justification, in support of their negative judgment of the reforms, which it is worth pointing out once more were begun under Nicholas I.

This is not the place to go into detail about the negative effects of the reforms, which have been described at length in a number of monographs. I shall therefore merely mention a few of the deficiencies that became apparent toward the end of the nineteenth century. The major shortcoming of the reform program was that it was based on a static world view, an erroneous judgment of the nature of modern society that gave short shrift to the dynamic forces unleashed by modernization. The most serious problem was implicit in the very terms of the emancipation decree. It is incorrect to argue, as many radical and Soviet historians do, that the amount of land given to the freed peasants in 1861 was woefully inadequate (in general, that is—there were of course many exceptions to the rule, to varying degrees). To be sure, the plots offered were seldom generous, but broadly speaking they were sufficient to enable peasants to provide for their immediate needs. But, before a dozen years had gone by, they became quite unsuitable for two reasons, at least one of which could not have been foreseen: namely, the sharp rise that occurred in the size of the population. The original plots proved inadequate for the needs of a rapidly expanding peasantry (and the rapid expansion was itself due in part to the traditional conception and organization of the peasant economy). Other important factors included the shortage of capital and the practice, traditional in the communes, of periodically redistributing plots, which impeded the introduction of new farming techniques and kept yields low. Thus the plots were underutilized and the peasants were constantly clamoring for more land. Ultimately this led to the peasant uprisings of the early twentieth century. For as the agricultural crisis worsened, there was but one solution acceptable to the peasants and to most leaders of public opinion: an equitable reapportionment of the land designed to put most arable soil in the hands of the peasantry.

Is it true, however, that land hunger was the major cause of the agricultural crisis and that failure to take this into account was the major defect of the 1861 reform? Objective analysis of the economic situation must await attention by a specialist in the subject, which I cannot claim to be. Nevertheless, I will hazard the guess that the real problem lay in the restrictions placed on peasant mobility. For fiscal and administrative (or police) reasons, the emancipation act delegated responsibility for maintaining law and order and collecting taxes to the rural commune. No peasant was allowed to leave his commune without first obtaining the consent of his fellow citizens. Such consent was not readily given, because the departure of any peasant meant that the existing tax burden would be shared by fewer people, so that the amount paid by each would automatically increase. The communes controlled the issuance of passports to peasants who took temporary work elsewhere and thus made sure that these workers would eventually have to return to pay their share of communal taxes. But this limited the mobility of workers and thereby assured a relatively cheap supply of labor to industrialists and large property owners who hired additional hands to help with the harvest.

Lack of mobility resulted in overpopulation of the agricultural areas of Central Russia (where the land was least fertile). It was the principal cause of the agricultural crisis and hampered the growth of a permanent urban proletariat (as well as settlement of outlying regions, especially Siberia). When the government finally took steps to promote mobility at the beginning of the twentieth century, conditions were far less favorable than they had been, and the intellectual and political climate was one in which land redistribution had become the major issue of the day. Neither the opening of Siberia to peasant colonization nor the relaxation of communal control could bring about the desired results sufficiently quickly.

The existing order of things made it inevitable that the reform of the local administration (the *zemstva*) would not be without shortcomings. The most energetic *zemstvo* officials, who worked closely with teachers, public health officials, statisticians, and technicians, naturally considered themselves to be the elected representatives of the nation. Accordingly, they had the presumption to attempt to coordinate their activities on a nationwide basis. In doing so they encountered opposition from the central government, which refused to countenance this logical development. *Zemstvo* officials were denied the right to make representations to the central authorities or even to act as consultants. The government was concerned to halt a process that might eventually lead to a constitutional monarchy, ending the personal authority of the sovereign. In effect it refused to recognize civil society or allow it to organize. Thus the reform of the *zemstva* led ultimately to a serious conflict between the state and the local elites representing a civil society still in the process of formation. This conflict paralyzed efforts to modernize rural life, improve hygiene among the peasants, teach new methods of farming, and so on.

Finally, all the reforms undertaken during the reign of Alexander II suffered from one major—and, in the circumstances, inevitable—defect: they were subject to the whim of the autocrat. Even reformers well-placed at court or in the administration depended on the emperor to hold special interests in check and to overcome the apathy, corruption, and inefficiency of the bureaucracy. Paradoxically, reforms intended to introduce modern economic relations and European political institutions in Russia ended by reinforcing the power and moral authority of the autocrat, which had been undermined by the defeat suffered in the Crimean War.

It is hardly surprising that a program of reforms as wide-ranging as the one put forward by the government of Alexander II could not have proceeded indefinitely without running into serious opposition. Its political success depended on the sovereign's continued enthusiasm. But that enthusiasm waned when the program was beset by practical difficulties. In addition, the attention of the emperor and the general public was distracted from the long and arduous task of carrying out the reforms by the Polish insurrection of 1863. This so frightened the Russian authorities that they began to doubt the wisdom of the liberal reform program. The international and domestic repercussions of the Polish uprising thwarted the progressive aspirations of establishment reformers. Still, the reform effort did not come to a halt: the *zemstva* and the new court system were put in place in 1864 and a major reform of the military was carried out in 1874. But the spirit was no longer the same: the confident optimism of the early days had evaporated.

After 1866 progress was slowed by bureaucratic apathy and by the emperor's lack of firmness. Little by little the government was persuaded by the arguments of conservatives and timid progressives that greater caution was in order and further reforms should be delayed. Meanwhile, new problems, mainly economic, came to light. Emancipation had ruined many noble landowners who had been unable to adapt to the new conditions. Lacking initiative and practical experience, many had failed to make wise investments with the capital distributed by the state as compensation for the loss of serfs and land. The inadequacy of the plots given to the peasants in Central Russia and the impediments to mobility of the rural population began to make their effects felt. Discontent among both peasants and the educated elite, particularly in the provinces, created a climate of latent hostility and grumbling opposition to further reform, and this made the government hesitant to enforce reforms already introduced and reluctant to extend them in any way.

But couldn't reform have continued on its own, independent of the government? Perhaps, but only if civil society had been able to organize itself quickly and effectively. As we have seen, however, it was in fact impossible for an autonomous, enterprising civil society to develop in a country where peasants were confined to their communes and subject to special laws and *zemstvo* officials were not allowed to work in concert or to organize nationally. The urban business elite, as distinct from the bureaucratic elite and the nobility, was still in its infancy. In the circumstances it is hardly surprising that a radical, revolutionary movement began to develop. Support for such a movement came from many quarters, including educated progressives disappointed by what the great reforms had achieved. Alain Besançon has shown how student unrest grew out of dashed hopes for rapid and radical social change and how students affected by this were drawn to socialist, materialist, and nihilist ideologies and clandestine revolutionary organizations.[2] Students who had failed in their attempts to bring moral and cultural leadership to the masses through propaganda and education turned next to out-and-out opposition. They rejected the existing system and all its reforms and instead placed their hopes in revolutionary change.

This is not the place to recount the history of the various revolutionary movements and groups that developed in Russia, of which Franco Venturi, among others, has provided a magisterial account.[3] It is important, however, to stress that the spread of a revolutionary movement that included groups practicing political terrorism could only reinforce the government's conservative, indeed reactionary, tendencies. The momentum of the reforms was broken, and the government's mistrust of the educated deepened, particularly since it was apparent that the revolutionaries and the radical intelligentsia were receiving protection and assistance from the academic, professional, and even business elites. The radicalized (and alienated) intelligentsia was used by both the gov-

2. Besançon, *Education et société* and, by the same author, *Les origines intellectuelles du léninisme* (Paris: Calmann-Levy, 1977), especially chap. 6; Abbott Gleason, *Young Russia: The Genesis of Russian Radicalism in the 1860s* (New York: Viking, 1980).

3. Franco Venturi, *Roots of Revolution* (London: Weidenfeld, 1960); Adam Ulam, *In the Name of the People* (New York: Viking, 1977).

ernment and the nonrevolutionary opposition as a pretext and a smokescreen. A dialogue of the deaf developed between the government on the one hand and educated leaders of civil society on the other; the latter group included professionals, businessmen, artists, and philanthropists, all of whom longed for greater freedom and autonomy and wished to be allowed to participate in political life.

The Balkan war and expansion into central Asia also helped to inflame public opinion and encourage political organization.[4] Just as the Polish insurrection had rekindled the flame of Russian chauvinism, so the war in the Balkans and the conquest of central Asia stoked the fires of imperialism and aggressive pan-Slavism. The nationalistic and imperialistic fervor was reflected in the press, in organizations such as the Red Cross and the Slavic Society, and in other patriotic activities. The popular enthusiasm frequently clashed with the government's cautious diplomatic attitudes and timid approach to colonial expansion, giving rise to the curious spectacle of dyed-in-the-wool conservatives organizing in opposition to the autocratic regime, of which they considered themselves to be the true ideological champions. Whatever practical success it achieved, this "right-wing agitation" did much to undermine the moral authority of the autocratic government. At the same time it stimulated curiosity in religious, metaphysical, and nationalistic (or traditionalistic) aspects of Russian culture, as a counter to the positivism and materialism of the radical intelligentsia; none of this helped to consolidate the regime, however.

After the war in the Balkans, revolutionary agitation intensified and, with the formation of the People's Will (Narodnaia Volia) group, turned toward political terrorism. Condemned to death by this group, Alexander II was assassinated on March 1, 1881, after more than a year of dramatic at-

4. For a recent interpretation and lengthy bibliography, see Dietrich Geyer, Der russische Imperialismus (Studien über den Zusammenhang von innerer und auswärtiger Politik 1860–1914 (Göttingen: Vandenhoeck und Ruprecht, 1977).

tempts on his life, just when he seemed ready to allow civil society a limited consultative role in the legislative process.

The reaction of the country was a far cry from what the radical and revolutionary intelligentsia had expected. Not only did the government succeed in arresting and sentencing to death all the members of People's Will, thus ending terrorism and revolutionary agitation for a decade, but public opinion also turned away from terrorist radicalism and indeed from political activisism in general, as people sought refuge in more "modest tasks" aimed at improving the standard of living of the masses. The governments of Alexander III and his son Nicholas II seized the opportunity to halt the progress of reform and, after several years of hesitation and delay, moved to undo some of what had been achieved, introducing what Soviet historians like to call the "counterreforms" of the 1880s and 1890s.

The Counterreforms

The counterreforms particularly affected the universities and the *zemstva.* Censorship and control over intellectual activity were tightened with the imposition of strict new regulations governing student life and the universities. The jurisdictions of the *zemstva* were curtailed and their activities placed under the direct control of the central government with the creation of so-called *zemskie nachal'niki,*[5] who were appointed by the minister of the interior and chosen among the local landed nobility. These measures reflected a determination to halt further development of civil society and to limit public participation in political life. Residents of town and country alike were placed under surveillance. Surveillance in the literal sense, by the arbitrary and tyrannical police, was

5. The *zemskie nachal'niki* (literally, "land captains") were responsible for local police and supervision of local administrative agencies.

also stepped up. Alexander III's government also sought support from sections of the population committed to militant, Great Russian, and Orthodox chauvinism. The autonomy and privileges that had hitherto been enjoyed by alien, non-Orthodox populations, modest as they had been, were now drastically curtailed and even revoked. A policy of all-out Russification was begun in the Baltic provinces, Poland, the Caucasus, and even Finland. The Jewish population, after enjoying a brief period of benign neglect that gave rise to the *Haskalah* movement and encouraged many of the younger generation to opt for cultural assimilation, was once again made the victim of administrative restrictions and harassment of a particularly harsh variety. Even worse, Jews suffered violence in the pogroms and, as their numbers grew without any corresponding increase in the size of the territory in which they were forced to reside, sank deeper and deeper into poverty.

Industrialization

In contrast to this rather bleak picture, the economic policies of the last two tsars did help to promote an industrial "takeoff" but at the cost of reviving and indeed exacerbating the agricultural crisis. Measures taken by ministers such as Witte helped to stabilize the financial situation and stimulated export of agricultural products and raw materials. These measures also raised Russia, whose economic potential developed extraordinarily quickly, to the rank of a world industrial power by 1895, thus dealing a hard blow to the agricultural sector of the economy. The resulting imbalance was pointed up dramatically by the great famine of 1891–92, which also revealed glaring defects in the government's social policies. The government was wrongly accused of not having done all that was needed to reduce the suffering of the populace and to prevent such a disaster from recurring. The famine, and the government's efforts to deal with it, reawakened social and civic commitment on the part of the elite. There was renewed agitation in the universities, and various occupational, social, national, and religious groups showed signs of becoming increasingly discontented and prone to violent demonstration.

The economic and social difficulties, aggravated by the arrival on the scene of a large, ill disciplined, and miserably poor industrial proletariat, heightened political tensions and raised expectations that the situation would soon deteriorate into one of overt crisis. The intellectual climate only encouraged this state of mind: leading developments of the time were the debates between Marxists and populists, the symbolist vogue in art and literature, the revival of religious thinking and idealistic metaphysics, and, finally, the *fin de siècle* atmosphere created by the writings of Nietzsche, Ibsen, and others.

The storm broke in the very first years of the twentieth century. The agricultural crisis led to sporadic peasant uprisings, riots in the cities, and conflicts between the government and non-Russian nationals, all of which turned informed public opinion against the government once and for all. Peasant rebellions and strikes were coupled with acts of political terrorism and with equally eloquent and impressive peaceful demonstrations of liberal and progressive views, as well as public speeches at banquets and university meetings. It is important to emphasize that professional associations provided, in their annual congresses and meetings, an institutionalized way of expressing public discontent. Former *zemstvo* leaders who had lost their platform in the wake of Alexander III's counterreforms took advantage of these new forums to orchestrate a political campaign against the conservative regime.

In the hope of defusing a situation that threatened at any moment to explode into revolution, the government of Nicholas II, in which Plehve was the dominant figure, conceived the unfortunate idea of dragging Russia into a war with Japan, which it was hoped would yield a quick victory. The government was counting on an outpouring of patriotism to put an end to social protest and political demonstration; these calculations proved to be sadly mistaken. The disastrous war pointed up all the material and moral shortcomings of the regime, and the economic sacrifices required by the war effort proved costly to both government and citizenry. Far from calming public opinion, the war sharpened discontent and brought on the revolution. Mutinies in the army and navy, combined with a campaign of dinner speeches, strikes, and peasant uprisings, culminated in October 1905 in a general strike that forced the government to beat a hasty retreat. Under pressure, Nicholas promised to allow legislative elections and the drafting of a constitution. This major concession produced the desired results, and calm was restored with the signing of the treaty of Portsmouth.

In the spring of 1906 elections were held for the Duma and Russia gained a new government that was constitutional in character. This is not the place to discuss the controversial question whether the government established in 1906 was truly constitutional or not. Autocracy was not formally abolished, and the emperor retained ultimate authority. Although suffrage was still restricted, the existence of an elected Duma did allow civil society to organize openly and take an active role in political life (political parties were legalized for the first time).

The first Duma was dominated by constitutional liberal sentiments, and its economic and social views were fairly moderate. The Duma saw its role more as one of harassing the imperial government than of cooperating with it. Conflict with the government led quickly to the dissolution of Russia's first elected legislative assembly. After several months of crisis, Stolypin, the prime minister, carried out what the public saw as a *coup d'état:* by changing the election laws, he secured election of a new Duma, more moderate and conciliatory than the old one, and subsequently took further drastic steps to put down violent uprisings that had developed, in the countryside and in various towns. By placing the country under martial law, Stolypin was finally able to restore order. Between 1907 and 1914 (indeed, until the eve of the 1917 revolution), Russia enjoyed a period of calm during which wounds began to heal, the process of modernization and industrialization resumed its course, and the government took steps to change the country's agrarian structure.[6] Intellectual and cultural life found their second wind, and the period was one of dazzling creativity in many areas. For the first time it was now Russia that set the tone for the West in style, taste, and spiritual values.

But the growing incapacity of the executive branch of government, the seditious attitudes of an influential segment of civil society, and worse revolutionary agitation than ever created a crisis atmosphere. The "social question" had lost none of its importance. The proletariat and peasantry continued to live under precarious conditions of utter poverty, and the slow improvements that were being made in their standard of living exacted a stiff price: sacrifice of age-old customs and traditions (most of the proletariat had peasant roots and remained tied to the countryside). The educated classes and "rooted" intelligentsia, hounded by the police and viewed with suspicion by the government, could not collaborate sincerely or effectively with the state. Stolypin and his successors therefore turned to the wealthy for support, relying on their nationalistic and patriotic sentiments, with the result that non-Russian elites turned against the regime.

By combining Great Russian nationalism at home with imperialistic chauvinism in foreign policy, the regime ingeniously contrived to get Russia involved in international diplomatic controversy in the hope of obscuring or playing down

6. See Malia, *Comprendre la révolution russe;* and M. Szeftel, *The Russian Constitution of April 23, 1906: Political Institutions of the Duma Monarchy* (Brussels, 1976).

its problems at home. In this way Russia became caught up in World War I, where it suffered defeats whose disastrous consequences made revolution if not inevitable then at least highly probable. The regime's death knell was sounded when the leaders of civil society and members of the elite who had remained loyal to the Petrine state began to see the court cliques and the incompetent bureaucracy as barriers to the domestic reform and mobilization of resources that were needed if anything was to be salvaged from the wreckage of war. An interruption of food supplies to the towns and a demonstration against the shortage of bread in the capital that degenerated into a riot triggered the collapse of the regime. The imperial government simply evaporated overnight when it lost what support it had left among organized groups within the society.

With this brief sketch of events in the period 1861–1917 out of the way, we are now in a position to take a closer look at the relationship between society and the state.

The Two Poles

Think of the social and political forces at work in Russia as forming a sort of ellipse. Within this ellipse there is both continuity and change. Think of the two foci of the ellipse as poles of continuity. In my view, these two poles should be thought of as bearing opposite charges: between them there is constant tension, conflict, a struggle to the death. Indeed, it was the tension between these two poles which determined, in large part, the relative positions of all the other particles in the system. Let us examine each of these two poles of continuity in turn.

At the first pole we find the figure of the autocratic sovereign, the emperor (and his immediate entourage). This was

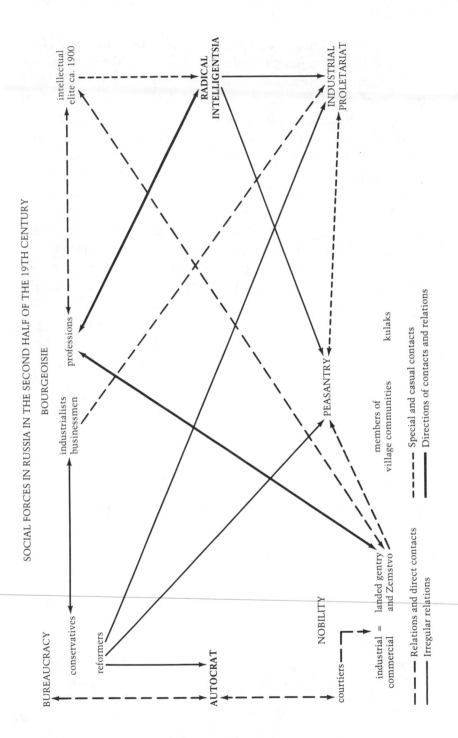

SOCIAL FORCES IN RUSSIA IN THE SECOND HALF OF THE 19TH CENTURY

BOURGEOISIE

intellectual
elite ca. 1900

RADICAL
INTELLIGENTSIA

INDUSTRIAL
PROLETARIAT

professions

industrialists
businessmen

PEASANTRY

members of   kulaks
village communities

conservatives

BUREAUCRACY

reformers

NOBILITY

landed gentry
and Zemstvo

AUTOCRAT

courtiers

industrial =
commercial

Relations and direct contacts   Special and casual contacts

Irregular relations   Directions of contacts and relations the cornerstone of the Russian political, social, and ideological system. The primary importance of the tsar's personal authority has been mentioned several times. The whole imperial system was embodied in the personal authority of Nicholas I, who, despite his fundamental conservatism and unwillingness to change, trained leaders and compiled information without which his successor could never have initiated his ambitious program of reforms. Again, it was the personal authority of Alexander II that overcame all resistance to those reforms—from the landed nobility, the bureaucrats, and high-ranking officials of a former era. And it was also the personal authority of this same Alexander II that later closed off the path to further progress and refused to allow the nascent civil society to assume an active public role and transform Russia into a moderate *Rechtsstaat*. And finally, it was again the personal authority of the two tsars, Alexander III and Nicholas II, that imposed the reactionary policy of counterreforms. This policy, stubbornly pursued by Nicholas II, was in large part responsible for the fact that the October 1905 manifesto did not succeed in creating a truly liberal constitutional regime: by protecting the autocratic power of the tsar and his bureaucracy, this policy led Russia into the revolution of 1917.

What is paradoxical, however, is that, over the course of the nineteenth century, the tsar's purely personal authority actually diminished. The distance between the emperor and Russian society steadily increased. Admittedly, people of the very lowest classes apparently continued to look upon the emperor as their benevolent father, at least until the bloody Sunday of January 9, 1905. But if they did so it was only by force of habit: no visible, symbolic, or ritual confirmation of this "political myth" was forthcoming from the monarch himself. The rest of the population—the educated classes, the urban proletariat, and the alien peoples—lost whatever was left of the belief in the sovereign's paternalistic and benevolent role and began calling for the establishment of a constitutional monarchy. As late as 1905 it was possible to believe that the poor workers, the children of peasant parents, continued to cherish a paternal image of the tsar, as is attested by the activities of Gapon and Zubatov. The order given by Nicholas II to fire on a crowd of unarmed people who had come to present their grievances and to beg for aid instantly destroyed what was left of the traditional myth.

To return for a moment to the central paradox, it is worth noting that it was the sovereign himself who, in the nineteenth century, took the initiative to change his traditional image. The emperors and empresses of the eighteenth century may have dressed in the European fashion and declared themselves, as their Western counterparts did—in homage to the Roman tradition—"sovereign emperors," yet they remained in contact with the people or at any rate with those who resided in the capital cities of the empire. The meeting between Grinev's fiancée and the empress in a public park was not merely the product of a sentimental novelist's imagination but something that might actually have occurred.[7] To the astonishment of foreign diplomats, Alexander I would stroll by himself through the streets of his capital. Then, too, in the eighteenth century, especially in the time of Peter the Great, Elizabeth, and Catherine II, the sovereign frequently took part in public celebrations and ceremonies and rubbed elbows with ordinary citizens. The same is true of coronations, marriages, baptisms, and funerals involving members of the imperial family. All nobles, even the most obscure and impoverished, had access to the court.

When Nicholas I came to power, however, a radical change took place, the beginnings of which can be traced back to the second half of the reign of Alexander I, though Alexander himself followed eighteenth century tradition and in any case

7. Grinev was the hero of Pushkin's novel *The Captain's Daughter*, the action of which takes place in the aftermath of the Pugachev rebellion in the reign of Catherine II.

had no domestic life to speak of.[8] Like his father, Paul I, Alexander was enthusiastic about military displays and parades, and the characteristic "parade mania" of Russia's rulers dates from his reign. But the new enthusiasm for parades was the sign of a very significant change: ceremonies such as the changing of the guard at the Winter Palace took the place of other public celebrations to which the entire population was invited. Gone were the public balls, the fireworks displays, the triumphal entries, and the like, which had traditionally been occasions for the monarch to appear in public and take part in popular festivities. Military parades separated the monarch from the spectators. Regiment after regiment erected a moving wall of troops between the emperor and his people, and woe unto anyone who dared cross that forbidden barrier.

Nicholas not only kept up this practice but added yet another element of separation: he closeted himself with his family in private life. Court life itself became less open, less public. Access to receptions and ceremonies became increasingly difficult. Daily life at court was adjusted more and more to the monarch's whims and family concerns. The emperor and empress, true to their ideas and temperaments, devoted themselves to raising and educating their children. Ceremony and etiquette of course continued to be an important part of their lives, and the emperor and his family were obliged to make regular appearances in public. Every Sunday there was a parade to and from mass, and on Easter Sunday there was a great ceremonial welcome. The emperor appeared in full pomp and circumstance on certain holidays (na iordan', birthdays, and so on), and there was also the imposing ceremony of coronation, which was held in Moscow. But the point remains: the solemnities were henceforth regulated in such

8. For what follows I am indebted, in part, to conversations with Richard Wortman of Princeton University, who is working on a study of the nature of autocratic power in the nineteenth century.

a way as to prevent contact between the people and their sovereign. The monarch could be seen only at a distance, and between him and the crowd were regiments on parade (this was also true to some extent of "public" functions at court).

It is tempting to argue that the sovereign's decision to attach primary importance to his family and his private life opened a breach between him and his people. The traditional image of the benevolent father faded away, while the even older Muscovite icon of the tsar as Christ's vicar on earth vanished altogether. Secularization in the eighteenth century, "privatization" in the nineteenth, destroyed the traditional popular conception of the Russian monarch. The tradition of personalized power withered and, just when it was needed for a vital political purpose, finally crumbled. It is equally tempting to blame the emperor personally for all the country's reverses and disasters and to reproach him for his isolation and for his ignorance of and lack of interest in his country's problems, when nothing was supposed to be done except by his express command.

Some writers have also exaggerated the role played by the emperor's personal friends and family members. But the favorites of the last emperors were no longer public figures like the favorites of the eighteenth century; yet, although they were merely the ruler's personal friends and companions, they have often been accused or suspected (not unreasonably in the case of Vyrubova and Rasputin) of exerting occult, and therefore presumably harmful, influence.

Nicholas II preferred to have as little as possible to do with court ceremonies and public appearances. When all is said and done, it seems accurate to say that Russia's last autocratic ruler lost his political authority when he took refuge from his country's problems in private life and lost contact with his people. He wanted to live the life of a bourgeois head of family, like the lives led by Louis-Phillippe or the King of Würtemberg, and not unlike constitutional monarchs in our own day. But by so doing he forfeited his personal authority and gave the *coup de grâce* to the myths and traditions on which the imperial system was based.

We come now to a second aspect of autocratic continuity. No autocrat, no matter how powerful or independent, no matter how much personal authority he wields, can rule without advisers and other functionaries. He may also call upon the services of his courtiers, who may or may not also occupy official posts. Finally, he will make use of his police—in Russia, the Third Section of the Imperial Chancellery and the National Police Corps (replaced at the end of the century by the notorious *okhrannoe otdelenie* or *okhrana*, literally the department of security but in fact the tsar's secret police). These police forces had responsibilities which they saw as exemplifying the personal character of the monarch's authority. In discharging these responsibilities they gathered information and dispatched inspectors (a sort of *missi dominici*) and *fligel' ad'iutantly*[9] to execute the sovereign's orders directly, bypassing the bureaucratic hierarchy and, if necessary, contravening its instructions.

Certain distinctions are in order, however, when it comes to considering the government's regular functionaries, those who formed the personnel of what we shall call, for the sake of convenience, the bureaucracy (though a better term is needed to cover the complexity of the imperial government). In a very interesting study soon to be published, the American historian T. Taranovski identifies two groups of functionaries, two bureaucratic hierarchies that rivaled each other for the favor of the monarch and the right to govern the country. Both groups survived till the end of the empire by allying themselves with different segments of society after a true civil society began to develop in Russia. One group (I use the term "group" rather than "party" because a party in-

9. See note 3 to chapter 6.

volves a higher level of intellectual and institutional cohesion than was achieved here) consisted of liberal reformers, the other of conservatives. It is not enough to label the two groups, however.

In the first half of Alexander II's reign, the more dynamic and influential of the two groups consisted of officials who had been trained and initiated into government service under Nicholas I. At that time they had developed a professional ethos that mandated service not simply to the emperor but to the country and its people, service intended to open the way to material and spiritual progress. To do this, they counted on the support of the sovereign to promote reform and push it through to completion, so as to liberate the creative forces latent in all the social orders. Once reform was underway, liberal reformers wanted to pursue the full program through to completion. They hoped to begin a dynamic process that would ultimately bring about a peaceful reordering of society, based on a "bourgeois" liberal social and economic system. They advocated a moderate *laissez-faire* economy that would develop the spirit of enterprise and individual initiative in all areas of Russian life. They felt that emancipation of the serfs would foster greater mobility and independence among the peasantry and that reform of the *zemstva* would lead to true local self-government. As for the economy, the liberal reformers hoped that modernization and industrial development could be accomplished without overlooking the interests of the agricultural sector. In the area of cultural policy, they were as liberal and progressive on such issues as education, censorship, etc., as was possible in the circumstances. Admittedly, they did not wish for an end to autocracy (on which they relied for support) or empire: their loyalty was not in question. Russia, they believed, could be transformed only with state leadership under the aegis of a benevolent, paternalistic ruler.

The second group within the bureaucracy was much more exclusive: it consisted of high-ranking dignitaries, many of "aristocratic" origin, who had been educated at court and trained for practical life in the military and who subscribed to reactionary principles that had been prevalent in the 1820s. This group had many contacts at court and indeed in some respects resembled a "court cabal." Curiously, however, in the 1870s and 1880s this group was most closely allied with the provincial governors, who saw themselves as personal representatives of the tsar and delegates of the central government and who were very much in the forefront of efforts to curb the activities of the *zemstva,* which were suspected of harboring radical republican sentiments. This group held the emperor to be sacrosanct and felt that reform had gone far enough. Time was needed for the country to assimilate and digest the changes before reexamining the situation. The conservative group had the support not only of a court faction and at times of Alexander II himself but also of wealthy nobles who felt that their property rights had been threatened and who wanted nothing to do with the *zemstva* or any kind of consultative representation.

When we look at the social background of officials belonging to each of these two groups, what we find is rather paradoxical: the majority of liberals belonged to the petty nobility and owed their positions entirely to state service. It seems only logical that they, like the *szlachta* of 1730 before them, should have been ardent defenders of autocracy and of the existing political system, which had enabled them to rise to positions of influence. The history of the eighteenth century and the logic of their social background both suggest that the members of this liberal group should have been hostile to any move toward a constitutional regime that would have accorded greater autonomy, independence, and influence to the general public, that is, to civil society. By contrast, the conservatives, many of whom were also of "aristocratic" origin, as logical successors to the *verkhovniki*[10] of 1730, should have become the champions of a policy that would have given this

10. The *verkhovniki* (literally, "top men") were members of the Supreme Privy Council, the highest de facto state organ under Catherine I and Peter II; they attempted to impose limits on Empress Anna's autocratic powers.

small group, reminiscent of the senatorial party under Alexander I, an influential role in creating a constitutional regime (based on birth, rank, and wealth) on behalf of an oligarchic elite. But their ideas in fact had little in common with such a constitutional position, as we have seen. Their worst fear was that the *zemstva*, led by wealthy provincial nobles, would succeed in bringing about a constitutional monarchy.

The existence of these two factions within the bureaucracy had very important consequences. Of the two, the liberal group was the more familiar with the country's needs. Its members had not only an objective appreciation of the situation but also knowledge of the intellectual and economic factors that had contributed to European progress, and they hoped to help Russia share in the benefits of that progress. The liberals favored a dynamic and pluralistic society and believed that government not only could but should place its trust in civil society. Had their advice been heeded, Russia would probably have proceeded more rapidly and more surely along the road to modernization. Among the members of the liberal group were statesmen and officials who tried valiantly, if not always skillfully, to forestall the kinds of conflict that ultimately led to disaster. But without the sovereign's full support they were helpless, since Russian society was not yet sufficiently organized to provide an independent power base. This was the liberals' great weakness. When it came to changing the political system, their hands were tied. Even their economic and cultural policies required the backing of the emperor. Nor could the liberals look to constitutional monarchy as a solution, since they could not openly ally themselves with social groups that shared their aspirations but wished for an end to autocracy.

The conservative bureaucrats relied almost exclusively on the tsar for their support and used the influence of court coteries and friends of the imperial family to translate the tsar's wishes into practice. They would have liked to see a return to the centralized government and despotic paternalism of

Peter the Great and Nicholas I but did not share the positive side of Peter's vision: the prospect of a powerful and prosperous Russian Empire, which, in the conditions prevailing in the nineteenth century, would have required a dynamic, pluralistic, independent, and creative civil society. But to have granted civil society enough freedom to achieve the government's economic and military objectives would inevitably have posed a threat to autocracy and bureaucratic control.

Since both liberals and conservatives styled themselves supporters of autocracy, the monarch remained the final arbiter, playing one group off against the other and deciding in favor of one or the other as he saw fit. As long as the sovereign was wise enough to pursue a flexible policy of reform that did not preclude progress altogether, things went reasonably well. This was the case in the first part of Alexander II's reign, as we saw earlier. But in the second half of the reign things started to go sour, partly for fortuitous reasons (the influence of the tsar's entourage on his peculiar personality), partly because of increasing economic and social difficulties. The problems became insuperable when a man of mediocre intelligence and narrow, reactionary views, like Alexander III, or a person whose apathy and weakness were almost pathological, like Nicholas II, came to the throne: in these circumstances the system led Russia straight to disaster. There was no escape: nothing short of violence was capable of breaking the vicious circle created by the rigid relations among the three principal elements of the imperial system. Autocracy had outlived its historical usefulness and thus helped to weaken the regime; its inertia, together with its inability to deal with the problems of war or with social and political conflict, contributed importantly to its final downfall in February–March 1917.

The radical intelligentsia constituted the second stable pole in the social and political configuration of the empire in the years 1861–1905. We have seen how, under Nicholas I, the alienated younger generation of the intellectual elite had refused to participate in practical life or to join the state service, and how some members of this generation then began to elaborate an ideology based on a "historiosophy" of Russia's past and a vision of its future, on a moral image of the Russian people and the role that it ought to play. Broadly speaking, this ideology, or rather this quest for an ideology, reflected the intelligentsia's need for certainty (its need to define its own position vis-à-vis history and the Russian people). Viewed in this way, the intelligentsia represented the crystallized consciousness of a specific *moment* in Russia's historical and eschatological evolution, the moment when the intelligentsia began to see itself in the role of guide, helping the people to assume its historical role of building the society of the future.

Although various intellectuals proposed various options and attitudes in this regard, this crystallization of consciousness at a specific moment and a specific relation to the people remained the common denominator of the intelligentsia, whose members shared an implicit conception of the historical process and of the nature (or character) of the Russian people. The dilemma facing the intelligentsia was the following: Was it correct to regard the historical process as following an ineluctable course, in which case passivity was the appropriate attitude to adopt while awaiting the inevitable dénouement, or was the proper attitude rather one of voluntarism aimed at deliberately transforming, in accordance with some rational plan, society and its economic underpinnings?

The younger generation of the elite generally inclined toward voluntarism and was therefore more radical than the previous generation. The "fathers," the men of the 1830s and 1840s, had been idealists, but their "sons" now turned toward philosophical materialism and from there moved easily into revolutionary activism and even terrorism in the hope of cutting through the Gordian knot of Russian history. They set about destroying the existing system in order to rebuild society on a completely new foundation. What explains this shift? In my view there were three main factors. First, the collective psychology of an entire generation underwent a radical change. Young intellectuals turned their backs on the philosophical idealism of their elders and enthusiastically embraced a rather simplistic form of materialism. They prostrated themselves before the god of science and adopted uncompromising voluntaristic attitudes that set them apart from the dreaminess and *Schönseelerei* of their elders. This change has often been explained in social terms: the younger generations of the intelligentsia, the nihilists of the 1850s and 1860s, seem to have come from a social background different from that of the previous generation. This was particularly true of the *raznoschintsy*, most of whom came from clerical families, whereas the men of the 1830s and 1840s belonged to the landed nobility.

Unfortunately, this argument is not entirely correct. In fact, the majority of the younger generation was also of noble descent. But the memoirs of those who took part in the change reveal that a psychological factor may have played an important part. The fathers of the nihilists, many of whom had been elevated to noble status because of services rendered to the state by their parents or grandparents, had held middle- to high-level posts in the government of Nicholas I, a closed and rigid regime which saw itself as enduring forever and which was based on unquestioning obedience to paternal authority—the cornerstone of discipline in the family and village, just as the emperor, the father of all, was the cornerstone of discipline in the nation as a whole. But the reverses suffered in the Crimean War revealed the underlying corruption and disorder and shook, possibly even destroyed, the patriarchal authority on which the regime was based.

Emancipation dealt the final blow: overnight, the authority of nobles and officials over the peasants disappeared, leaving the "fathers" without a role to play and undermining their moral authority. Thus they were no longer in a position to serve as role models for their children who renounced them. The rebellion against everything the generation of the 1830s and 1840s had stood for—its values and ideals—was complete. Everything that had once been held in high esteem now came under attack.

This sociopsychological explanation, adequate perhaps in itself, is not the only one available, however. An objective factor must also be taken into consideration, namely, changes in Russian higher education. Once advanced education in a specialized field became an essential prerequisite for any career worthy of the name, whether in the state service or in a profession, all young men of good family, whether noble or not, as well as ambitious youths of humbler origins, flocked to the universities. For the first time, these young students found themselves in unfamiliar surroundings (perhaps even in an unfamiliar place), separated from their families and aware of their isolation from the people. Deprived not only of comfort but also of good company, students were forced either to join existing circles *(kruzhki)* or to start new ones.

The *kruzhki* perpetuated the traditions of the eighteenth and early nineteenth centuries, creating a highly emotional, all-embracing atmosphere and demanding intellectual and spiritual orthodoxy of their members. The type of social life that existed in the circles facilitated indoctrination of new members by old ones and by those able to assert some sort of intellectual, social, or moral dominance. Created by and for the students, whose identity and moral certitude had been shaken if not shattered by their fathers' moral, social, and economic demise, the circles played a crucial role in the radicalization and philosophical and political indoctrination of the younger generation. Since, in Russia as in other countries, the universities (whose influence extended even to the high schools and *gimnazii*) continued to shape the minds of the young down to the end of the empire, the tradition of the circles and the tyrannical fascination they held for young minds also endured.

Yet the circles would have found it much more difficult to fascinate young minds so totally, or to spread radical ideology so easily, had it not been for the educational policies of the government. The attitude of university administrators toward the students, along with the harsh conditions in which young scholars were forced to live and about which the authorities showed themselves incapable of doing anything, helped to make the circles more attractive than they might otherwise have been. Censorship and disciplinary policies were handled clumsily (to put it mildly), and the government stubbornly bucked the intellectual tide of Europe by insisting that the university curriculum continue to emphasize subjects of no practical value, which only exacerbated the tensions. Even worse, the government either impeded or prohibited the development of civil society and refused to allow technical data collected by the *zemstva* to be put to practical use. Students felt that they could do nothing for their country or their fellow men unless they entered the government service (which in any case preferred to hire graduates of the technical schools maintained by certain ministries, particularly the ministries of the army and navy). But most students were unwilling to accept a position in the government because they prefered to maintain their independence and intellectual freedom. Thus a radical, indeed revolutionary, spirit was handed down from generation to generation of university students. In these circumstances the students drew sympathy from the educated and professional elites, which offered financial aid to the circles and protection from the police, even to groups engaged in terrorist or revolutionary activity.

The schematic outline given above corresponds best to the 1870s generation of nihilists and radicals. Yet in large part it remains valid for the next several decades. It is important to point out, however, that the radical intelligentsia was a fringe group, a small part of the educated (or semi-educated) elite which refused to take an active part in government or established social life. It was a group that remained aloof from the rest of society, permanently awaiting radical change through social revolution. Hence it required not just a political program but an ideology (whether of a scientistic, Marxist, or romantic populist stripe). For ideological reasons or, more rarely, out of awareness of Russia's desperate poverty, the radical intelligentsia hoped that the reforms inaugurated by the emancipation of 1861 would lead to a complete overhaul of Russia's society, economy, and political system. It opposed any compromise that fell short of this goal, any progressive program of moderate reform, and refused to take any part in the civil society that was just coming into being. The intelligentsia therefore rejected the political programs of the *zemstva*, which aimed at achieving a constitutional regime without resolving the issue of the social structure.

Inevitably, the alienated radicals saw the autocratic regime, which persecuted them mercilessly, as their main enemy. Their hatred of the regime was unrelenting, violent, and complete; nothing short of autocracy's total destruction, regardless of the cost to society, would have satisfied them. In this respect, not so much the action but the thinking of the radicals had a totalitarian cast *avant la lettre*. Outrageous intolerance and dogmatism were characteristic features of the radicals' collective mentality, corresponding to the narrowness and brutality of the autocratic regime that they fought with admirable selflessness and dedication. Just as autocracy could not change owing to the political role it played in the system described above, so the radical intelligentsia too was condemned to remain forever the same (notwithstanding superficial changes of ideology and tactics): thus the autocratic tsar and radical intelligentsia formed two opposite poles of Russian society, which we have been calling poles of continuity. Why? Because the factors that had been present when the intelligentsia first came into being in the 1850s and 1860s remained and, but for minor changes, continued to produce the same effects. In the absence of a strong and highly organized civil society, and without any autonomous form of political life (which permitted autocracy to endure), the alienated intelligentsia inevitably lived on, rising again and again from its ashes, replenishing its ranks from the universities, and training would-be professional revolutionaries, "Pugachevs with degrees," whose existence had been predicted by Joseph de Maistre.

The Society Between the Poles

We have, then, two fixed poles: at one extreme the autocracy, at the other the alienated intelligentsia of radicals and revolutionaries. Between these two fixed poles lay a society in flux, and autocracy and intelligentsia alike attempted to gain support from various of its constituents. The time has now come to take a closer look at this society, beginning with the nobility, which had been, legally and culturally, the preeminent class in Russia society since the time of Peter the Great.

During the reign of Nicholas I this class was definitely split into two parts: a court "aristocracy" consisting of an increasingly professionalized class of government officials (discussed above), and a "landed nobility," which played a more or less important role in economic and cultural life in the provinces. The landed nobility included both those nobles whose primary concern was their own private life and those who aspired to a public role in the zemstva. For the majority, emancipation came as a rude shock. The less wealthy nobles were practically ruined by it. Many got out while they could and either obtained some kind of post in the bureaucracy, entered a profession, or learned a technical specialty whose outlook and interests they made their own.

Recent studies have shown that nobles who acquired new

attitudes through professional associations took an active part in efforts to achieve economic progress and to distribute the benefits thereof to all classes of society; ultimately, they sought and obtained influence over decisions pertaining to their chosen professions. Since the tsar and the bureaucracy stubbornly opposed political activity by representatives of professional groups, conflict between these men and the regime was inevitable. At first the disputes were purely technical (how best to ensure the public health or educate the inhabitants of a particular village, for example). But their scope quickly widened in reaction to government censorship and control, and in the end the professional associations turned radical. Such politicization of course could be directed only at the regime, even if association members remained, as individuals, loyal and patriotic subjects. In the turmoil surrounding the famine of 1891, the Russo-Japanese War, and the revolution of 1905, the professional associations were ranged with the opposition and some even joined forces with the revolutionary parties.

Nothing will be said here about those nobles who sank into poverty and lost their social status (like the family of Raskolnikov and other ruined nobles in the works of Dostoyevsky). Those who survived the crisis attempted to transform themselves into a class of landlords, living on the profits of their estates and hoping to put enough aside to provide their children with the education necessary to pursue a career in one of the professions, in the universities, in business, or in the bureaucracy. Many of these noble landlords held official posts in the *zemstva*, but not necessarily the key posts.

At first sight it may seem odd that the state was not more favorably disposed to efforts by this class to set itself up as a rural elite interested in farming and in the *zemstvo* administration. But the government was concerned with the peasants, not the nobles, whose interests it believed had been adequately safeguarded by the emancipation act. The economic policy pursued by Witte, first introduced by his predecessors

Bunge and Vichnegradsky at the ministry of finance, favored the industrial over the agricultural sector and hurt farmers, peasants, and nobles alike. Mistrust and antagonism between the bureaucracy and the landed nobility, whose origins can be traced back to Nicholas I, were thus made worse by the emancipation and still worse by the economic policies subsequently adopted by the government.

Aware of the dangerous alienation of the landed nobility, which posed a particular threat in the economic conditions of the period 1880–90, the autocratic government changed its attitude and attempted to develop a firm base of support among the noble landlord class by assigning it responsibility for rural police and supervision of the *zemstvo* institutions and by attempting to improve its economic situation. An agricultural bank was established for the benefit of the landlord class, and tariff protection was extended to farm products. With these measures Alexander III and Nicholas II hoped to "reestablish the nobility" and at the same time to secure a political base for themselves. This new nobility was defined primarily in terms of economic interests and centered in the countryside. But the government's last-ditch effort to win its support came too late. Many nobles were by this time no longer engaged in agriculture, and it was utopian to think that the small minority that remained on the land could stem the tide of change, when much of the arable land was being transferred at an ever-increasing pace into the hands of wealthy merchants and peasants. Moreover, by favoring noble landowners who carried relatively little weight economically, the government harmed the peasantry and did even worse damage to non-noble entrepreneurs engaged in a variety of businesses.

There is no doubt, finally, that industrialization was proceeding apace and that the government was forced to devote a good deal of attention to industrial problems at a time when, from a social and political standpoint, it should have been more concerned with the crisis of the peasantry. The policy of favoring the landed nobility was not without dangers and ambiguities of its own, as the crises of 1905 and 1907 clearly indicate. In attempting to strike a balance between the rural nobility, the peasantry and industry, the government failed to secure the unconditional support of the nobility, which had meanwhile formed its own pressure group, the Council of the United Nobility *(soviet obiedinennogo dvorianstva)*, which was particularly influential in the south and southwest, where noble Russian landlords were in conflict (or competition) with Poles, Ukrainians, and Jews. As a condition of its support for the Stolypin government, the Council stipulated that the government must adopt a chauvinistic Great Russian policy, which had the effect of alienating other nationalities and of encouraging foolhardy diplomacy.

The attitude of the landed nobility remained ambiguous. Although it professed loyalty to the tsar (and the belief that it was in fact loyal was central to its psychology and political convictions), that loyalty was severely tested, beginning in 1911, by the peculiar personality and behavior of Nicholas II and by the activities of his entourage. Nor did the landed aristocracy ever overcome its distrust, not to say hatred, of the bureaucracy, which neither would nor could grant all its favors exclusively to the nobility. The conflict between nobility and bureaucracy caused difficulties for the Duma leadership and prevented the tsar from securing the unquestioning support of the landed nobility, whose political importance he and his entourage in any case overestimated.

Any responsible government, of course, labors under the obligation to devote its attention first and foremost to the most numerous class of society: in the case of Russia, this was the peasantry. There were two fundamental problems in this regard: first, peasants constituted a special class in the eyes of the law, and second, their mobility was limited. These two factors were responsible for the serious agricultural crisis of the late nineteenth and early twentieth centuries. The whole situation was in large part a product of the complementary attitudes of the government and the educated elite. The government, as was inevitable, treated the peasants as their masters had treated them when they were serfs, while the educated elite looked upon them as helpless children who required education and guidance before they could reap the benefits of civilization and culture.

In this connection, it is useful to note the ambivalent attitude of the government and (for different reasons) the educated elite, especially the intelligentsia, toward industrious peasants who had the talents needed to make money—peasants to whom other peasants (and, following their example, the rest of society) referred as kulaks. The educated elite wanted no part of the kulaks, for two reasons. First, there was no place for the kulaks in the Slavophile image of the rural commun (mir), supposedly a village in which harmony and love reigned supreme and inequality of wealth could only prove detrimental. The kulaks stood for selfish individualism and materialism, and these were incompatible with the community ideals (sobornost') promoted by Slavophile intellectuals and agrarian socialists. By contrast, the Marxists, who counted on the disintegration of the communes to hasten the transition to capitalism, looked upon the kulaks as agents of historical progress, even while dismissing their scale of values as contrary to the Marxist ideal. Second, Russian intellectuals subscribed to an egalitarian and idealistic ethic and looked upon self-interest and the pursuit of profit as reprehensible in themselves. The quest for wealth was evil as such, and the kulaks were the worst possible example of such a quest, because they grew wealthy at the expense of their relatives and neighbors, fellow members of the commune.

It is hardly surprising, therefore that the agrarian problem was approached, as a social as well as a political issue, from the standpoint of the poor peasants (bedniak). The compassion and concerns of both government and intellectuals were focused on them. It was out of the question even to think of weakening the communes, which guaranteed that the poor peasants would receive at least enough land to live on; nothing could be done to change this, even if it meant limiting the acquisitiveness and productivity of the wealthy kulaks. Until the beginning of the twentieth century, the *mir* remained the only acceptable basis for a solution of the agrarian crisis: the state would accept no other solution for administrative and fiscal reasons, and the intellectuals would accept no other solution for ethical reasons. It took the peasant uprisings and the revolution of 1905 before Stolypin and his collaborators found the courage to take the bull by the horns and allow the commune to be broken up, thus taking the risk of relying on the kulak to meet the country's agricultural needs.

Legally and culturally, the peasants remained on the sidelines as a civil society took shape in Russia toward the end of the nineteenth century. Of course, the educated classes and the government ought to have seen that, unless the peasants were integrated into civil society, Russia would never become a prosperous, progressive, and liberal country (remember that peasants accounted for 80 to 85 percent of the population[11]). Yet the attempt was made by every possible means to keep the peasantry isolated from capitalist society, even though this meant subjecting much of the population to grinding poverty. This was doubly unjust. In the first place, the peasants were deprived of a fair share of the benefits of progress (however modest they may have been). In addition, they were kept from coming into contact with modern Russian civilization, since this was an offshoot of industrial capitalism.

In this respect the situation in Russia differed sharply from that of other European countries. When the peasants finally began to stir, they took the traditional route of anarchic re-

11. V. Leontovitsch, *Geschichte des Liberalismus in Russland* (Frankfurt-am-Main: Klostermann, 1957).

bellion accompanied by arson, pillage, and occupation of the land. They did not agitate for "modern" reforms that would have granted them the freedom to move about the country and to own land. They did not ask for direct aid or subsidies to improve their farming methods, attend to their health needs, or educate their children. Stolypin drew the necessary conclusions, wiped the slate clean, and started fresh. He was the first Russian statesman who attempted to treat the peasants as citizens on a footing of equality with the emperor's other subjects—a businessman whose business happened to be farming. His policy might warrant favorable judgment had conditions in Russia at the time been more or less "normal" and stable.[12]

The industrial proletariat, which first emerged in the last quarter-century of the imperial regime, was closely linked to the peasantry. In fact, the proletariat did not develop as a mass phenomenon in Russia until the last few decades of the nineteenth century, and rapid growth did not come until the decade preceding World War I. The birth of the proletariat in Russia, as everywhere else, was difficult and fraught with conflict. For our present purposes it will suffice to say just a few words concerning the place of this new class in Russian society.

It is worth noting that, even as late as 1905, the majority of industrial workers remained in close contact with the rural peasantry. Many worked only part time for industry and returned to their villages to lend a hand in the harvest and other heavy chores. For legal and tax purposes these workers were under the jurisdiction of their native communes. Their

12. The effects of Stolypin's agrarian reform are a matter of controversy, currently under investigation from a number of different angles. For a survey and an interesting interpretation, see T. Shanin, *The Awkward Class. Political Sociology of Peasants in a Developing Society, Russia 1910–1925* (Oxford: The Clarendon Press, 1972).

wives and children usually remained in the village, cultivating their own plots or working on a family plot under the direction of a grandfather or older brother. Such workers retained the mind set, the behavior, and the judgment of the peasant. Still, even though workers were not yet fully integrated into the city's social and cultural life, their ties to the village grew weaker and weaker as time went by, and they found themselves increasingly alienated from the peasantry without yet having found a place in any other group or segment of Russian society. Nevertheless, their political opinions and concerns, insofar as they showed signs of having any, seem to have been identical to those of the peasantry (as is shown by the results of elections to the first few Dumas).

By 1905 or so it becomes possible to identify a true "hereditary" urban industrial proletariat—that is, a class of workers born in the cities whose only option was to seek work in industry. This development is especially clear in heavy industries that required a skilled labor force (such as iron and steel). Workers, especially foremen, accepted the values of the industrial system. Their attitudes, habits, and customs were marked by Western influences to an even greater extent than those of merchants, shopkeepers, and clerks. Workers did their best to climb the social ladder and integrate themselves into the Western-style world created by industry. The radical intelligentsia looked upon the industrial work force as fertile ground for political organizing and offered workers intellectual leadership, which they presumably needed because of their "objective" social and political position.

Because of the backwardness of the Russian economy, educational and living standards of Russian workers did not measure up to the standards set by more highly developed countries. Though less wretched and discontented than the peasants, Russian workers enjoyed only a small fraction of the benefits that capitalist industry had already begun to bring to Western societies. The situation was made even worse by the fact that economic development in Russia, whether as a result of deliberate planning or natural evolution, gave priority to heavy industry and to the production of basic machinery and infrastructure, with production for consumption trailing behind. Revolutionaries therefore had an easy time persuading workers that capitalism was their enemy. Even the proletarian elite (which still lived and worked in undeniably wretched conditions) subscribed to revolutionary radicalism, as is shown by the wave of strikes and labor disputes that began to develop in 1912. There seems to have been no place in Russia for Fabianism or even for revisionist Social Democracy of the sort that developed in Germany. The radical Marxist intelligentsia found in the Russian proletariat the ideal audience for its ideology.

This brings us to the bourgeoisie, a social class that was still in the process of formation on the eve of the Revolution. Here I am using "bourgeoisie" in the nineteenth-century sense to mean the class consisting of wealthy merchants, industrialists, and financiers. Little is known about this class, and it is hard to say what the bourgeoisie was like around 1900, when it first entered the public arena with the expectation of exerting political influence and playing a public role. Research now under way will, I hope, provide us with a more accurate picture and a better understanding of the bourgeois class. For the time being, the best we can do is to mention a few of its more prominent characteristics.

The Russian bourgeoisie had no clear definition in terms of its professional composition and no distinctive legal status. Unlike the term "merchant," which did refer to both an occupation and a legal status, the words "industrialist" and "banker" had no such precise reference. Bankers, in fact, could choose to belong to almost any group they wished. Furthermore, members of the bourgeoisie were far from sharing a common set of interests (indeed, division within the Russian bourgeoisie was far sharper than in the West). The interests

of, say, textile merchants and manufacturers conflicted with
the interests of those responsible for planning and managing
heavy industry. There was constant tension between traditional merchants and old-line manufacturers on the one hand
and modern-minded financiers and captains of industry on the
other.

The state's position in this conflict was far from clear. At
times it seemed to encourage modern industry, but when
representatives of the traditional merchant and manufacturing groups made their case with a great show of patriotic and
nationalistic fervor, the government apparently reversed its
position. It is true that, by 1880, modern industry had become strong enough to press its own case and win out against
the arguments of the traditionalists. But this led only to increased conflict between the industrialists on the one hand
and the landed nobility and proletariat on the other.

Again the state vacillated. It had no wish to harm the landed
nobility, but neither did it wish to harm the interests of the
industrialists, even though it had little sympathy for bourgeois entrepreneurs. At the same time, the government,
banking on the proletariat's peasant origins and religious and
patriotic feeling, adopted a paternalistic attitude toward industrial workers similar in many respects to its attitude toward the peasantry. Well before such relatively advanced
countries as France, Russia adopted progressive factory legislation.

Unfortunately, enforcement of the factory laws was lax. At
times the government responded to the needs of the industrial proletariat against the wishes of the bourgeoisie, as in
the area of urban legislation. This did not prevent it from energetically defending industrial interests, however, particularly those of major corporations that attracted capital from
abroad. The government was indecisive in part because it was
concerned with defusing social tensions resulting from the
concentration of large numbers of exploited workers in urban
slums, in part because of the traditional lack of sympathy on

the part of many officials and other educated people for the materialistic values of bourgeois capitalism.

Curiously enough, many wealthy heirs of business fortunes shared these attitudes and turned against their fathers' values. Declaring themselves enemies of materialism and capitalism, these young men embraced the arts or became involved in radical politics. It was not until the eve of World War I that a few representatives of the commercial and industrial bourgeoisie decided that the time had come to take an active role in public life and formed associations and parties not only to defend their economic interests but also to reform a system whose collapse many had begun to fear. During World War I this movement acquired an institutional base with the founding of the Union of Cities and the Union of Industry. Although a good deal of energy was devoted to the cause and the movement was able, in the wartime climate, to exert some influence, the attempt came too late to prevent the collapse of the system. It is worth noting that the imperial government did nothing to encourage this elite fringe group in its efforts to develop a public role, despite the group's enormous importance for Russia's economic development.

In the last fifty years of the imperial regime, the "national problem," i.e., the situation of non-Russians living within the borders of the empire, took on new significance and became one of the crucial issues of the new century. The subject is too vast to be covered even in outline. The best we can do here is to touch on the aspect of the problem that was most significant from the standpoint of relations between the society and the state. The Russian Empire had from the beginning more or less deliberately pursued a policy of cultural and social integration. As long as this policy was applied to nations deemed to rank below Russia in level of civilization, it worked rather well. But with the conquest and assimilation of peoples and nationalities whose level of civilization was equal to, if not greater than, Russia's, problems arose.

The indigenous elites agreed to integration for material,

social, and political reasons, but the lower classes, which expected none of these advantages, balked. Resistance developed wherever the native language, religion, and culture were strong enough to support ethnic consciousness and a sense of identity. Consequently, in the second half of the nineteenth century the traditional policy of social and cultural integration ceased to work and lost some of its luster.

As the alien populations entered into trade with a more advanced economy, they developed a class whose education and way of life drew its inspiration from national linguistic and religious traditions. The members of these new social strata, who had been introduced by the Russians to the nationalist ideas of Western romanticism, naturally began to call for greater administrative autonomy, and for practical and political recognition of their cultural particularity. The imperial government responded to these demands with a chauvinistic policy of cultural and religious "Russification." This short-sighted approach only exacerbated the conflict and increased resentment on the part of native elites, which had been taught in Russian schools to respect cultural and intellectual independence and tradition. The native elites thus came to advocate a new kind of nationalism and demanded not only recognition of their cultural particularity but also the right to organize autonomous national institutions and organizations.

The conflict became even more virulent toward the end of the nineteenth century and reached a peak after 1905, when the discriminatory Russification policy was stepped up under pressure from various Russian groups fearful of losing their dominant position at the regional level. National conflict was yet another factor contributing to the disintegration of the empire, damage from which might have been limited had the government been willing, while there was still time, to allow the formation of autonomous intermediary bodies to represent the various nationalities.

The Silver Age

The last quarter-century of the empire of the tsars saw an extraordinary flourishing of the arts, literature, and intellectual achievement of many kinds. For the first time Russian works began to attract attention in other countries. Thus Russia finally contributed its share to contemporary thought and civilization, as it continued to do even after the Revolution thanks to the émigrés. The flourishing cultural life is a factor that must be taken into account in any attempt to understand the relations between society and state in the years preceding the collapse of the Russian Empire, for the very intensity and fecundity of cultural life in Russia encouraged change and influenced the course of events.

For our purposes the educated elite may be divided into two groups: the professional elite and the independent artists and writers. This does not mean that there were no points of contact between the two groups. On the contrary, there were many such contacts, especially in literature and the humanities. Broadly speaking, however, the two groups held different conceptions of public life and politics, even though both shared a deep-seated aversion to the autocratic regime.

Members of the liberal professions, along with many engineers, chemists, etc., were torn between two conceptions of their role. Their outlook had been shaped by the alienated intelligentsia, to which many had belonged in their youths, and they had absorbed the intelligentsia's moral and social values without necessarily accepting its ideological commitment. Hence they had a highly developed sense of their social mission and responsibility to the people. They saw their primary obligation as one of helping the people (and above all the most wretched) to achieve a decent standard of living, to acquire an education, and to improve standards of health and sanitation. Unlike the alienated radicals of the intelligentsia, however, these trained professionals had practical knowledge of Russian realities, and they hoped to put this knowledge to use in order to bring about gradual change without violent upheaval. This is the group that Martin Malia has so aptly described as the "rooted" intelligentsia.

The great majority of these men were also state or *zemstvo* officials, however. They were therefore subject, indirectly at any rate, to governmental discipline. They felt constant conflict between their duties to the government and their duties to the people, to say nothing of disputes over matters of taxation and budget. The government demanded obedience from its officials and insisted that its technical and fiscal decisions be carried out, for otherwise it would have been at the mercy of its technical advisers and its margin for maneuver would have been severely limited.

Conflict was especially common between the administration and the medical profession; between teachers and the Holy Synod, which was pursuing its own aggressive educational policy at the parish level and sent missions to non-Orthodox groups, including Old Believers; and between the ministry of justice and lawyers, who sometimes pleaded on behalf of clients by blaming social conditions and psychological predispositions rather than adhering to the strict letter of the law. As we saw earlier, such conflicts helped to politicize the professional associations that represented members of the rooted intelligentsia and complicated collaboration between the administration and various social and public service agencies. As a result, many private charitable organizations were established, especially after 1905, with money contributed by businessmen and members of the aristocracy, and, chiefly in the cities, these took the place of state social agencies, health departments, and educational authorities. But the activities of these charitable organizations were impeded by state regulation and censorship, to the great displeasure of the donors and professionals involved.

It is clear, then, that professionals agreed to support the state only on condition that they be allowed to work toward improving the general welfare without undue government interference. But under Alexander III and in the early years of Nicholas II's reign, and again after 1907, the state looked with suspicion upon any private initiative in the social realm, so that conflict was inevitable. The professional elite (the rooted intelligentsia) sympathized politically with the alienated radical intelligentsia, since the radicals, focused as they were on the general welfare, supported the professionals' efforts in this regard. To be sure, there is no dearth of instances in which professionals collaborated with state officials to resolve some crisis or deal with some specific issue, but on the whole, and particularly in regard to the overall shape of government policy, top officials and leading professionals found themselves in opposite camps, with little hope of reconciliation.

Around 1900 there began to appear, for the first time in Russia, men who considered themselves professional artists, men of letters, and "thinkers" (philosophers, lay theologians, scholars, etc.). These men devoted themselves exclusively to their discipline or art; they held no other position, played no role in society, and frequently lived on what they earned from sale of their works. Hence they too were members of the rooted intelligentsia. Here, however, we are mainly interested in the intellectual, philosophical, and moral (or political) attitudes of this new group. The blossoming of Russian culture at the beginning of the twentieth century was an extraordinarily dazzling phenomenon, affecting every aspect of the arts, literature, philosophy, and science. Practitioners in each of these areas were determined to go their own way. Artists insisted on the autonomy of aesthetic values. Scientists insisted that knowledge and rational inquiry were ends in themselves. Philosophers turned a critical eye on standards of truth and value. In metaphysics there was a return to philosophical idealism. The materialistic positivism that had held sway over the radical intelligentsia since 1850 and still commanded the allegiance of the revolutionaries was definitively abandoned.

Last but not least, there was a reaction against the intrusion of social and political concerns into philosophy and art. An end had come to the need for intellectuals and artists to concentrate on political, economic, and social themes. In short, the new generation had sounded the death knell of the repentant *intelligent,* who had long ago taken the place of the repentant noble; younger intellectuals began to take their place in Russian civil society (even if their art was unfettered by any aesthetic law and their metaphysics began with a repudiation of reason).

Thus a split developed between the innovative elites (the rooted intellectuals) in the arts, literature, science, and philosophy, and the alienated, politicized, traditional radical intelligentsia. Striking proof of this is provided by the impassioned debate that attended the publication of the collection of articles, *Vekhi (Landmarks).* The antipolitical stance adopted by the intellectuals and artists associated with this book amounted to a declaration of independence, a disengagement from ideological commitment, and a determination to return to reality and to face up to it in a positive way. Once freed from the grip of politics, the authors held, scholarship, science, philosophy, and theology were able to share in the exciting ferment that has characterized intellectual life in the West in this century.

Enthusiasm for logic and speculation and emphasis on the spiritual and metaphysical value of the creative act in art, science, or literature (apart from the success of that act) reflect a liberation of the Russian spirit: one is struck by the extraordinary variety of the creative outpouring, by the audacity of formal experimentation, by the sheer volume of new ideas, themes, and theories. Beyond all the variety, however, is one common denominator: rejection of philosophical positivism and bourgeois materialism. Just as, in Europe, symbolism, neo-Kantianism, and the "fin de siècle" aesthetic and spirit represent a rejection of the philistinism of industrial civilization, so the artists and intellectuals of Russia's Silver Age were rejecting a civil society that had been erected on a basis of capitalist materialism and nothing else. The avant-garde looked forward impatiently, though not without trepidation, to the end of "bourgeois" civilization. Many minds seem to have been overwhelmed by the apocalyptic climate. Some expected the coming apocalypse to take a religious form: the coming of Christ would be heralded by the appearance of an Antichrist. Others expected it to be political: revolution would bring power to the people, to the peasants and proletarians, and the dawn of a new era, a new civilization. In the meantime anything was possible, everything was permissible, and many members of the avant-garde adopted anarchism as a doctrine and a way of life, thus limiting the extent to which they could become "rooted" members of society.

Thus the leading innovators of the early twentieth century, for all that they opposed the traditions of the radical intelligentsia, were no defenders of the status quo. At best they were hesitant supporters, but often outright enemies, of the nascent civil society that industrialization and "modernization" had produced in Russia. Their attitude toward the imperial regime was one of hatred and contempt, because the government supported the most bourgeois and materialistic aspects of Russian culture while persecuting iconoclasts and free spirits. The reinstitution of stricter censorship in 1907 did not prevent purely artistic and literary publications from reaching the public, however, despite the social and political attitudes of the avant-garde. What is more, the appearance of works by poets and writers of peasant and proletarian origins served only to harden the intellectuals' negative attitudes toward the regime. Like the radical intelligentsia, the avant-garde looked forward to the regime's collapse, which they hoped would inaugurate a period of unfettered creativity and provide an opportunity to impose its aesthetic values and standards on the new society that would emerge after the revolution or the apocalypse, whichever it might be.

Taking a broad view of all these developments, we see, then, that Russian civil society never produced an "ideology" of its own in the sense of a coherent set of values, principles, and practices that might have served to guide its participation in the political life and economic development of the country. Civil society fell apart before it had a chance to develop an autonomous corporate structure. It lacked a firm intellectual and spiritual basis and was still seeking its own norms and values, its own philosophy. Without a genuine intellectual and cultural program of its own, civil society lacked the means to resist those who advocated starting over with a clean slate. By one of history's ironies, the innovative ferment of the early twentieth century in art, literature, and philosophy left Russia without the guidance of a political philosophy. The influence of anarchism, the concern with the apocalypse, and the eclecticism of moral thinking upset the equilibrium of the educated elite. Civil society was left to the mercy of the radicals and nihilists in politics and culture. The political and economic collapse led to intellectual collapse as well, thus clearing the way for the triumph of ideology, which alone seemed to offer a coherent guide to action.

To conclude, then, social groups were constantly tossed back and forth by the social, cultural, and political forces unleashed by the process of modernization. (See the accompanying diagram for a schematic indication of the forces at work; the diagram is necessarily oversimplified, because it leaves out geographical, chronological, and dynamic factors that affected the pattern of change). No stable new pattern ever developed despite the ever accelerating pace of change, which overwhelmed a society not yet highly organized and still unprepared for such violent upheaval.[13] The poles of continuity, the autocratic tsar and the radical intelligentsia, limited the degree to which society could adapt to these

13. To this situation may be applied the phrase "crisis without alternatives," which Christian Meier has used to describe the final years of the Roman Republic. See his *Respublica amissa. Eine Studie zur Verfassung und Geschichte der späten römischen Republik*, 2d ed. (Frankfurt–am–Main: Suhrkamp, 1980).

changes and kept society fragmented. Thus a strong, autonomous civil society was never able to develop. The lack of autonomous representative bodies, combined with the growing inability of the autocracy and the intelligentsia to offer guidance, led to gradual paralysis of the system and created a void that ultimately engulfed the imperial regime.

IMPORTANT DATES

1645–1676 Reign of Alexis Mikhailovich
1649 Law Code *(Ulozhenie)*
1682–1689 Regency of Sophia
1694 Beginning of Peter's personal reign
1698 Revolt of the *streltsy*
1700–1721 War of the North, concluded by treaty of Nystad
1703 Founding of St. Petersburg
1711 Creation of the Senate
1714 Law on single inheritance
1720 General Regulation concerning "colleges"
1722 Table of Ranks
1725 Founding of the Academy of Sciences
Death of Peter the Great
1729 Birth of Sophie von Anhalt-Zerbst
1730–1740 Accession of Anna. "Constitutional" crisis
1731 Founding of the Corps of Cadets
1741–61 Reign of Elizabeth
1744 Sophie's departure for Russia and Orthodox baptism. Becomes Catherine. Marriage to Peter of Holstein, Elizabeth's nephew and heir to throne
1762 Exemption of the *dvoriane* from compulsory state service.
Coup d'état and accession of Catherine II.
1767–1768 Legislative Commission
1775 Statute on provinces
1785 Charters of nobility and cities
1796 Death of Catherine II
1796–1801 Reign of Paul I
1801–1825 Reign of Alexander I
1802 Creation of ministries
1803 Decree creating "free agriculturists"

1804	First statute on universities
1809–1810	Speransky's reform plans
1811	Institution of Council of State
1812	Napoleon I invades Russia
1813–1815	War with Napoleon continues
1816–1818	Serf emancipation in Baltic provinces
1819	Founding of the University of St. Petersburg
1821	Creation of the secret Societies of the North and South by the future Decembrists
1825	Decembrist uprising (Dec. 14)
1825–1855	Reign of Nicholas I
1826	New statute on censorship. Creation of the Third Section of the Imperial Chancellery
1833	"Codification" of the law
1835	Statute on the universities
1854–56	Crimean War
1855–1881	Reign of Alexander II
1861	Emancipation of the serfs (Feb. 19)
1861	Peasant uprisings in various provinces. Students movements in St. Petersburg, Moscow, and other cities
1863	Uprising in Poland, Lithuania, and Byelorussia New statute on universities
1864	Reform of local administration. *Zemstva* Judicial reform Educational reform
1874	Military reform. Introduction of compulsory military service
1881	Assassination of Alexander II (March 1)
1881–1894	Reign of Alexander III
1889	Introduction of the *zemskie nachal'niki* Agitation in the universities
1891	Great famine on the Volga
1893–1899	Russia's industrial "takeoff"
1894–1917	Reign of Nicholas II
1898	Founding of Russian Social Democratic Party
1901	Founding of Russian Socialist-Revolutionary Party
1901–1904	Rise of the revolutionary movement
1904–1906	Russo-Japanese War
1905	Revolution Red Sunday (Jan. 9) October Manifesto (Oct. 17)

1906	First Duma. Stolypin's agrarian decree
1910–1911	Stolypin's agrarian reform
1911	Assassination of Stolypin
	Election of fourth Duma
1914–1918	World War I
1917	February Revolution
	Abdication of Nicholas II (March 2)

BIBLIOGRAPHICAL INTRODUCTION

This select list is meant as an introduction and guide to further reading; it contains primarily recent monographs in English, whose bibliographies are particularly useful. The list is arranged topically, although the categories are not necessarily strictly delimited.

BIBLIOGRAPHIES AND SERIALS

Clendenning, P. and R. Bartlett. *Eighteenth Century Russia: A Select Bibliography of Works Published from 1955–1980.* Newtonville, Mass.: ORP, 1981.

Crowther, P. A., ed. *A Bibliography of Works in English on Early Russian History to 1800.* Oxford: Blackwell, 1969.

Istoriia SSSR: Annotirovannyi perechen' russkikh bibliografii, izdannykh do 1965 g. 2d ed. Moscow, 1966.

Istoriia SSSR: Ukazatel' sovetskoi literatury za 1917–1952 gg. 2 vols. Moscow, 1956–1958.

Shapiro, D. *A Select Bibliography of Works in English on Russian History, 1801–1917.* Oxford: Blackwell, 1962.

Simmons, J. S. G., ed. *Russian Bibliography, Libraries and Archives (A Selective List of Bibliographical References for Students of Russian History, Literature, Political, Social and Philosophical Thought, Theology and Linguistics.)* Oxford: Hall, 1973.

Most Important Serials in Western Languages

Cahiers du monde russe et soviétique. Paris.

Canadian American Slavic Studies (and its affiliates: *Russian History, Soviet History*). U.S.A.

Forschungen zur Geschichte Osteuropas. West Berlin.
Jahrbücher für Geschichte Osteuropas. German Federal Republic.
Oxford Slavonic Papers. England.
Slavic Review. U.S.A.
Slavonic and East European Review. England.

GENERAL HISTORIES OF RUSSIA

Auty, Robert and Dimitrii Obolensky, eds. *Companion to Russian Studies,* vol. 1: *An Introduction to Russian History.* Cambridge: Cambridge University Press, 1976.
Florinsky, M. T. *Russia: A History and an Intepretation.* 2 vols. New York: Macmillan, 1954.
Istoriia SSSR s drevneishikh vremen do nashikh dnei. 1st series. 6 vols. Moscow, 1966–1968.
Kliuchevskii, V. O. *Kurs russkoi istorii.* 5 vols. Moscow, 1956–1958.
Miliukov, Paul, Charles Seignobos, and L. Eisenmann. *History of Russia.* trans. by Charles Lam Markmann. 3 vols. New York: Funk & Wagnalls, 1968.
Pipes, Richard. *Russia Under the Old Regime.* New York: Scribner's, 1974.
Seton-Watson, H. *The Russian Empire, 1801–1917.* Oxford: Clarendon Press, 1967.
Stählin, Karl. *Geschichte Russlands von den Anfängen bis zur Gegenwart.* 4 vols. Berlin, 1930–1939.
Stökl, Günther. *Russische Geschichte.* 3d ed. Stuttgart: A. Kröner, 1973.

COLLECTIONS OF ARTICLES

Black, C. E., ed. *The Transformation of Russian Society.* Cambridge: Harvard University Press, 1960.
Blackwell, W. L. *Russian Economic Development from Peter the Great to Stalin.* New York: New Viewpoints, 1974.
Cherniavsky, M., ed. *Structure of Russian History.* New York: Random House, 1970.
Geyer, D., ed. *Wirtschaft und Gesellschaft im vorrevolutionären Russland.* Cologne: Kiepenheuer and Wietsch, 1975.
Haimson, L. H., ed. *The Politics of Rural Russia, 1905–1914.* Bloomington: Indiana University Press, 1979.

Harcave, S. *Readings in Russian History.* 2 vols. New York: Crowell, 1962.

Lederer, I. J., ed. *Russian Foreign Policy.* New Haven: Yale University Press, 1962.

Nichols, R. L. and T. G. Stavrou, eds. *Russian Orthodoxy Under the Old Regime.* Minneapolis: University of Minnesota Press, 1978.

Pintner, W. McK. and D. K. Rowney, eds. *Russian Officialdom: The Bureaucratization of Russian Society from the Seventeenth to the Twentieth Century.* Chapel Hill: University of North Carolina Press, 1980.

Pipes, R., ed. *The Russian Intelligentsia.* New York: Columbia University Press, 1961.

Ransel, D. L., ed. *The Family in Imperial Russia.* Urbana: University of Illinois Press, 1978.

Simmons, E. J., ed. *Continuity and Change in Russian and Soviet Thought.* Cambridge: Harvard University Press, 1955.

Treadgold, D. W., ed. *The Development of the USSR: An Exchange of Views.* Seattle: University of Washington Press, 1964.

Vuchinich, W. S., ed. *The Peasant in Nineteenth-Century Russia.* Stanford: Stanford University Press, 1968.

MUSCOVY

Besançon, A. *Le tsarévitch immolé.* Paris, 1967.

Cherniavsky, M. *Tsar and People.* New Haven: Yale University Press, 1961.

Kliuchevsky, V. *Course in Russian History. The Seventeenth Century.* New York: Times Books, 1972.

Vernadsky, G. and M. Karpovitch. *A History of Russia.* Vol. 5.: G. Vernadsky, *The Tsardom of Muscovy, 1547–1682.* 2 vols. New Haven: Yale University Press, 1969.

REIGNS

Peter the Great

Kliuchevsky, V. *Peter the Great.* New York: Vintage Books, 1961.

Pavlenko, N. *Petr Pervyi.* Moscow, 1975.

Sumner, B. H. *Peter the Great and the Emergence of Russia.* London: English University Press, 1950.

Wittram, R. *Peter I, Czar und Kaiser.* 2 vols. Göttingen. Vanden-hoeck & Ruprecht, 1964.

Catherine II

De Madariaga, I. *Russia in the Age of Catherine the Great.* New Haven: Yale University Press, 1981.
Raeff, M., ed. *Catherine the Great: A Profile.* New York: Hill and Wang, 1972.

Paul I

Ragsdale, H., ed. *Paul I: A Reassessment of His Life and Reign.* Pittsburgh: University International Center, 1979.

Alexander I

McConnell, A. *Tsar Alexander I. Paternalistic Reformer.* New York: A.H.M., 1970.

Nicholas I

Lincoln, W. Bruce. *Nicholas I, Emperor and Autocrat of All Russia.* Bloomington: University of Indiana Press, 1978.

ADMINISTRATION, GOVERNMENT

Amburger, E. *Geschichte der Behördenorganisation Russlands von Peter dem Grossen bis 1917.* Leyden: Brill, 1966.
Eroshkin, N. *Istoriia gosudarstvennykh uchrezhdenii dorevoliutsionnoi Rossii.* 3d ed. Moscow, 1983.
Lincoln, W. B. *In the Vanguard of Reform: Russia's Enlightened Bureaucracy, 1825–1861.* DeKalb: Northern Illinois University Press, 1982.
Orlovsky, D. T. *The Limits of Reform. The Ministry of Internal Affairs in Imperial Russia 1801–1881.* Cambridge: Harvard University Press, 1981.

Raeff, M., *Michael Speransky, Statesman of Imperial Russia*. 2d ed. The Hague: Nijhoff, 1961.

Raeff, M., ed. *Plans for Political Reform in Imperial Russia*. Englewood Cliffs, N.J., Prentice-Hall, 1966.

Starr, S. F. *Decentralization and Self-Government in Russia*. Princeton: Princeton University Press, 1972.

Weissman, N. B. *Reform in Tsarist Russia: The State Bureaucracy and Local Government, 1900–1914*. New Brunswick: Rutgers University Press, 1981.

Wortman, R. S. *The Development of a Russian Legal Consciousness*. Chicago: University of Chicago Press, 1976.

Yaney, G. L. *The Systematization of Russian Government*. Urbana: University of Illinois Press, 1973.

PEASANTRY

Blum, J. *Lord and Peasant in Russia from the Ninth to the Nineteenth Century*. Princeton: Princeton University Press, 1961.

Confino, M. *Domaines et Seigneurs en Russie vers la fin du XVIIIe siècle*. Paris, 1963.

———— *Systèmes agraires et progrès agricole*. Paris-La Haye, 1969.

Emmons, T. *The Russian Landed Gentry and the Peasant Emancipation, 1861*. Cambridge: Cambridge University Press, 1968.

Field, D. *The End of Serfdom: Nobility and Bureaucracy in Russia, 1855–1861*. Cambridge: Harvard University Press, 1976.

Gerschenkron, A. "Agrarian Policies and Industrialization, Russia, 1861–1917." *The Cambridge History of Europe*, 2(2):706–800. Cambridge: Cambridge University Press, 1965.

Robinson, G. T. *Rural Russia Under the Old Regime*. Berkeley: University of California Press, 1969.

Shanin, T. *The Awkward Class. Political Sociology of Peasantry in a Developing Society, 1910–1925*. Oxford: Clarendon Press, 1972.

TOWNS AND URBAN CLASSES

Coquin, F.-X. *La Grande Commission législative (1767–1768): Les Cahiers de doléance urbains*. Paris-Louvain, 1972.

Hamm, M. F., ed. *The City in Russian History*. Lexington: University Press of Kentucky, 1976.

Hittle, J. M. *The Service City, State and Townsmen in Russia, 1600–1800*. Cambridge: Harvard University Press, 1979.

Rieber, A. J. *Merchants and Entrepreneurs in Imperial Russia*. Chapel Hill, University of North Carolina Press, 1982.

Zelnik, R. E. *Labor and Society in Tsarist Russia*. Stanford: Stanford University Press, 1971.

THE ECONOMY

Blackwell, W. L. *The Beginnings of Russian Industrialization, 1800–1860*. Princeton: Princeton University Press, 1968.

Gerschenkron, A. *Europe in the Russian Mirror*. Cambridge: Cambridge University Press, 1970.

Lyashchenko, P. *History of the National Economy of Russia to 1917*. New York, 1949.

Pintner, W. McK. *Russian Economic Policy Under Nicholas I*. Ithaca, Cornell University Press, 1967.

Portal, R. "The Industrialization of Russia." *The Cambridge Economic History of Europe*, 6(2):801–874. Cambridge: Cambridge University Press, 1965.

Tugan-Baranovskii, M. *Russkaia fabrika*. Moscow, 1938.

NOBILITY

Dukes, P. *Catherine the Great and the Russian Nobility*. Cambridge: Cambridge University Press, 1967.

Jones, R. E. *The Emanicipation of the Russian Nobility*. Princeton: Princeton University Press, 1973.

Manning, R. T. *The Crisis of the Old Order in Russia: Gentry and Government*. Princeton: Princeton University Press, 1982.

Meehan-Waters, B. *Autocracy and Aristocracy: The Russian Service Elite of 1730*. New Brunswick: Rutgers University Press, 1973.

Raeff, M. *Origins of the Russian Intelligentsia in the Eighteenth Century Nobility*. New York: Harcourt Brace, 1966.

CHURCH

Ammann, A. M. *Abrisse der Ost-slawischen Kirchengeschichte*. Vienna, 1950.

Freeze, G. L. *The Russian Levites. Parish Clergy in the Eighteenth Century.* Cambridge: Harvard University Press, 1977.

―― *The Parish Clergy in Nineteenth Century Russia: Crisis, Reform, and Counter-Reform.* Princeton: Princeton University Press, 1983.

Kartashev, A. V. *Ocherki po istorii russkoi tserkvi.* 2 vols. Paris, 1959.

Pascal, P. *Avvakum et les débuts du Raskol: La crise réligieuse au XVIIe siècle.* 2d ed. Paris-La Haye, 1963.

Frieden, N. M. *Physicians in an Era of Revolution and Reform, 1856–1905.* Princeton: Princeton University Press, 1981.

EMPIRE

Allworth, E., ed. *Soviet Nationality Problems.* New York: Columbia University Press, 1971.

Coquin, F.-X. *La Sibérie. Peuplement et immigration paysanne au XIXe siècle.* Paris, 1969.

Geyer, D. *Der russische Imperialismus (Studien über den Zusammenhang von innerer und auswärtigen Politik, 1860–1914).* Göttingen, 1977.

Nolde, B. *La formation de l'Empire russe.* 2 vols. Paris, 1952–53.

DIPLOMATIC HISTORY

This form of history has been much neglected in Russian historiography. The best summary introduction is to be found in the standard histories of Europe (e.g., *Cambridge History of Modern Europe*) and the classical monographs on European diplomatic history in the eighteenth and nineteenth centuries.

INTELLECTUAL HISTORY AND REVOLUTIONARY MOVEMENTS

The best way to approach these vast topics is to turn to the original works of Russian political and social thinkers, the most important of which are available in translation. The handiest introduction (and bibliographical guidance) is to be found in the following anthologies:

Edie, J. M., J. P. Scanlan, and M.-B. Zeldin, eds. *Russian Philosophy.* 3 vols. Chicago: Quadrangle, 1976.
Raeff, M. *Russian Intellectual History: An Anthology.* New York: Humanities Press, 1978.
Segel, H. B., ed. *The Literature of Eighteenth-Century Russia. A History and Anthology.* 2 vols. New York: Dutton, 1967.
Zenkovsky. S. A. *Medieval Russia's Epics, Chronicles and Tales.* New York: Dutton, 1974.

General Surveys

Besançon. *A Les Origines intellectuelles du léninisme.* Paris, 1977.
Florovskii, G. *Puti russkogo bogosloviia.* Paris, 1981.
Malia, M. *Alexander Herzen and the Birth of Russian Socialism.* Cambridge: Harvard University Press, 1961.
Masaryk, T. G. *The Spirit of Russia. Studies in History, Literature and Philosophy.* 2 vols. New York, 1955.
Szamuely, T. *The Russian Tradition.* London: Secker & Warburg, 1974.
Ulam, A. *In the Name of the People. Prophets and Conspirators in Prerevolutionary Russia.* New York: Viking Pre..s, 1977.
Venturi, F. *Roots of Revolution.* London: Weidenfeld, 1961.
Vucinich, A. *Science in Russian Culture.* 2 vols. Stanford: Stanford University Press, 1963.
Walicki, A. *The Slavophile Controversy.* Oxford: Oxford University Press, 1975.
Zenkovsky, V. V. *History of Russian Philosophy.* 2 vols. London, 1953.

Marxism

For the history of Marxism in Russia, besides the many biographies of Lenin, Trotsky, and Stalin, see in particular:

Ascher, A. *Pavel Axelrod and the Development of Menshevism.* Cambridge: Harvard University Press, 1972.
Baron, S. H. *Plekhanov: The Father of Russian Marxism.* Stanford: Stanford University Press, 1963.
Keep, J. H. L. *The Rise of Social Democracy in Russia.* Oxford: Clarendon Press, 1963.

Kindersley, R. *The First Russian Revisionists: A Study of Legal Marxism in Russia.* Oxford: Clarendon Press, 1962.

Pipes, R. *Struve: Liberal on the Left, 1870–1905.* Cambridge: Harvard University Press, 1970.

—— *Struve: Liberal on the Right, 1905–1944.* Cambridge: Harvard University Press, 1980.

Walicki, A. *The Controversy Over Capitalism: Studies in the Social Philosophy of the Russian Populists.* Oxford: Clarendon Press, 1969.

INDEX